# The Daily Telegraph
# BOOK OF IMPERIAL AND
# COMMONWEALTH OBITUARIES

For my ever supportive wife, Rita

# The Daily Telegraph
# BOOK OF IMPERIAL AND
# COMMONWEALTH OBITUARIES

Edited by
## David Twiston Davies

Frontline Books, London

*The Daily Telegraph Book of Imperial and Commonwealth Obituaries*
This edition published in 2009 by Frontline Books,
an imprint of Pen & Sword Books Ltd,
47 Church Street, Barnsley, S. Yorkshire, S70 2AS
www.frontline-books.com

Copyright © Telegraph Media Group Limited, 2009

ISBN: 978-1-84832-524-1

For more information on our books, please visit
www.frontline-books.com, email info@frontline-books.com
or write to us at the above address.

Printed in the UK by the MPG Books Group

# CONTENTS

# INTRODUCTION

IT IS LONG since children's eyes lit up at mention of the Empire. Once it was the pride of the British nation, exercising a stewardship of those under its protection that justified a leading place on the international stage. Later it was judged to have been a conspiracy of exploitation, a symbol of all that was stuffy and old-fashioned. Both views contain elements of truth, an inevitable reflection of imperfect human nature.

Yet the Empire and its successor, the Commonwealth, have not been bettered by any alternative international body. Neither the United Nations, with its selective focus on an anonymous international agenda, nor the European Union, with an ever-constricting web of legislation, satisfy the human spirit as this strange creation of unwitting genius did – and still does. The days of redcoats marching down dusty tracks to establish new nations in the glow of *Pax Britannica* have passed. But those who still live in the Queen's realms enjoy not only the reassurance of a common loyalty but a shared language, a history, constitution, legal system, and, not least, a sense of humour.

In the light of a worldwide economic breakdown, the result of a naïve belief in unremitting progress and a scant regard to lessons of the past, the continuing value of Empire and Commonwealth is plain.

No attempt is made here to explain the distinction between Empire and Commonwealth beyond that the one implies direct supervision and the other locally established government which grew out of it. The individuals described here were conscious in at least some measure of the Crown and the British tradition, even if they reacted against its pinpricks at times with varying degrees of creative irritation.

The Empire came into existence for reasons that ranged from economic need to fears for security, a wish to learn more of our world and a desire to aid those who were less fortunate. Most important it inspired not only those who left Britain's shores in search of opportunities to better themselves but also persuaded those they encountered around the world to join them in their task of building nations.

The variety of ways in which the resulting partnerships worked successfully, and sometimes unsuccessfully, is illustrated in this collection of 92 obituaries published in *The Daily Telegraph* between 1991 and early 2009. Their subjects range from Dan Leahy, who encountered a Stone Age tribe in New Guinea and lived to see it served by supermarkets, to the Maharajah of Kutch, one of India's last ruling princes, as well as the widest variety of politicians. Sir John Dring was a firm district officer on the North West Frontier, where fierce tribesmen rarely take their fingers off the trigger. Sir "Rag" Pillai made a successful switch from the elite Indian Civil Service to the post-independence government of Pandit Nehru, while Sunil Dutt was an icon of the modern age, a film actor and minister.

As always, democracy arrived hand in hand with comedy. P. V. Rao was the Prime Minister who liberalised the Indian economy before being brought down by allegations of corruption; he then became a figure of fun for Indians in London who wondered if the sexually explicit passages in a novel he published in his seventies were based on personal experience. Helen Suzman, for long the sole opponent of the Afrikaner regime in the South African Parliament, had a rapier-like wit that brought to mind the great Prime Minister David Lloyd George. The Canadian minister Jack Pickersgill was a parliamentary strategist so slick that he gave birth to the word "pickersgillian", meaning too clever by half. New Zealand's Prime Minister, Sir Robert Muldoon, had an impressive grasp of finance, but the electorate grew tired of his pugnacity after he punched a heckler. While Bill Wentworth, the Australian MP, successfully lobbied for the standardisation of the states' railway gauges he so exasperated his opponents with his anti-Communist diatribes that two Opposition members wearing white coats appeared in the chamber and tapped him on the shoulder, as if summoning him back to the asylum.

A rougher political tradition is to be found in the Caribbean, where the left-wing Michael Manley reduced Jamaica to an economic disaster area when he first obtained power, but showed he had learned by his mistakes in his second term as Prime Minister. Sir Eric Gairy, leader of GULP (the Grenadian United Labour Party), had a rival party leader imprisoned in a dungeon below his feet to hear him speak; he was eventually ousted while in New York to warn the UN about the dangers of unidentified flying objects. When Dame Eugenia Charles, the Dominican Prime Minister, invited the Americans to save Grenada from Gairy's even more disastrous successor, it confirmed the suspicion that women make the best leaders in the Caribbean.

If much of Africa's experience of democracy has turned out disastrous, thanks to tribal loyalties this has not been for want of trying. Sir Michael Blundell did much to aid a peaceful transfer of power to black rule in Kenya and to aid its farming economy. Sir Garfield Todd, a Christian missionary and Prime Minister of Southern Rhodesia, parted early from his settler colleagues and supported Robert Mugabe, who then deprived him of the vote. Mugabe's rival Joshua Nkomo sadly concluded that a nation could win freedom without its people becoming free. In Uganda, Idi Amin butchered his people but demonstrated a comic talent that never failed to amuse while it horrified the British public. Perhaps most surprising was Hastings Banda, the self-appointed Life President of Malawi; a former London doctor he valued the Classics, wore morning dress in his red Rolls Royce and started a public school in the bush.

If they were driven by the spirit of *uhuru* ("freedom") others, such as Ratu Sir Kamisese Mara in Fiji were all too aware of the ill-consequences of being forced into independence. King Taufa'ahau Tupou IV of Tonga, the world's heaviest and only Methodist monarch, had some reason for his genial reluctance to sanction a headlong rush for democracy, though an unwise financial decision led to trouble for his successor.

If Time marches forward relentlessly, instincts and opinions travel at differing speeds. Looking at the way some peoples were precipitately forced into independence one realises that Britain's greatest fault may lie less in the half-conscious way it acquired an empire than in the precipitate manner it abandoned one.

A striking example of the gossamer line, which links the Queen's subjects, was revealed by Royce Frith, the Canadian High Commissioner in London. He won the dominion new cheers when he thanked West Country fishermen for supporting their Canadian counterparts in the North Atlantic against Spanish rivals while John Major's government upset all parties concerned by an inept attempt to steer a central course.

The assumptions of politicians and journalists notwithstanding, it would be a mistake to suppose that the peoples of the Empire and

Commonwealth were solely concerned with politics. Some were called to be lawyers, such as the distinguished Malaysian judge Tun Mohamed Suffian, whose Norfolk-born wife Bunny was a leader of Kuala Lumpur society. Sir Lionel Luckhoo, was "the Perry Mason of the Caribbean", and Ralph Lownie, a Kenya magistrate, had a man to polish his chamber pot. Others were clergy, such as the Reverend Robert Philp, who preferred to read the Bible in Kikuyu and was a model missionary in Kenya and the Right Reverend Howell Witt, a flamboyant Bishop of Bathurst, New South Wales, who wondered why God had elevated him and liked to dress up as "The Duchess of Dingo Creek".

The lure of adventure against the wide background of Empire exercised a powerful pull. Sir Edmund Hillary took up climbing in New Zealand, and found fame thrust upon him after conquering Mount Everest; Dudley Magnus became an amateur swagman "on the track" during the Depression in the Australian bush; Andrew Macpherson spent a holiday from school in Ottawa mapping the last unexplored part of the Eastern Arctic. Bunny Allen was the last of the great white hunters, with an irresistible lure for such film stars as Ava Gardner and Grace Kelly; and Jill Lowe swapped a divorcée's single life in Pimlico for marriage to a peasant farmer in Rajasthan.

Set against the tapestry of Empire even those born in the colonies who had conventional careers can seem to be imbued with exotic light. Sir Roy McKenzie was a chainstore owner and multi-millionaire philanthropist in New Zealand who liked to be known as a "community volunteer". R. M. Williams founded a clothing company, which marketed "Outback Chic" around the world while the Earl of Egmont was a contented Alberta farm boy until the *Daily Express* rang his father in 1929 to say they had inherited £325,000. For all the disadvantages with which he was born perhaps the most remarkable was Hamilton Naki, a gardener at the Groote Schurr hospital in Cape Town who secretly became one of South Africa's most brilliant surgeons as an assistant to Christiaan Barnard.

Among the great cultural figures are Sir Sidney Nolan who, rooted in the traditions of both Britain and Australia, created the most striking paintings of the Outback. "Prince" Mbarga was a Nigerian singer whose one hit "Sweet Mother" sold 13 million copies across the globe. Geoffrey Kendal, the actor-manager and father of the actress Felicity Kendal, devoted decades to performing Shakespeare all over India.

Yousuf Karsh was the Armenian refugee to Canada who took the most arresting photographs of Winston Churchill and Her Majesty the Queen.

Lastly there were the women, who stood back from male activities yet still exercised strong influence. Lady Barlow organised a declaration of loyalty that was signed by four-fifths of the population of Newfoundland and fiercely denounced the attacks of British tabloids on the monarchy. Lady Khama, the London secretary whose marriage to Sir Seretse Khama, the future President of Botswana, caused an unseemly political furore, became known as "the Queen Mother" to Botswanans, Victoria Opoku-Ware, chief wife of the King of the Ashanti, was a leader of Ghanian society and Queen Susan of the Albanians, an Australian grazier's daughter, married a throneless Balkan monarch.

WHEN the late Hugh Massingberd and I, his deputy, set about creating *The Daily Telegraph*'s first proper obituary section in 1986, with its own space and place in the paper every day, we recognised that we had two main stories to cover. One was the two world wars and the other the Empire. At first it was a strain to fill two columns every day, with only the uneven material in the office library to draw upon and contributors who were initially slow to grasp what was required. Nevertheless Hugh's enthusiasm, bubbling humour and rich fund of recondite knowledge turned what hard newsmen had regarded as a frivolous distraction and the graveyard of journalistic ambition into a triumph that not only became one of the most popular parts of the paper but inspired obituaries columns throughout the great centres of the old Empire. Five volumes so far have been devoted to the Armed Forces, but this is the first book dealing with our second great subject.

As the daily space allotted to the section increased we took on David Jones, a writer with the sharpest pen, who was to succeed Massingberd as editor in 1994. Since the early records were carelessly kept, it is impossible to identify everyone who contributed to this volume. But among them are the column's subsequent editors, Kate Summerscale, Christopher Howse, Andrew McKie and now Harry de Quetteville, aided by Jay Iliff and Roger Wilkes. There was also a team of part-time writer-editors who worked on the desk several times a week. They included Robert Gray, Claudia FitzHerbert, Will Cohu,

George Ireland, Georgia Powell, Philip Eade, James Owen and Katharine Ramsay, all of them enjoying the invaluable aid of the department's successive secretaries Martine Onoh, Diana Heffer, Teresa Moore and Dorothy Brown, my invaluable support as Letters Editor for many years. Among the outside writers who have contributed to this necessarily arbitrary selection are Charles Allen, Dean Godson, Amit Roy and Edward Fox; Geoffrey Hattersley-Smith and Fred Langan; Suzanne Twiston-Davies; the late Philip Warner; James Shipman; Sue Steward, Neil Snowden, Patrick Marnham and Chris Munnion; Martin van der Weyer; David Bowman, Nicholas Usherwood, Nick Squires, Rupert Allason and Captain Peter Hore; the late Keith Chalkley; and Philip Snow.

Mention should be made not only to Gavin Fuller, the paper's librarian, but also Brian Coulon, the picture librarian who enabled this to become the first obituaries book to be published with photographs. Lastly, Will Lewis, like his predecessors as the paper's Editor, is thanked for continuing support.

Whether or not they are fully conscious of the significance of their contributions, all have celebrated an empire which, the great Indian writer declared, was greater than that of Rome.

*David Twiston Davies*
Chief Obituary Writer
The Daily Telegraph
1 1 1 Buckingham Palace Road
London SW1W 0DT

# THE INDIAN SUBCONTINENT

~

## Lieutenant-Colonel Sir John Dring

LIEUTENANT-COLONEL SIR JOHN DRING (who died on June 16 1991, aged 87) was a frontiersman when there was only one frontier with a capital F – British India's north-western border with Afghanistan.

He was Assistant Commissioner at Peshawar in the late 1920s during the troubles instigated by Abdul Ghaffar Khan and the Red Shirts, which led him to survive three assassination attempts, as the bullet marks on his "Tin Lizzie" helmet bore witness. A restful period as Assistant Political Secretary to the Viceroy, Viscount Willingdon, was followed by a return to the border as Deputy Commissioner at Dera Ismail Khan and secretary to the province's governor.

In 1940 Dring was posted to South Waziristan when a number of Mahsud tribes were in open revolt. He received the rare distinction for a political officer of a mention in despatches for making the best of a military campaign in which, he said, "everything went wrong". His part in the operation, for which he felt unfairly blamed, had begun when a light aircraft deposited him at dusk outside Razmak fort to join a force setting out for tribal territory. By nightfall the entire column was pinned down by fire, and had suffered heavy casualties.

"It was the worst frontier incident for many years," he remembered. "The hostiles got above the military picquets, and disaster followed. All the wires were cut and I spent no less than four and a half weeks in a hole in the ground utterly cut off." Nevertheless a peace treaty was negotiated at a tribal *jirga*, and reparations were paid.

As the drive towards Indian self-government gathered pace, Dring's work took him increasingly into the higher echelons of the North West Frontier government, and included a vexatious spell as Deputy Commissioner at Peshawar, under a Congress government.

When Pakistan gained independence at the end of the Raj in 1947, Dring elected to stay on as a caretaker for some months before being offered the Prime Ministership of the princely state of Bahawalpur. He remained for four years, employing his diplomatic skills to convert a feudal khanate into a democratic state with its own ministers and assembly.

Arthur John Dring was born in Calcutta on November 4 1902 into a Raj presided over by Lord Curzon. As the son of Sir William Dring, a *burra sahib* in the East India Railways, young Johnnie enjoyed many privileges, including rail travel in his father's carriage, which was fitted up with dining saloon, bedrooms and bathrooms.

The boy was sent home to be educated at Winchester and Sandhurst before coming back to India in 1922 to join the Guides Cavalry, the North West Frontier Province's premier corps. Already a keen horseman – "I don't remember a day when I didn't go riding," Dring later recorded – he became an enthusiastic polo player and, for some years, Master of the Peshawar Vale Hunt. Riding to hounds imported from England, the P.V.H. chased jackals, which he considered better sport than foxes. From the Guides he was recruited in 1927 into the elite Indian Political Service. An exacting apprentice-ship in the field was followed by a spell in the secretariat, before he went to Peshawar.

When Dring finally left the subcontinent, in 1952, the Colonial Service put his knowledge of Muslim and tribal culture to good use by asking him to organise plebiscites in the northern regions of Togoland, Nigeria and the Cameroons. By now an arthritic hip severely restricted his riding; nevertheless he agreed to make up a Wykehamist four at a polo match at Kaduna, in northern Nigeria. He stuck gamely to his pony, but at the end of the chukka had to be prised from his mount and given morphine.

In 1957 Dring came home, where he chaired the Havant bench and the Hampshire Police Authority and was Deputy Lieutenant. Like many other prematurely retired colonial servants, he channelled his essential energies into the cultivation of roses.

John Dring was appointed CIE in 1943 and KBE in 1952. He married, in 1934, Marjorie Wadham, with whom he had two daughters. After her death he married Deborah, widow of Major-General J. S. Marshall and daughter of Major-General Gerald Cree.

# The Maharajah of Kutch

THE MAHARAJAH OF KUTCH (who died on June 21 1991, aged 81) ruled his state in western India for six months until it was absorbed into independent India.

Before succeeding to the *Gadi* (royal couch) in February 1948, the Maharao Madansinghhji Vijayrajji, as he was, had been regent for a year during his father's ill-health, when he failed to see eye to eye with Lord Mountbatten. The Viceroy proposed that Kutch, as the most senior princely state in India, should lead the way in signing the instruments of accession to the Indian Union. "You are going to throw us to the wolves," protested the Maharao. But, recognising the inevitable, he accepted the Viceroy's assurances that the rights of the princes would be protected.

The events of the next few months proved his fears right – "before the ink was dry", he later declared. Unable to bring himself to sign away his recently acquired powers, the new Maharajah employed his Prime Minister to surrender the state on his behalf. In 1971 came what he regarded as the final breach of faith when Indira Gandhi broke the pledge given by her father, Pandit Nehru, by abolishing the maharajahs' remaining rights and privileges.

Madansinghhji Vijayrajji Sawai Bahadur was born on October 10 1909, into the Jadejas, an ancient Rajput royal clan which traced its ancestry back to the moon by way of Krishna, and had ruled Kutch for more than a millenium. This was as much due to geography as to the Jadejas' martial prowess, since much of the kingdom comprised the desert salt-marsh known as the Rann of Kutch: it proved as impenetrable to Pakistani tanks in the 1971 Indo-Pakistan War as it had to the first Muslim invaders eight centuries earlier.

Young Madansinh spent his early years under the strict tutelage of his grandfather, Khengarji II, an autocrat who ruled for more than 60 years. At an early age he was removed from his parents' care to be brought up in the austere and feudal surroundings of the maharajah's palace in the state capital, Bhuj. There he was educated as a Rajput prince, with additional schooling from British tutors.

Before Madansinh was in his teens he was betrothed to a princess of Kishengarh, a matter over which he was not consulted. "I was shown a picture of my bride," he recalled, "but she didn't look like her picture at all."

Madansinh inherited a great love of sport, and became a champion pig-sticker, playing a leading role in the regional Gujerat Cup and Salmon Trophy meets as a leading exponent of the over-arm stab rather than the more usual British under-arm thrust. From his British tutors and sporting coaches he acquired a great fondness for tennis, playing for India at Wimbledon several times in the 1930s.

Both Madansinh's grandfather and his father, who became maharajah in 1942, were rulers of the old school, dedicated to resisting British "interference" and to opposing Gandhi and the Independence movement. Though a friend of Pandit Nehru, he inherited from his family a deep distrust of all politicians, and regarded Indian politics as "a dirty game, not a place for a scrupulous man".

None the less he was persuaded by Mountbatten that he could best serve his country as a diplomat. After a spell with the Indian High Commission in London from 1951 he spent the next decade as Indian ambassador in Norway, Chile and Colombia.

Following his retirement from public service in 1962, the Maharajah divided his time between his stately Vijay Vilas Palace in Kutch and a modest cottage in Mayford, near Woking. Although a man of great wealth, he was of modest demeanour and habits. A large part of his inheritance was surrendered voluntarily to the Indian exchequer in 1948, and he donated 100 kilograms of gold to the Indian war fund at the time of China's invasion of Assam in 1962. Growing increasingly disillusioned with Indian politics after the events of 1971, he spent most of his time in England, where he had Centre Court seats reserved for him at Wimbledon every summer up to his 80th year.

Despite their early differences, the last Maharajah and Mountbatten became good friends, and in later years he often drove over from Woking to Broadlands, Mountbatten's home outside Romsey. At one of these meetings he reminded the former Viceroy of the pledges that he gave, and which had been broken. "Lord Mountbatten laughed and said 'You were right. I was wrong.' It took a great man to say that."

~

## Sir Raghavan Pillai

SIR RAGHAVAN PILLAI (who died on March 31 1992, aged 93) held positions of the highest level in both the Raj and independent India.

The son of an administrator, Narayan Raghavan Pillai was born of *nair* (warrior) stock on July 24 1898 at Trivandrum, in the state of

Travancore and Cochin. He was educated at Madras University, where he took a first in English and then, against his parents' wishes, borrowed money from them to go to Trinity Hall, Cambridge. There he gained firsts in both natural sciences and law and met Edith Minnie Arthurs, to whom he was engaged for seven years before they could afford to marry.

Like many patriotic Indians of his generation, Pillai faced two choices: either to join the Congress Party, or to enter the Indian Army or the Indian Civil Service. Although Indians had been allowed to join the ICS since 1858, and a handful had sat its fiercely competitive examinations, few passed. However Pillai came second and, in 1922, was sent as Assistant Commissioner to the Raipur District of the Central Provinces, where he learned "on the job" the art of administering to the needs of half a million people. He spent half the year in the saddle, touring villages to collect revenues, dispense justice as a magistrate (with the power to send miscreants to prison for up to two years) and to inspect opium dens.

In 1927, he was appointed Assistant Collector of Customs in Madras, and the following year he and his fiancée evaded the ban on mixed marriages by going to Pondicherry in the south to marry under French law. The next year he was Deputy Director of Commercial Intelligence at Calcutta, and in 1932 he became Deputy Secretary to the Commerce Department of the Government of India, where he remained until the end of the Raj 15 years later.

Pillai's insistence on specialising in commercial affairs enabled him to avoid the tough political decisions, such as suppressing Congress, which the generalists in provincial postings were forced to implement; and along the way he earned a reputation as a first-rate draftsman.

As the Second World War approached he was intimately involved in efforts to develop Indian industry for war production, when its under-developed arms and textile industries were required to supply substantial quantities of ammunition and tents to British forces in the Middle and Far East.

After Independence, Partition and the departure of most of the British and Muslim cadres from the ICS, Nehru, the new Prime Minister, who had previously been less than sympathetic to the ICS, came increasingly to depend upon men such as Pillai, who embodying the Service's traditions of discretion and loyalty had no difficulty in serving a new master. "His business", one observer noted of Pillai, "is to do a good job, whether the job is the procuring of animal manure or the crushing of nationalism or the nursing of village sports."

In 1948, Pillai became India's Commissioner-General for Economic and Trade Affairs, with the rank of ambassador, and led the Indian delegation to the talks on the General Agreement on Tariffs and Trade (GATT). As head of the first Indian mission in Europe, he laid the groundwork for the development of the Indian Foreign Service. On one occasion when two ships built for the Bombay Steam & Navigation Company were launched in Belfast, he used coconuts instead of champagne at the ceremony. He also made sure that the Indian swastika, which symbolises good luck, was marked on the side of the vessels.

Pillai was then appointed Cabinet Secretary and, despite aspersions on the "patriotism" of ICS officers (often from those whose ideological loyalties lay with Peking or Moscow), he upheld the service's tradition of neutrality. After three years he became Secretary-General of the Ministry of External Affairs, or Permanent Under-Secretary.

Pillai loyally implemented Nehru's policies of anti-colonialism and non-alignment. He accompanied him to China in 1954 and the following year when the Russian leaders Bulganin and Khruhschev paid a official visit, Nehru, who was widowed, asked Edith Pillai to sit near him; she wore a sari for the occasion.

Pillai was also prominent in attempts to achieve a solution to the Kashmir dispute. When he retired as Secretary-General in 1960 he was given the Padma Vibhushan, the second-highest Indian honour; and in the Lok Sabha (India's Lower House) Nehru paid an extremely rare tribute to a civil servant, saying that Pillai's departure created "a certain blank". Nehru also paid him the honour of asking him to witness his will.

In 1961 Pillai became the first Indian chairman of GKW (the Indian subsidiary of GKN). As the doyen of Indian civil servants, he was recalled six years later to preside over the report of a commission on the future of the Indian Foreign Service. Then, anxious to escape the limelight, he and his wife retired to London, where they lived in a flat at Buckingham Gate and then at Hans Place.

"Rag" Pillai was appointed CBE in 1937, CIE in 1939 and KCIE in 1946; he was elected an honorary Fellow of Trinity Hall in 1970. His wife died in 1976, and he was survived by their two sons.

# Raja Bhalindra Singh of Patiala

RAJA BHALINDRA SINGH OF PATIALA (who died on April 16 1992, aged 81) dominated India's sporting scene for more than four decades.

A scion of the most powerful royal family in the Punjab, he was a toweringly handsome Sikh with a passionate belief in the amateur sporting ethic. So it was fitting that he should have become the elder statesman of the International Olympic Committee, to which he was elected in 1947.

Raja Bhalindra Singh was born on August 9 1910 at Patiala's royal Sikh household, some 150 miles north of New Delhi, and nicknamed "Prince Peter". His father, Maharaja Bhupinder Singh, was accorded a 19-gun salute by the Raj since Patiala was the largest of the Punjab's princely states.

After entering into alliance with the British Governor-General, Lord Minto, in 1809 Patiala aided the Raj during the Gurkha Wars, the Indian Mutiny, the Afghan Wars and later the two world wars.

Maharaja Bhupinder Singh, who decreed that "wine, fish, meat, alcohol and plenty of sex were good for the soul", entertained the Prince of Wales at his Motibagh Palace in 1921 and took him for a duck shoot during which a plethora of birds was dispatched. The Maharaja was renowned for his sexual and sporting prowess. He had 365 wives and was master of the Patiala Tigers, the world's highest-handicap polo team. He was also a devoted cricketer, a talent he passed to Bhalindra, his second son, and maintained a permanent box at Lord's.

While Yaduvendra, his elder brother, succeeded as Maharajah, Bhalindra was accorded the title of Raja, a style he continued to use after royal nomenclature was abolished by Mrs Gandhi.

He was educated at Aitcheson College for Chiefs in Lahore, and Magdalene College, Cambridge, where he was given a trial in the seniors' match, when his bowling enabled him to take five wickets for 40 runs. On the strength of this he was included in the team against Northamptonshire, his only first-class match in England, in which he scored two and seven runs. However, he played 12 matches for Southern Punjab and Patiala and, as a middle-order, right-hand batsman in 1943–4, made 392, including 109 for Southern Punjab against Northern India; he also took 25 wickets for an average of 27 runs.

Singh also served as Home and Education Secretary in Patiala during the Second World War. A decade after all Indian princely states were merged to form the Union of States in 1948, he was elected to serve Punjab's legislative assembly for four years.

A member of the organising committee of the inaugural Asian Games held in New Delhi in 1951, he became President of the Amateur Athletic Federation of India two years later. In 1959, he followed his brother, father and his grandfather in becoming head of the Indian Olympic Association, staying in the post until 1975 and then, after a five-year gap, returning to it for a further five-year stint, during which he was one of the principal organisers of the 1982 Asian Games in New Delhi.

Singh feared professionalism would kill popular interest in sport, producing robots running up and down breaking records. In later years, he somewhat modified this view and came to accept that without professionalism sporting movements, especially the Olympics, could not grow.

But he remained a fierce opponent of the politicisation of sport. In 1968 he threatened to pull the Indian contingent out of the Asian Games in Bangkok after overt attempts by government officials to interfere in selection procedures.

Singh also took a close interest in hockey and athletics, particularly cross-country running. In his later years he lamented the falling standards of hockey in India, as the national team declined from a position where it had consistently won the Olympic gold medal to one where it failed to qualify for the finals. "Indian hockey", he said, "is dying in colleges and universities, and unless these bases are rebuilt India cannot hope to win in any arena."

A legendary host, who entertained guests with an old-world style and charm, he was an excellent cook. He would spend hours preparing dishes created from recipes handed down by ancestors, who had once maintained the most lavish tables in the subcontinent. His one regret, he said, was that he had never written a cookery book. He was a keen rider and tennis player as well as a lover of Indian classical music. His earthy humour endeared him to athletes, and helped him to deal with obdurate bureaucrats.

He was survived by his second wife, a son and three daughters.

## Allan Arthur

ALLAN ARTHUR (who died on May 22 1998, aged 82) was the sixth generation of his family to work in India, joining the Indian Civil Service from Cambridge in 1937 and becoming Deputy Commissioner of Attock District, based at Campbellpur, seven years later.

*Arthur showing Pandit Nehru around the ruins of Multan after the riots of March 1947.*

The district included the great Mughal fort which dominates the point at which the Grand Trunk Road crosses the Indus, the boundary of the Punjab and the North West Frontier Province, and Arthur greatly enjoyed touring on horseback when excitement was generated by the obstreperous Abdul Ghaffar Khan, leader of the anti-British Red Shirts.

In 1946, he was made Deputy Commissioner of Multan, an area of 6,000 square miles with a population of 1.5 million; as its 31-year-old ruler, he was little older than Alexander the Great when he was wounded assaulting Multan in 326 BC. The region's population was predominantly Muslim, and no sooner had the League's agitation subsided than fanatical Hindu and Sikh leaders provoked violence, resulting in communal riots of great ferocity in March 1947. At one point Arthur found himself incongruously wearing morning dress at a police station with a howling mob outside. The military had been summoned and, as there was nothing more to be done until rescue arrived, he positioned himself in full view of the mob and calmly read the newspaper. The tension eased, and the ringleader later admitted to Arthur that the rioters' will had been sapped by this display of British phlegm, which later earned him an MBE.

Allan James Vincent Arthur was born in Calcutta on September 16 1915. As a baby he narrowly missed being torpedoed by a German U-boat in the Mediterranean when travelling to England. At the end of the Great War his family returned to India, where Allan remained until, aged nine and still happily illiterate, he was dispatched to a prep school in Kent. Thereafter he saw his mother every other year, his father every four or five years. He spent the holidays with aunts and cousins.

On being sent to Rugby, he was advised to take up swimming to strengthen a weak heart. So keenly did he do so that he became captain of swimming and then, at Magdalene College, Cambridge, captain of the university team. In 1937 he swam in the Universities Games in Paris.

On first arriving in the Punjab, he was sent for training to Amritsar, his only posting in what, after partition, became India. He was initially impatient with the prejudices of the British ruling class, but this was tempered by an appreciation of the heavy workload of the district officer and the benefits of British administration.

After 18 months in Amritsar, Arthur was transferred to Lahore as a first class magistrate and personal assistant to the Deputy Commissioner. In April 1941 he was appointed sub-divisional officer of the hill station at Murree, where he progressed to try murder cases. Nine months later he was posted to Kasur, where an old Mughal tomb served as his courtroom.

Following Independence, he was asked to stay on by the governments of both Pakistan and India; the rajah of one small hill-state asked him to be his *diwan* (chief minister). But Arthur decided, in common with most of his colleagues, to leave.

The next year he was accepted by the Sudan Political Service with his ICS seniority intact, subject to passing exams in Law and Arabic. Arthur arrived in Sudan in January 1949 to take over almost at once as District Commissioner, Khartoum. The most important project with which he became involved was a gigantic operation of slum clearance and social resettlement in Khartoum South. This initially aroused fierce opposition from landlords, but was greeted with enthusiastic approval on completion.

In 1951, Arthur was appointed District Commissioner at Shendi, a rural area of 15,000 square miles on the Nile. His role there was broadly similar to that in Khartoum, but tribal quarrels and land disputes formed much of the legal casework while violent crime also kept him busy. His severe but consistent approach to sentencing recidivists earned him the sobriquet "Abu Khamsa" – "Father of the Five Years".

Three years later, Arthur became Deputy Governor of the Northern Province. But his contract was soon terminated as the country prepared for independence in 1956; and, with reservations, he accepted his father-in-law's offer of a job with the family firm of sugar merchants. It proved to be an opportune time to join the business, as wartime controls were being dismantled and the market was ripe for expansion. Arthur's energetic and affable approach, together with his integrity and canniness, led him ultimately to become chairman of the company from 1972 to 1975.

In later life, he concentrated on local politics, being Mayor of Chelmsford in 1977 and, from 1978 to 1985, Vice Lord Lieutenant of Essex. When he made a last trip to India in 1997, for the 50th anniversary of Independence, as president of the Indian Civil Service (Retired) Association, he thought the country little changed.

Tall and broad-shouldered, with an imposing presence and little self-doubt, Allan Arthur was a decisive and highly effective administrator who enjoyed life for both its challenges and pleasures. He married first, in 1940 (dissolved 1948), Joan Heape. He married secondly, in 1949, Dawn Drake; they had two sons and two daughters.

~

# Geoffrey Kendal

GEOFFREY KENDAL (who died on May 22 1998, aged 88) promoted, with his wife Laura Liddell, one of the most romantic endeavours in theatrical history: a touring company that criss-crossed India for more than 20 years offering professional productions of Shakespeare and other English classics in colleges and towns as well as the remotest villages.

The adventure inspired the James Ivory–Ismail Merchant film *Shakespeare Wallah* (1965), which featured the Kendal family. But while the film showed a company struggling to hold audiences as the imperial tide receded and the lure of the cinema increased, Geoffrey Kendal never lost his belief that India provided "the best audience for Shakespeare in the world".

His enthusiasm as an actor-manager sustained the discomfort and strain of constant travel through India: by car over the roughest roads, by train in overcrowded carriages during floods, monsoons and unbearable heat. To let off steam he would break into extraordinary rages which his family would insist on regarding as purely theatrical. Fortunately Laura Liddell was not only a superb actress, but also a calming influence, who made light of combining her peripatetic theatrical career with bringing up their two daughters, Jennifer and Felicity. The two tasks were hardly separable: Jennifer had made her stage debut in England, while still a baby, as the changeling boy in *A Midsummer Night's Dream*; 12 years later in India, Felicity succeeded her in the same part.

As the girls grew up it seemed more likely that Jennifer would become the star, for Felicity treated the whole business as a frivolous game. In the event Jennifer married the Indian actor Shashi Kapoor, with whom she helped to found the Prithvi Theatre in Bombay. Before her early death in 1984 she had won acclaim as the lonely Anglo-Indian schoolmistress in her husband's film *36, Chowringee Lane* (1981). Felicity Kendal, meanwhile, had become a leading performer in Britain, both on television and in the theatre. But her beginnings remained etched in her mind. "I remember the hard slog," she wrote, "and the fun, the constant laughter and jokes that helped to keep us going when the adventure got a bit uphill. And I remember my parents' determination to keep going: never to give up or settle down or heaven forbid buy a house, but to continue to the next town, the next season, the next generation."

The harsh touring life under the constant threat of financial disaster would occasionally be interspersed by the lavish hospitality of such hosts as the Nizam of Hyderabad, who put at their disposal not merely a princely set of apartments, but also his Pontiac and chauffeur. At

Travancore the Kendals were greeted by a red carpet and garlands and taken to their island lodgings in the Maharajah's barge. In general, though, the company had to make do with the absence not only of habitable lodging, but adequate stage facilities. The Kendals were thus obliged to rely on their principal virtue as actors: an old-fashioned capacity to speak their lines clearly and comprehensibly.

The company, Shakespeareana, inspired many Indian recruits who went on to make the theatre their career. "Let Shakespeare keep India and Britain united!" proclaimed an admirer, and for a quarter of a century after the end of the Raj the Kendals fulfilled that ideal.

Geoffrey Kendal was born Geoffrey Bragg at Kendal, Westmorland, on September 7 1909, the son of a clerk at a woollen mill and a schoolteacher. He discovered his vocation in amateur dramatics, and when Sir Frank Benson's company toured in the area was employed as a spear-carrier in *Richard II*. But instead of offering a permanent job, Benson confined himself to a recommendation to keep fit: "Do you play hockey?" he demanded.

So Bragg began his career in an engineering company. Sacked, he succeeded at 19 in becoming assistant stage manager with the Morecambe Rep. His experiences of this period, reminiscent of J. B. Priestley's *Good Companions* or Mr Crummle's troupe in *Nicholas Nickleby*, are vividly caught in his autobiography The *Shakespeare Wallah* (1986).

Bragg's breakthrough came when he joined the Edward Dunstan Shakespeare Company, which staged the Bard in small towns. At first he feared the worst. "A more motley crew I had never seen anywhere," he wrote. "My heart sank. Had I really let myself be dragged down to the depths simply because of a romantic notion to play Shakespeare?" He soon discovered his mistake. "All my experience to date was as nothing to what I was learning now," he continued. "These were the real pros, real gods that I had fallen among at last." Better still, one of them was Laura Liddell.

In 1933, when the company temporarily disbanded, Geoffrey Bragg and Laura Liddell decided to form their own troupe. After marrying at Gretna Green, they persuaded their parents to lend them £200, and founded the Bragg-Liddell Company. About this time Bragg changed his name to Kendal. The company's first season, at the Connaught Theatre, Worthing, proved a disaster; and they did little better in Scotland or the north of England.

On the outbreak of the Second World War, Kendal volunteered as an engineer in the Merchant Navy, but then he and Laura both joined ENSA, the organisation that entertained the troops. In this way they had their first glimpse of India, embarking on a six-month tour in the thriller *Gaslight*.

Back in Britain, they realised that the prospect for touring companies was grim, and determined to return to India to play Shakespeare in schools and colleges. Thereafter the Kendals felt unsettled whenever they were out of India, and were always anxious to discover ways and means to return.

Their luck changed markedly when they met the Earl and Countess Mountbatten on Malta. Shortly afterwards they were back in India, being received by Pandit Nehru. They also toured Hong Kong, Singapore and Malaya, but always preferred Indian audiences. In the 1960s, after both daughters had left the company, they established themselves in Delhi with a 90-minute programme which they took round schools and colleges.

Not until the 1970s did the Kendals leave India. In England they showed that their appetite for touring remained unsatisfied, and still seized every opportunity to return to their old haunts.

They gave their last performance in India in 1985, when they played in *Dear Liar* at the Prithvi Theatre in Bombay, and were feted by three generations of fans. In 1991 they received the Sangeet Nataki Academy Award for services to the arts in India. Laura Liddell died the following year.

## Nirad Chaudhuri

NIRAD CHAUDHURI (who died at Oxford on August 1 1999, aged 101), was a prodigiously learned writer with the outspoken belief that Britain's abandonment of India in 1947 was the most shameful act in its history. Delighting in the paradox of such sentiments issuing from an Indian, he severely criticised the snobbery and narrowmindedness of British rule yet castigated, even more forcefully, the venality and corruption which made modern Indians unsuited to self-government.

His love affair with Britain was all the more remarkable because he only visited it for the first time at the age of 57, when he was the guest of the British Council and the BBC for five weeks. The result was *A Passage to England* (1959), a series of evocative essays about his experience as a well-read, sceptical brown man who sought and found "the reality of Timeless England".

*Chaudhuri attending his first cricket match at Oxford at the age of 92.*
(Simon Walker)

The son of a small landowner and magistrate, Nirad Chandra Chaudhuri was born at Kishorganj in East Bengal (now Bangladesh) on November 23 1897. Queen Victoria's Diamond Jubilee had just been celebrated; the Empire was at its apogee.

Young Nirad had no contact with either Englishmen or anglicised Indians, but he was so steeped in English history and literature that, at the age of 10, a neighbour found him walking along a country road reciting Nelson's signal before the Battle of Trafalgar: "England expects every man will do his duty."

He went to Calcutta University and then into the military accounts department of the Government of India. But, chancing on Matthew Arnold's poem *The Scholar Gipsy*, he threw up a career for the perils of freelance journalism. He wrote articles and edited a literary journal. Unlike most young journalists, however, he also continued to study rigorously until he was not only steeped in Sanskrit and Prakrit texts, but equally familiar with English, French and Classical literature.

To the surprise of his family, when he reached his thirties he asked his father to choose him a bride in the Indian tradition, only specifying that she must be intelligent and from the right class. When he was first alone with Amiya Dhar after their marriage in 1932, he was reassured to discover that, although his bride did not then share his love of Western classical music, she knew how to spell Beethoven. They had three children and remained together until her death in 1994.

To make ends meet, Chaudhuri became literary assistant to a reclusive ornithologist who only expected him to talk, and secretary to Sarat Bose, the barrister brother of the nationalist leader Subhas Chandra Bose. This brought him into contact with leading politicians. He was not impressed. Gandhi was negative and fuelled by hatred; the anglicised Nehru's political views seemed to be derived from Hampstead, and his artistic taste from Heal's of Tottenham Court Road.

When Sarat Bose was imprisoned in 1941, Chaudhuri took a full-time job with All-India Radio in Delhi. Wearing Western dress for the first time, he had nominal charge of Bengali broadcasts, but devoted most of his energies to writing a regular war commentary in English for translation into India's other languages. Despite occasional incidents of racial prejudice shown by white staff, the war made Chaudhuri an Englishman in every way but birth, he recalled. He was so impressed by Winston Churchill's wartime speeches that he placed the great man's photograph alongside a reproduction of the *Mona Lisa* in his study.

When Japan entered the war, many Indians forecast a Japanese invasion. This led him to tell his wife that, if they were attacked, he would kill her and their three sons, set their house on fire and die fighting. "My wife trusted my judgment," he recalled. "In any case she was not the person to take hypothetical dangers seriously."

By the end of the war, Chaudhuri was so westernised that he even began to develop a discriminating taste for claret. But he was under no delusion about the damage done to Britain by the election of the Labour government in 1945. He was so concerned that he sent an article to *The Daily Telegraph* warning about the folly of appeasing nationalists; it was not published.

Chaudhuri finally lost his job after the publication of *The Auto-biography of an Unknown Indian* (1951), which described his life up to 1921 with the assurance and pace of a great Victorian. There were laudatory reviews in London from such literary luminaries as Harold

Nicolson, John Raymond and Sir John Squire, while Churchill told his family that it was one of the best books he had ever read. In India it was reviled by all but the British-run *Statesman* of Calcutta. Not the least reason was its dedication: "To the memory of the British Empire in India, which conferred subjecthood on us but withheld citizenship; to which yet every one of us threw out the challenge: *Civis Britannicus sum*, because all that was good and living within us was made, shaped and quickened by the same British rule."

On going freelance again, he found that his fellow countrymen felt little inclination to take work from a troublemaker, who really had been a little-known Indian. Staff at the British High Commission remained aloof. He stayed afloat financially only through a job translating a regular newsletter into English for the French embassy in Delhi.

However, with his new reputation, he caused a mild sensation among British readers by daring to attack the political and social accuracy of E. M. Forster's novel *A Passage to India* in the magazine *Encounter*. News that Forster, who had been kind to him on his visit to Cambridge, was deeply hurt led Chaudhuri to postpone a sequel examining the book as a work of fiction; but he held privately that it was the worst novel about India ever written by an Englishman.

Chaudhuri caused even greater offence in India with *The Continent of Circe* (1965). In this he argued, as a lapsed member of the Hindu faith, that Hindus were a European race on whom the Indian climate had exercised such an adverse influence that they contained a streak of insanity. The book won the Duff Cooper Memorial Prize in London. At the presentation ceremony Field Marshal Sir Claude Auchinleck declared that it would have completely changed his attitude to India if he had been given it at the start of his career in 1903.

Despite being 72, Chaudhuri had strong reason, therefore, to move to Britain in 1970, where his son Kirti, historian of the East India Company, was a lecturer in Asian Economic History at London University. Chaudhuri said that the British climate wrought an immediate improvement in his health. He took a semi-detached Victorian house in Oxford and slipped smoothly into a life of two cultures while studying the Indian manuscripts in the Bodleian Library.

He became a familiar figure in the town, walking around in cloth cap and tweed sports jacket, while at home he continued to wear his familiar *dhoti*, rising before six each morning to begin his four-hour working day. If writing in Bengali he would squat in bare feet on his study floor; but for English he sat on a chair to use a portable typewriter on a table, carefully sounding out in his mind what he was going to say in Macaulayan English.

Although Chaudhuri proved a continuing fascination for television documentary-makers his views could hardly have been less fashionable. He took a distinctly dim view of "Swinging London"; he dubbed the Permissive Society "the Permanent Rut". Even the Falklands War could not sway his genial pessimism since he predicted that Mrs Thatcher's victory would prove no more significant than that of Queen Boadicea.

Chaudhuri's study in 1974 of the 19th-century Oxford scholar Friedrich Max Muller demonstrated his extraordinary comprehension of British and Indian civilisations. It was followed by *Clive of India* (1975). This notably unprejudiced study of an always controversial figure came to few surprising conclusions, except that Clive was temperamentally the closest figure in English history to Napoleon.

As he got older, Chaudhuri lost none of his assurance. When his second volume of autobiography *Thy Hand, Great Anarch!* came out in 1988, three years after he had completed the writing, it ran to almost 1,000 pages. He had resolutely refused to cut any of the digressions, whether fascinating or not, saying the book could come out in full posthumously, if necessary.

Not the least pleasure of his last years was the respect paid to him in India by a younger generation which was now disenchanted by the nationalist leaders who had gained power in 1947. He found a readership for three volumes in Bengali on the decline of the region's culture and, claimed, with great satisfaction, to command the largest fees for a journalist on the subcontinent.

He also took to writing elegant letters to *The Daily Telegraph* in which he reflected on the follies of British attitudes to race relations, spoke up for a classical education and castigated his fellow Indians – with whom he had little contact – for showing no interest in European painting or opera. While declining to make a public attack, he declared in private that Salman Rushdie, author of the notorious novel, *The Satanic Verses*, was "a low scribbling adventurer". Even Lord Tebbit's cricket test for the suitability of immigrants failed to ruffle his composure. An appreciation of *The Wind in the Willows*, Stilton cheese and opera would be surer tests of Englishness, he wrote. When

*The Sunday Telegraph* invited him to watch his first cricket match at the age of 92, he made an elegant figure in a well-cut suit.

His spirits were high as he approached 100, for which he could offer no explanation since he had no expectations of an after-life. He took immense pride in the fact that his last book in English *Three Horsemen of the New Apocalypse*, written in his 99th year, was published three days before his 100th birthday. In it, Chaudhuri predicted that all civilisation would be destroyed in the next 200–400 years because of the way that televisual culture destroyed all natural cultures.

His views took little account of the economic factors with which historians like to prove that a country's decline is inevitable. But believing that the British Empire in India was even greater than that of Rome, he recognised that the heritage of Britain would remain the dominating cultural beacon in its former Empire long after the last redcoat had departed.

A tiny, frail-looking man, with a manner suggesting a hummingbird, he was appointed an honorary CBE in 1992, yet suffered surprising neglect from Oxford. He received an honorary doctorate at 92 and was given a party for his 100th birthday by Trinity, but he was never given dining rights at a college, perhaps because of the relentless flow of his conversation. This worried him little: "When you realise that you are going to leave this world via the Oxford crematorium, dining rights are a trifle."

~

# Iris Portal

IRIS PORTAL, the writer Iris Butler (who died on November 9 2002, aged 97) was the younger sister of the Conservative minister "Rab" Butler, and excelled as a biographer after a kaleidoscope of experiences in India.

Her best book, *The Eldest Brother: The Marquess Wellesley 1760–1842* was published in 1973. Wellesley was Governor-General of India, Foreign Secretary and Lord Lieutenant of Ireland, yet was outshone at every turn by his younger brother, the Duke of Wellington. Perhaps as a consequence, he tended to view his own triumphs with distaste and bemoaned the fields he had never conquered.

The first full biography of Wellesley since 1895, the book drew on a trunk full of unpublished letters written by the Marquess to his mistress Hyacinthe, which had been lent to Iris Portal by Field Marshal

Lord Carver, a kinsman of the Wellesleys. Philip Ziegler wrote that its great strength was that it laid bare Wellesley's private life and related it convincingly to the public image. Correlli Barnett chose the book "without hesitation" as his Book of the Year, praising it for delivering Wellesley "from the colossal shadow of his brother" and presenting him "as a fascinating blend of ability and vanity".

Iris Mary Butler was born at Simla on June 15 1905, the daughter of the future Sir Montagu Butler, who had passed top in the Indian Civil Service exams of 1896, and his wife Ann, whose Scottish Presbyterian family had Indian connections stretching back to the 17th century.

Two and a half years younger than Rab, Iris later complained that while she was regularly smacked by their austere Aberdonian nanny "Rab never was." When they were small, their father was Settlement Officer at Kotah, which entailed camping throughout the cold weather, and moving from village to village to assess the land. The family followed with a train of camels carrying tents, furniture and crockery, and Iris and Rab in a cart pulled by two ponies, Peter and Polly. Their parents rode everywhere on horseback, sometimes switching to elephants to cross rivers.

Each day at sunrise, the children would be bundled into quilted Rajput dressing gowns, and taken to the next stopping place. "An advance party would have struck a few tents for us," Iris recalled, "and we would get there in time for a late breakfast. Then my father would set up his table for petitions and we would be turned out with our toys to play among the tents, with nanny keeping an eye on us."

In the evening, the parents would go out to shoot something extra for meals. Iris remembered being made to stand with a rifle by a bear which had been shot, a frightening experience because she was unsure that it was dead: "The smell of the bear and the cordite of the rifle made a great impression on me. One had toy bears and it seemed so sad that the bear should be shot." In his memoirs, Rab recalled how the Maharao of Kotah, a kindly figure known to his people as "the Breadgiver", had given him and Iris four splendid stuffed animals on wheels called Bear, Lion, Elley and Dog.

The camping ended in 1909 when their father was posted to Lahore. Then it was parties with other British children, and picnics in formal Mughal gardens. There Iris's sister Dor (the geographer and writer Dorothy Middleton) and Jock (who was killed with the RAF during the Second World War) were born.

In 1911 Iris, her siblings and their mother went to England to live at Bourton Manse, on the Butler family estate near Shrivenham, Berkshire. The girls went to a boarding school on the south coast, but although both showed marked ability, there was no suggestion that they should go to university; all the money was needed to send Rab, and later Jock, to Cambridge. Instead, after being presented at Court, Iris returned to a very social life in India.

During the next two summers at Simla, Iris Butler never thought about anything but amusing herself: "It was excessively gay. My record was 26 nights dancing running, at the end of which I had to attend an official dinner that my mother was giving and was severely reprimanded for falling asleep in the middle when talking to a very woolly old judge." Since rickshaws were deemed too extravagant she rode everywhere, with her dress hitched around her waist, and always met the same people. "Everyone knew rather too much about everyone else's affairs, and it was a staple topic of conversation what was going on, who was going out with so-and-so."

In 1926 Gervas Portal, of Gardner's Horse, became ADC to her father, who was by then Governor of the Central Provinces. Portal hoped to shoot tiger in the Seeone jungle immortalised by Kipling. He shot two, fell in love with Iris and married her in 1927. The couple's first four years of married life were spent at Meerut, where the Sepoy Mutiny had begun in 1857. Iris Portal recalled: "On the gates of the bungalows were plaques which said, 'Here Mrs So and So and her three children were killed and thrown down a well.'"

In the early 1930s Gervas Portal commanded the Governor's bodyguard in Bombay, where his wife immersed herself in welfare work among the young soldiers' families, to the consternation of other memsahibs. Subsequent postings took them to Poona, Bihar and Hyderabad, where he became Comptroller of the Household of the younger son of the Nizam.

One day Iris Portal was taken by her friend Princess Niloufer, wife of the Nizam's younger son, to the palace basement. There stood rows of tarpaulined lorries with flat tyres but loaded with precious stones and gold coins. This was part of the Nizam's plan for removing some of his wealth from the country in the event of a revolution; but he had then lost interest in the risk.

Around this time Iris Portal fell from a pony trap and fractured her skull. During her long convalescence, she was visited by another friend, the Begum Shah Nawaz, who sacrificed a black cockerel in her bedroom to speed her recovery.

After the outbreak of war, Iris Portal began nursing in Delhi, then followed her husband to Ranchi to work in a military hospital on the border with Burma. The conditions were grim, but she only had to leave the operating theatre once when the surgeon said: "Drop that leg in the bucket, nurse."

She finally left India in 1943 on a ship which had to dodge U-boats. When her husband followed in 1946, they settled in the wilds of north Norfolk, where she was active in the St John Ambulance, the Royal British Legion, as County Commissioner of the Guides, and on the county council's education committee. She also wrote and reviewed for the *Eastern Daily Press*. At Christmas, there would often be Indian friends to stay; they loved coming, although in the unheated house, they would have gladly joined the family in taking it in turns to change in the airing cupboard.

After Gervas died in 1961 and their daughters had grown up, Iris wrote her first book, *Rule of Three* (1967), a study of Queen Anne and her favourites, Sarah Churchill and Abigail Hill. Nigel Dennis was fiercely critical in *The Sunday Telegraph*, taking the author to task for her purple prose and "wonderfully confused passion for similes that are often funny but never quite exact". But the book sold well, and she was soon at work on *The Viceroy's Wife: Letters of Alice, Countess of Reading, from India 1921–1925* (1969), which was far more favourably received. *The Daily Telegraph*'s critic praised her "admirable introduction" and her running commentary, "which while skilfully interpolated is never intrusive".

Despite her limited formal education, Iris Portal had an encyclopaedic knowledge of English literature, and it was a brave person who sought to out-quote her on Shakespeare, Kipling, Thackeray or Shelley. She was deeply interested in eastern theology, but was most notable for her concern for others; never forgetting a birthday or a name, and always wanting to rush to the support of anyone in trouble.

# Jill Lowe

JILL LOWE (who died on August 19 2004, aged 67) swapped life in Pimlico for marriage to a peasant farmer in the mustard fields of Rajasthan.

By the time she was in her early fifties, Jill Lowe had brought up five children in London, survived bankruptcy and divorce, and was working as a tourist guide. One winter she went travelling in India and ended up on a driving tour of Rajasthan, for which she was the only taker. Her driver, Lal Singh Yadav, a widower 10 years her junior, proved an informative and charming guide, and she soon felt "a magical, inexorable cord" drawing her to him. Their clandestine trysts surprised her almost as much as they shocked the staff at the hotels in which they stayed.

By the time Yadav made an unscheduled detour to his family farm, Jill Lowe was smitten. She met his mother, brothers, sisters-in-law, uncles, aunts, nephews, nieces, cousins and their children, who lived at the compound, in addition to other relatives in the village. There was no furniture at the farm except for the charpoys on which they sat and slept. Power cuts meant there was nothing to do after dark. The family washed where the water buffaloes drank, and the nearest telephone was 15 miles away. On her first night there she shared a room with Yadav, his nephew and a baby. The lavatory was the mustard field, which was especially public after the harvest, and she was constantly pestered by inquisitive children. When one of her daughters came to stay several years later, she shared a room with 27 others.

Among many alien customs in her new life, Lowe learned not to kiss Yadav in front of his sister, to touch his eldest brother's feet in greeting and to cook and clean while Yadav loitered at the bus stop drinking whisky with his friends. She put up with the contempt of those Indians who considered her liaison with a mere driver outrageous, and survived almost being lynched after Yadav was involved in a road accident.

But the sheer strangeness of the environment entranced her. Each summer she went back to London to see her family and to earn money since Yadav had lost his part-time job as a taxi driver and showed no inclination to find another. In the autumn she returned to India, where she and Yadav would set off by Jeep on long and unpredictable journeys around the country. They set up a travel company under the name Safaris in India, offering a 40-day driving tour between Delhi and Kanyakumari. But the venture folded after Yadav fell for one of their clients.

Jill Lowe and Yadav were married in 1993, having visited a Brahmin to establish an "auspicious" date. They bought a necklace (the Indian equivalent of a wedding ring) at a bakery-cum-jeweller and married at the Chausath Yogini Temple in Nagpur.

Many of her British friends remained bemused by the path she had chosen. But if there were moments when she despaired of her new husband and her adopted country, Lowe never doubted "the peace of mind and freedom from worry" which they offered her. She remained obsessed by Yadav, and he by her. His contradictions reflected those of his country: he was superstitious yet secular, unflappable and fatalistic, and generally optimistic, though with depressive tendencies. He was extraordinarily generous but would quibble over a rupee; his acts of selfishness were tempered by his undiluted charm. He loved an Englishwoman but refused to eat English food. He adored all children, but lived apart from his own. Although an intensely lovable companion when he was around, he was often absent for long stretches.

Jill Lowe was born in London on July 31 1937. Her grandfather, Francis Lowe, had made a fortune building terraces in Birmingham before becoming MP for Edgbaston, chairman of the Conservative Party and Father of the House of Commons. He was offered a peerage, which his wife bade him refuse on the ground that they "lacked a place in the country"; but he accepted a baronetcy. Jill's father, Arthur, represented Britain in the Davis Cup and was runner-up in the Men's Doubles at Wimbledon in 1921.

She was educated (hopelessly by her account) and spent a year in Italy before returning home to become a debutante. At the Oxford and Cambridge Boat Race she met her future first husband, Peter Gibbons, a trainee barrister; she was 20 when they married in 1957. Converting to Roman Catholicism, she had four daughters and a son. But after 16 years her husband went bankrupt, the marriage broke down, the bailiffs claimed the house and many of their possessions; after a nervous breakdown she thought about committing suicide.

Things began to look up, though, when she told the Headmaster of Downside, Dom Raphael Appleby, that she would have to remove her son. He smiled and said: "I see no reason why 499 other boys cannot take care of the 500th." The nuns at St Mary's, Shaftesbury, where her daughters were at school, went further, providing her with a room and a job; her duties ranged from sewing to escorting sixth-form girls to dances at neighbouring boys' schools and ensuring they all returned.

Sister John saved altar wine for her because "you worldly people need a cocktail before Sunday lunch", and when she left after two years the Reverend Mother invited her to a farewell dinner that consisted of bacon, baked beans and vintage claret.

Returning to London, Jill Lowe bought a dilapidated property in Pimlico, where she took in lodgers. To support her children, she became a freelance guide and worked at the British Museum and Harrods. In 1989, when her youngest daughter left home, she let out the flat and embarked on the trip on which she met Yadav. She chose India because it was cheap and she wanted to prove to her former boyfriend, who had left her "for a house-sitting job in Notting Hill Gate", that she could cope in the East.

In 2003 Jill Lowe's memoir, *Yadav: A Roadside Love Story*, which was published by Penguin to great acclaim in India, was described by William Dalrymple as "a remarkable, honest, funny and frequently moving love story".

—

## P. V. Narasimha Rao

P. V. NARASIMHA RAO (who died on December 23 2004, aged 83) was the Prime Minister of India between 1991 and 1996, when he took the considerable risk of lifting trade barriers and opening up an over-protected country to free trade. The gamble paid off. If India, along with China, seems to be well on the way to becoming one of the economic powerhouses of the 21st century, much of the credit is due to Rao. In introducing his reforms, he was ably assisted by his quiet but focused Finance Minister, Manmohan Singh.

Although economic liberalisation had started with his predecessors, Indira Gandhi and her son Rajiv, Rao accelerated the pace when he took over as India's ninth Prime Minister on June 21 1991, a week before his 70th birthday. By Indian standards this was not particularly old, but he had been in semi-retirement for the previous 18 months and had packed his large library in preparation for a life of scholarly seclusion in Hyderabad.

Rao was brought back from the political wilderness by the assassination of Rajiv Gandhi, who had held power, lost it and seemed to be on his way back to the prime ministership when he was blown up by a female Tamil suicide-bomber during an election campaign. Since his mother, too, had been assassinated in 1984, there were real

*Rao was infuriated to be asked by an Indian in London if an erotic passage in his novel was based on imagination or memory.* (AP/Ajit Kumar)

worries that Indian democracy might be derailed.

With the country in turmoil, the Congress Party turned to Rao as a stop-gap leader at a time when India was facing its worst economic crisis since Independence in 1947. Inflation was running at 17 per cent, and the country had some £50 billion of foreign debt. But, having won the election, Rao stayed on to drag the Indian economy from the old to the new.

In his personal demeanour he was an austere, erudite man with a long history of service to Nehru as well to his daughter and grandson, having served as foreign and defence minister as well as chief minister of his own state, Andhra Pradesh. This explains why the country was so shocked when he was convicted in 2000 of bribing four MPs to support his government in a no-confidence motion in 1993. He was given a three-year prison sentence, the first prime minister to be thus humiliated; but, because of the time taken over the appeal, he spent no time in jail. A court later quashed the charges against both Rao and his co-accused, but his reputation remained tarnished.

After stepping down as Prime Minister, Rao wrote a long English-language novel, *The Insider*. Although a dense book about land reform, it was billed as "the novel that tells the explosive truth about Indian politics". But it attracted some notoriety because of a sexually explicit passage, which seemed completely out of character with his dour, unsmiling image. When he launched the book at the Nehru Centre in London, an Indian woman was unwise enough to ask: "Mr Prime Minister, is the sexy passage from your imagination or your memory?"

Rao angrily replied: "I never thought NRIs [Non-Resident Indians] could be so despicable."

In recognition of Rao's international stature, Madame Tussaud's made a waxwork model of him, one of only a very few Indians who have been so honoured. But when he stood next to his model for the unveiling, as is the custom, a British journalist remarked unkindly: "The wax model looks livelier." Later, when Rao was going through the bribery scandal, Madame Tussaud's removed the model in favour of one of the Bollywood superstar Amitabh Bachchan.

Pamulaparti Venkata Narasimha Rao was born on June 28 1921 at Karimnagar in Andhra Pradesh, where his Brahmin family had a large farm. After taking degrees in science and law at Osmania and Nagpur universities, P. V., as he was known, became a reporter with a weekly newspaper.

In 1957 he was elected to the Andhra Pradesh legislative assembly, where he was to retain his seat for the next 20 years. In 1962 he became a minister in the state government, and nine years later was made Chief Minister. In this post he put a limit on the size of agricultural holdings, alienating large landowners in the process, even though he himself gave up all but 120 of his 1,200 acres of property (thus providing some dull material for his novel). In 1974, he was appointed general secretary of the Congress Party's national governing committee, and three years later he was elected to the Lok Sabha, the lower house of the Indian Parliament.

Rao backed Indira Gandhi after the Congress Party split into rival factions in 1969, and also when she imposed a two-year "state of emergency" in 1975. When she returned to power in 1980 he became her External Affairs Minister. Although he apparently disliked travelling, he was well-suited to the job in other respects, speaking seven Indian languages as well as English, French, Arabic, Spanish and Persian.

He had the tricky job of maintaining a close relationship with the Soviet Union, India's long-time ally, while expressing strong disapproval of the Russian invasion of Afghanistan. There was also the fall-out from the Iranian revolution, which overthrew the Shah and ushered in the ayatollahs. Next door in Pakistan, General Zia ul-Haq had started the process of Islamisation which was to lead in time to a more fundamentalist country and the emergence of the Taliban in Afghanistan. Still, Rao kept open channels of communication with Pakistan by visiting the country on several occasions and meeting its leaders.

In July 1984 he became Home Minister, responsible for the police and internal security. When Indira Gandhi was shot by her own Sikh bodyguards over the Indian Army's military action at the Golden Temple in Amritsar, her son Rajiv moved Rao to the Defence Ministry and then to the Ministry of Human Resource Development, where his responsibilities included education. In July 1986 he was given additional responsibility for health and family welfare before Rajiv Gandhi invited him to return to Foreign Affairs; he remained in that post until December 1989.

After Rajiv Gandhi's assassination 18 months later, for India's alleged interference in Sri Lanka, the Congress Party tried to persuade his widow, Sonia, to become its president. When she refused, Rao was offered the job as a compromise figure who could unite the party during the election campaign that had been interrupted by the murder. But, afterwards, it was clear that Rao was a serious candidate for not only party leader, but also Prime Minister.

Although he had undergone heart surgery, he was unanimously elected, and found himself head of a minority government. Rajiv Gandhi had begun the process of turning India into a free market economy, and Rao promised to continue in the same vein: "We owe it to ourselves, to our party, and to the country to implement [Gandhi's programme] to the hilt," he declared in his acceptance speech.

To deal with the crisis, Rao immediately advocated austerity measures. "We cannot tolerate waste, inefficiency, and indifference to quality, in the public sector or any other sector," he said. Interest rates were raised and the rupee devalued; farm subsidies were cut; regulatory controls were jettisoned while defence spending was cut and half of India's public sector, including the banks, was privatised. All his reforms, he said, were "part of a long process of liberalisation, bringing India into line with the changes, the opening up, in the rest of the world around us".

In 1996 Rao was defeated in the general election because of the persisting allegations of corruption. He was forced to resign as party president, and that December he was compelled to stand down as the Congress Party's parliamentary leader because of the scandal. Two years later Congress refused even to select him as a candidate in national elections because of his failure to stop the razing of the Babri mosque by Hindu zealots in 1992; then in 2000 came the bribery case in which he was accused of paying bribes totalling £545,000 to four

MPs in return for their supporting his government in a crucial no-confidence vote in July 1993. The MPs, who belonged to regional parties, had hidden the money in personal and party bank accounts, it was claimed. A case was lodged against Rao when one of them decided to give evidence in return for immunity from prosecution. He was briefly put under "house arrest" before being eventually cleared.

A widower for many years, Rao was survived by three sons and five daughters.

~

## Mildred Archer

MILDRED ARCHER (who died on February 4 2005, aged 93) played an important part with her husband, W. G. Archer, in reviving interest in the art of India after Independence in 1947.

When they returned home after more than a decade in Bihar province, where Bill Archer had served with the Indian Civil Service, he took charge of the Indian section of the Victoria and Albert Museum on being assured that he would have plenty of time to write books in office hours. But, when asked to catalogue "a few miscellaneous paintings" at the India Office Library in 1954, he was so busy that he suggested his wife instead.

During the next quarter century, Mildred Archer turned up a wealth of material which became the basis for a series of authoritative studies of the British, Hindu and Muslim painters, whose work varied according to locality and the different tastes of princely rulers, officials and military officers.

On arrival at the library in Whitehall, "Tim" Archer (as Mildred was known) was handed some tattered albums of paintings which had belonged to the East India Company, and given a stool in a small room where staff made the tea. As she worked away on a draining board, it occurred to her that the collection was surprisingly meagre for one that had been acquired over 150 years, and she started to look for more items. Poking around in corners and cupboards in rooms adjacent to the Reading Room, she came upon numerous dusty, brown-paper parcels containing largely unidentified portfolios of engravings and drawings on paper and mica.

She also found work by Chinese artists from Canton and sketches of Java collected by India's first Surveyor-General, which had been

*Mildred Archer enjoyed travelling in a basket carried by a tribesman in the Naga Hills when studying anthropology with her husband.*

stuffed up a chimney to prevent the soot falling down. In the "Iron Room", where printed books were stored in racks on rails suspended from the ceiling, she found 27 volumes sent home by the Marquess Wellesley, the Governor-General of India and elder brother of the 1st Duke of Wellington. The job was not without risk, since she could have been squashed between the careering racks; so the cry would go up, "Are you inside, Mrs Archer?"

The result was a steady stream of books, which impressed critics. When Terence Mullally reviewed *The Natural History Drawings in the Indian Office Library* for *The Daily Telegraph* in 1962 he wrote: "No professional art historian with a string of degrees from continental universities could have done the job better, but it remains a formidable achievement of the dedicated amateur."

Mildred Agnes Bell, the daughter of two teachers, was born on December 28 1911 and met her future husband just before going up to St Hilda's, Oxford, where she read history and enjoyed the left-wing ambience. The couple became engaged when Archer came home on leave, but they had to wait a further two years to wed because the Indian Civil Service disapproved of married junior staff. When she arrived in Bihar, where Bill was a district officer, Tim Archer had read E. M. Forster's *A Passage to India*, and was bristling with disapproval of the British community's fixation with club life and bridge; later she modified her criticism.

The couple went on tour for weeks at a time, attending village ceremonies and visiting places that they were later to recognise in pictures. They enjoyed the richness of Indian life, such as seeing an old woman pulling a piano strapped to her head, and having to tie a rope to tree trunks after their car's brakes failed going downhill.

While they were staying at Ranchi, Tim Archer was asked to stand in for some local schoolteachers, and was bemused to discover that she had to use Robert Louis Stevenson's *Child's Garden of Verses*. Fuming afterwards that the lines "And I can hear the thrushes singing / In the lilacs on the lawn" meant nothing to children who had never seen a thrush, she was persuaded to produce three textbooks, employing images familiar to Indian pupils.

On moving to Purnea, she took on an *ayah* to look after their young son and daughter. She started to borrow books from the Imperial Library in Calcutta and began to talk to the old families, who had once run profitable indigo plantations but now reminisced over silver teapots about "the good old days".

When Bill Archer was put in charge of the 1940 census in Bihar, they moved to Patna, where they became friends of the barrister P. C. Manuk, a collector of miniatures who prompted them to start collecting themselves. This eventually led to Tim's first book, *Patna Painting* (1947), the first study of the East India Company's art collection.

After the outbreak of war, the atmosphere in India became increasingly tense, and Bill found himself locking up old friends. When he and his wife visited one young woman in jail, they discovered that she had been sent by the Congress Party to investigate "the atrocities of Butcher Archer" following a riot in which some men had been killed; they gave her a copy of the *New Statesman*.

Then, shortly before Independence, Bill was transferred to the Naga hills, where he had the opportunity to indulge his anthropological interests among the tribes, who clung to their traditional ways so tenaciously that Tim found herself travelling in a basket on the back of a tribesman.

On returning to England, the Archers pursued their parallel careers, co-operating on books in which Bill supplied a dash of poetic flair that complemented Tim's methodical prose. Their work included *Indian Painting for the British* (1955), which is still the standard survey of the subject; *Tipoo's Tiger* (1959), an account of the celebrated musical sculpture that eats a British officer; *Indian Architecture and the British* (1968); *Indian Popular Painting* (1977) and *Indian and British Portraiture* (1979).

After Bill Archer's sudden death in 1979, Tim Archer continued to work on further books, co-operating with John Bastin, Ronald Lightbown and others. In addition to the articles and prefaces which she periodically wrote about the artists Thomas and William Daniell, who toured India in the 1790s, she produced, with Toby Falk, *Indian Miniatures in the India Office Library* (1981) and *India Revealed: The Art and Adventures of James and William Fraser 1801–35*. Her last work, *India Served and Observed* (1994), was a collection of autobiographical writings she and Bill had produced.

With Robert Skelton, of the Victoria and Albert Museum, she undertook a survey of the works of art to be found in official buildings in India; they recommended that none should be thrown out, and expressed reservations about the introduction of air-conditioning in the Indian climate. Tim Archer was appointed OBE in 1979.

## Sunil Dutt

SUNIL DUTT (who died on May 25 2005, aged 75) was one of the best-loved stars of the Indian cinema and, during his last year, his country's Sports Minister.

*Dutt addressing prostitutes on one of his yearly visits to a red light area of Bombay for the Hindu festival of Raksha Bandhan.*
(AP/Sherwin Crasto)

The story of Sunil Dutt, or "Duttsaab", as he was respectfully called, began in 1957 when Mehboob Khan's *Mother India* was released. The black-and-white film, a four-hankie weepie with a well-crafted storyline, reflected the utopian ideals of Nehru's socialist India and the struggles of the masses.

Dutt was perfect as Birju, the angry rebel, while the role of his single mother was played by Nargis, one of the most hauntingly beautiful of India's actresses, whom Dutt was to marry. The film, in which the mother is forced to kill her son, who has chosen a path of violence, has become one of the great classics of Indian cinema, and is sometimes ranked with *Gone with the Wind*. It was screened at the Cannes Film Festival in 2004 as part of its season of classic films, and then went on general release in French cinemas. In Britain, it is shown regularly at the National Film Theatre and on television.

Dutt was said to have rescued Nargis from a burning set and, although he was a Hindu and she a Muslim, their romance soon became the talk of India. After marrying, they became an iconic Bollywood couple, claiming the friendship of such figures as Jimmy Carter, who obligingly responded by calling Dutt "the Robert Redford of India".

The Dutts had two daughters and a son, Sanjay, who followed his father into films with *Rocky* (1981), and has since played the tough guy in numerous Bollywood movies. But he proved an endless worry. After bombs rocked Bombay in 1992, when some Muslim groups were apparently retaliating for the destruction by Hindu militants of the Babri Masjid in Ayodhya, a gun was found in Sanjay's home, and he was arrested. Dutt stepped down as an MP and put his professional career on hold for several years to campaign for Sanjay's release.

Just before Nargis died of cancer in 1981, she made her husband promise to campaign on behalf of victims of the disease. Devastated by her death, he kept the promise, reduced his film commitments and worked tirelessly for the Nargis Dutt Cancer Foundation. At one stage, when the Pakistani cricketer Imran Khan wanted his help for his cancer hospital in Lahore, Dutt flew to Birmingham for a fund-raising function. Although he was an Indian and Imran a Pakistani, Dutt summed up his view of life: "Disease and suffering have no religion and no nationality. My work encompasses mankind."

He was born Balraj Dutt on June 6 1929 at the village of Khurd in Jhelum district, now part of Pakistan. But after Partition in 1947 his mother told him: "Those who wallow in the past only learn to hate and do not move ahead in life." So he set off for Bombay, where he went to Jai Hind College, and joined Keymers, a British advertising agency, to supplement his income. He became a radio announcer on Radio Ceylon, and made the acquaintance of leading figures in the film industry.

In deference to his mother, Dutt waited to graduate before making his first film, Ramesh Saigal's *Railway Platform*, for which he changed his name because there already was a Balraj (Sahni) in the film industry. His good looks immediately turned him into a national heartthrob, and he was to have plenty of work for the next 40 years. Among his many roles, he was a simpleton in *Padosan*, a rich lawyer in *Waqt*, a dacoit in *Reshma Aur Shera* and a villain in *Geeta Mera Naam*.

In 2003 he made a brief appearance in the popular *Munnabhai M.B.B.S.*, as his son's father who discovers that the boy he thinks is a doctor is really a small-time gangster. Dutt was also noted for his adventurous and unconventional approach as the director of some well-received films, including *Yaadein*, in which he played the sole character.

His standing was further increased by a concern for public issues. Once, when upset by the turmoil caused by the terrorism in Punjab in 1987, he walked all the way from Punjab to the Golden Temple in Amritsar. This form of political activity, called *padayatra* ("journey on foot"), was intended to arouse the conscience of the nation. When Dutt spoke about India, he would quote the *Bhagavad Gita*, the Hindu holy book: "You are just expected to perform your duties and not to expect any rewards. As a citizen of India, I am concerned with giving my best."

Dutt entered politics in 1984 at the request of the Congress leader Rajiv Gandhi. He won Bombay North West, but because of his son's problems did not stand in the 1996 and 1998 elections, though he returned to the Lok Sabha (lower house of Parliament) in those of 1999, 2000 and 2004. On being appointed Minister for Youth Affairs and Sport when Congress returned to power in 2004, Dutt was responsible for ensuring that India was well prepared to stage the Commonwealth Games in 2010. His expectations for India were clear at the Olympics in Athens, when he was upset by the poor performance of the national hockey team, and was furious when two weightlifters tested positive for drugs. The best he could say after India had won a solitary silver medal was that India's performance was "not bad".

Some 50 years after he had left, Dutt returned for the first time to his ancestral village, where the warmth of his reception was testament to the following that the big names of Bollywood have in both India and

Pakistan. "The entire village was at the roadside to welcome me as they would a long lost son," he recalled. "Older women addressed me as 'Ballya', the name of my childhood … When I told them my mother had passed away, they wept. That moment, I realised emotions are similar it is how we use them that differentiates us."

~

# Nigel Hankin

NIGEL HANKIN (who died on November 30 2007, aged 87) went to India as a captain in the British Army in 1945, fell in love with the country and decided to stay; in 1992 he published *Hanklyn-Janklin*, a glossary of Indian English described as a "Stranger's Rumble Tumble Guide to Some Words, Customs and Quiddities Indian and Indo-British".

Hankin conceived the idea for the book in 1982, when a doctor, newly arrived at the British High Commission in Delhi, gave him a list of words and terms he had read in an Indian English-language newspaper but could not understand, such as "Eve-teasing" (sexual harassment).

The problem, as Hankin observed in his book, was not new: "Almost 150 years ago Sir Charles Napier had a similar difficulty: '1844, Headquarters, Kurrachee, 12th February. The Governor unfortunately does not understand Hindoostanee, nor Persian, nor Mahratta, nor any other eastern dialect. He therefore will feel particularly obliged to … officers … to indite their various papers in English, larded with as small a portion of the to him unknown tongues as they conveniently can, instead of those he generally receives namely Hindoostanee larded with occasional words in English."

Hankin's work, now in its fourth edition, paid homage to *Hobson-Jobson*, a glossary compiled in 1886 by Colonel Henry Yule which captured the effect that Indian languages had had on English and on the offspring that resulted from the miscegenation.

Thus, alongside definitions of such familiar terms as chit, loofah, bungalow and kedgeree, browsers of *Hanklyn-Janklin* might discover that the word "prepone" is "a recent and felicitous Indian-English word formation: the antonym of postpone"; and that the slang term "goolies" derives from the Hindi word *goli*, meaning medicine pill, and that it entered English from British railway travellers who would hear the station vendors hawking "Beecham Sahib's goolies". But Hankin's guide was less a glossary of terms than a picaresque ramble through the British experience of the subcontinent; it included much off-beat detail about the customs, rituals and idiosyncrasies that make India a source of fascination and amusement for Western visitors.

The curious concept of "anticipatory bail", for example, is described as "a provision unique in the world's judicial codes, whereby in anticipation of a criminal accusation a person may apply to a court for bail; if granted and the charge is made, he will be exempt from police custody". In an entry on "thugs" or "thuggees" the gangs of brigands whose ritual strangulations horrified the Victorians before they were put down through the efforts of Major-General Sir William Sleeman, Hankin noted that one village in the heart of thuggee country renamed itself Sleemanbad in his honour; the name remained in use until at least 1989. Meanwhile Hankin advised unwary visitors that the term "passenger train" when used in India is "as listed on the timetable a train that most passengers would prefer to avoid".

Nigel Bathurst Hankin was born at Bexhill, Sussex, on March 14 1920 and brought up by his grandmother after his father's early death. He spent the Second World War in the Army in Britain and North Africa before being posted to Burma in 1945.

He arrived in India as the war ended and, by the time the country gained independence, had decided to stay on. Hankin moved to New Delhi, where he soon became a familiar figure, his gangling frame dwarfing a Vespa motor scooter, or emerging, spider-like, from a motorised rickshaw. In the early postwar period he ran a mobile cinema. He then worked for many years for the British High Commission, where his odd jobs often included taking diplomats and their wives on tours of the city.

After his retirement in 1986 Hankin became a freelance guide for foreign visitors, conducting tours for which he charged 2,000 rupees (about £25) per person. The tourists also had to treat him to lunch at the Oberoi Maidens Hotel. What became known among the cognoscenti as "Nigel tours" tended to bypass the main tourist sites in favour of the teeming bazaars and spice markets of Old Delhi, soda stalls, small shrines, cremation grounds and neglected relics of the Raj, including Coronation Park, now the resting place for statues of imperial servants. Places on these tours were sought-after but difficult to obtain, as Hankin possessed neither an internet site nor a telephone. He always asked his tour guests not to mention how to get in touch with him, though the determined could contact him by leaving a note at the Mughal Gate of the High Commission. Independent travellers, he advised, should learn the Hindi word *chalo* ("go away") which "comes in handy every time beggars harass foreigners for bakshish".

Hankin returned to Britain for a holiday in 1982 but was bored after a few weeks, and never wanted to go back. He kept few family ties. "My brother came to India once," he recalled. "He thought there were too many Indians." But Nigel Hankin never "went native", remaining, in looks and mannerisms, an English gentleman and an amused and detached observer of the Indian scene. He never married, but had his *chai* and newspaper brought to him every morning by an old retainer who served him for more than 40 years.

~

## Benazir Bhutto

BENAZIR BHUTTO, the former Prime Minister of Pakistan (who was assassinated in a suicide bombing at Rawalpindi on December 27 2007, aged 54) restored democracy to her country in 1988 after 11 years of military dictatorship.

Her glamorous looks and fluent English led to a sustained love affair with Western politicians and journalists, many of whom had known her at Harvard or Oxford. For those with the standard Western prejudices against the Islamic world, she had the added assets of a pronounceable name and a tolerant religious outlook. She did not organise anti-American rallies or issue *fatwas* against

*Benazir Bhutto arriving to address her last public rally in Rawalpindi the day she was assassinated.* (AP/Mohammad Javed)

best-selling authors (despite Salman Rushdie's lampooning of her as the "Virgin Ironpants" in his novel *Shame*).

She was seen to greatest effect on the campaign trail, where she was renowned for her hectoring speeches and raucous motorcades. Face to face she could appear somewhat haughty, not unlike her role model Margaret Thatcher. However, in Pakistan she was often far less popular than her foreign press made out. To her opponents she was more British than Pakistani, more Western than Eastern. Her Urdu, although fluent, was ungrammatical, while her Sindhi, the mother tongue of her family, was almost non-existent. It was also said that she lacked a coherent political philosophy and tended to dissipate her energies on party politicking. During her first 20-month spell as Prime Minister, from 1988 to 1990, she failed to pass a single piece of major legislation, largely due to the constraints imposed on her by a hostile and still-powerful military.

The second time around, in 1993, she had the full backing of the Army, and managed subsequently to install a party loyalist, Farooq Leghari, as President. Her tight monetary policy produced a dramatic reduction in the budget deficit, pulling the country's economy back from the brink of collapse, and earning it a clean bill of health from the International Monetary Fund and World Bank. The massive inflow of foreign investment gave rise to expectations of a new era of economic development for Pakistan. Her offer of lucrative packages for foreign investors garnered contracts for infrastructure projects worth many billions of dollars. And her privatisation programme was commended for its transparency and broad ownership approach.

But Benazir Bhutto failed to honour her election pledge to end the politics of confrontation, and progress often became mired in petty disputes with the opposition, or was hijacked by minority interests who constrained her grip on power. She became increasingly reliant on the Establishment and cut off from the masses, despite the populist origins of her party. The strongest backlash was provoked by her attempts to control the press and manipulate the judiciary. The appointment of judges on the basis of loyalty to her party caused massive damage to the Pakistani bench's already dwindling credibility, not to say her own.

Benazir Bhutto also failed to defuse the sectarian and ethnic conflict in Karachi, Pakistan's largest city, where the murder rate was often running at more than 10 a day and the hapless provincial government had to rely on the Army to maintain law and order.

Her main interest was always foreign policy; she became the most widely-travelled Prime Minister in Pakistan's history. But while trips abroad earned her a high international profile and helped attract foreign investment, they did little to improve matters internally, where her political footing became increasingly shaky.

Benazir Bhutto was born on June 21 1953, the eldest child of Zulfikar Ali Bhutto, who was Prime Minister of Pakistan (initially West Pakistan) from 1970 until 1977. Before Pakistan's first land reforms in 1958 the Bhutto family were among the largest landowners in Sindh province. Benazir grew up in their spacious Karachi residence, 70 Clifton. She had a British governess, and went to the Presentation Convent, run by Irish nuns, and then to the Jesus and Mary at Muree.

Her reputation for bossiness stemmed from childhood when she would direct a stream of imperatives at her younger brothers. The first Bhutto woman not to wear a *burqa*, she always claimed to have been her father's favourite (the source of a bitter dispute with her brother Murtaza and mother Nusrat).

At 10 she was sent to boarding school in the pine-covered former British hill station of Murree. "For the first time I had to make my own bed, polish my shoes, and carry water for bathing and tooth-brushing," she wrote in her autobiography.

In 1965, during her second and final year there, India and Pakistan went to war over Kashmir, the road to which ran straight through Murree. The Tashkent Treaty that followed the 17-Day War, in which Pakistan's President Ayub Khan relinquished all of the gains made by his army, disgusted Zulfikar Bhutto, who promptly resigned as Foreign Minister. Two years later, in 1967, he formed the PPP, whose simple populist slogan "*Roti, Kapra, Makan*" ("Bread, Clothing, Housing") became a rallying cry for millions of poor Pakistanis. Benazir, then 14, enthusiastically joined up, the start of a lifelong political affiliation.

At 17, she was admitted to study comparative government at Harvard, aided by a recommendation from the economist J. K. Galbraith, a friend of her father's. "I was amongst a sea of women," she later wrote, "who felt as unimpeded by their gender as I did." From there she went to Lady Margaret Hall and then St Catherine's College at Oxford, where she was remembered as a glamorous and cosmopolitan Asian girl about town, known to her friends as Bibi or Pinky. She drove to lectures in a yellow MG, and spent her winters in Gstaad and summers on the Cannes lido. She had a penchant for royal biographies, slushy romances and 1970s easy listening, and liked nothing better than browsing in Harrods, a habit she retained throughout her life. Yet indications of her hard ambitious side surfaced when she stayed on an extra year to become President of the Union.

Benazir Bhutto's unquestioning reverence for her father, who was Prime Minister throughout her time at Oxford, was to be a source of ammunition for her later political opponents. Although hugely popular when he swept to power in 1970, Zulfikar Bhutto became an arrogant despot, with a reputation for rigging elections and torturing political opponents. Stripped of power in 1977, he was executed at Rawalpindi Central Jail in 1979 on the orders of General Zia, following a grossly unfair trial for corruption and conspiracy to murder an opposition politician. Benazir Bhutto had her last meeting with her father a few hours before he was hanged, separated by a heavy metal grille. "I pleaded, begged with them to let me embrace my beautiful father for the last time. They refused. We parted without being able to touch. But I did not cry. Daddy told me not to."

After launching a campaign to clear his name and topple Zia, Benazir Bhutto and her mother spent years in jail or under house arrest at Al-Murtaza, their country estate in Larkana. "Each incarceration is just adding a layer of anger," she wrote in her diary. In 1984, Zia allowed her to travel to London for treatment for medical problems that were probably exacerbated by the conditions of her imprisonment. She took a flat in the Barbican, and here worked at rebuilding the organisation of the PPP around herself and preparing for an election.

Her two brothers, Murtaza and Shahnawaz, meanwhile, had turned to terrorism. In Beirut, under the guidance of Yasser Arafat, they formed the Pakistan Liberation Army, later renamed Al-Zulfikar ("The Sword"). Its biggest achievement, the hijacking of a Pakistan International Airlines flight in 1981, gave Zia a pretext to crack down on the PPP, and Benazir was forced to distance herself from her brothers. Shahnawaz was mysteriously poisoned in his apartment in Cannes in 1986, but Murtaza remained a thorn in her side.

In October 1993, Murtaza announced his intention to return to Pakistan from exile in Damascus to contest the elections that brought Benazir's party back to power. Benazir's mother, at that time chairman of the PPP, endorsed his decision and campaigned for him, often against the official PPP candidate. But she was soon dumped as PPP chairman. "I had no idea I had nourished a viper in my breast," she said of her daughter. Many predicted mass defections to Murtaza, but in the event he won only one provincial assembly seat. When he flew in to Pakistan from Syria in early November, he was promptly arrested at the airport on terrorism charges. In September 1996, Murtaza was shot dead in a gun battle with police in Karachi.

Benazir Bhutto showed greater pragmatism, even ruthlessness, in her second government. "This time," she said, "I won't listen to the sloppy liberals." She acted more cautiously in her relations with the military while directing a campaign of harassment against anyone who opposed her, including judges, journalists and government officials. In November 1996, with the economy in crisis, her party split and the country in turmoil, President Farooq Leghari (her own appointee) dismissed her government.

She consented to a traditional arranged marriage in 1987. Her family's choice of Asif Zardari, a member of the Sindhi feudal elite, did her no favours politically. When they first met, Zardari was a womaniser on the fringes of Karachi society, known chiefly for building a disco in his home to woo the party set. Benazir Bhutto told her Oxford friends at the time that she thought he cut a ridiculous figure with his bushy moustache and macho image.

Zardari's reputation as a dodgy businessman was cemented by his remarkable transformation from a bankrupt into a fabulously wealthy man shortly after marrying Benazir, earning him the tag "Mr Ten Percent". Nevertheless, Benazir Bhutto stood by him, appointing him to her cabinet in 1996. After her second government fell, a stream of real and dubious corruption and criminal charges was brought against him, keeping him in jail without trial for eight years. When further charges were brought against him in 1999, he was jailed while Benazir was out of the country, and thereafter she based herself in Dubai and London. For much of this time, she was preoccupied with a series of lawsuits against her and Zardari that were primarily designed to end her political career.

In October 2007, under pressure to restore democracy, President Musharraf held secret talks with Benazir Bhutto in Abu Dhabi on sharing power, though they reached no agreement. Corruption charges against her were dropped, and she went back to Pakistan a few weeks later, planning to contest elections that were promised for January 2008.

Her return was characteristically flamboyant: millions attended her first act on arrival, a pilgrimage to the tomb of Muhammad Ali Jinnah, Pakistan's founder and first President, though the spectacle was marred when a suicide bomber, aiming at her, killed 140 spectators and injured hundreds more.

She and Zardari had two daughters and a son.

# Michael Charlesworth

MICHAEL CHARLESWORTH (who died on April 24 2008, aged 89) became a successful Principal of Lawrence College in Pakistan but devoted most of his life to Shrewsbury School, with which he was associated for more than 70 years.

Lawrence had been founded near Ghora Gali, in the foothills of the Himalayas, as a school for the children of British other ranks in the 19th

*Charlesworth met a village boy on the Deccan Plain who recited Kingsley's poem "O Mary, call the cattle home across the sands of Dee".*

century. But, after evolving into a more exclusive establishment and a teacher training college, it had developed difficulties following the partition of India.

By 1960, when Charlesworth arrived, the British boys had gone, and he was the seventh headmaster in 14 years. He lived in some luxury with six servants, one of them a sweeper in charge of emptying thunderboxes. There was no running hot water until the British Council provided a special heater. On his first night Charlesworth killed a rat in his chest of drawers.

He encountered more problems: first there was a notice in the *Pakistan Times* offering 100 rupees reward for a lost pupil; then 12 *dhobis* (laundrymen) camped on the lawn demanding more pay; a matron was found to be falsifying tailors' bills; and one of the nurses was discovered to have had an abortion in the school hospital.

An internecine war had broken out among the teaching staff, which Charlesworth could do little to solve as a head who was subject to the Ministry of Education in Lahore. But with the aid of the Governor of West Pakistan (who was subsequently shot in his bed by his son) Charlesworth gradually obtained independence. He gave the school back its sporting self-respect by joining in games, and raised standards in the Cambridge board exams. As the Christian head of a Muslim school he used the common ground between the religions to read prayers at the daily assembly that were God/Allah centred, except on Fridays when the Second Master was in charge. Never drinking alcohol in front of Muslims, he raised money for the building of a mosque and ensured that the boys attended for the compulsory sunset prayers.

After five years, however, he found himself suspected of spying during the India–Pakistan War when he made rounds to supervise the air-raid precautions during the blackout; it was muttered that he had been in India during the Second World War. Nevertheless, his services were appreciated in both Britain and Pakistan. He was appointed OBE, and the main road through Lawrence College was named Charlesworth Avenue after him.

Michael Lindsay Charlesworth was born on January 31 1919, the son of a prep school headmaster, and went to Shrewsbury as "new scum" at 13. The school offered no science, no art, little music, and was governed by an ethos that seemed to be a mixture of the Rule of St Benedict, the court etiquette of Louis XIV and the regime of H.M. Prisons; as a result it had developed a powerful sense of identity.

At Magdalen College, Oxford, Charlesworth did some acting and had his Christian commitment strengthened by tutorials with C. S. Lewis. After two years he left to join the Royal Artillery, which sent him to India. On the voyage out he was appointed ship's bugler, with instructions, in the event of a torpedo attack, to stand by the captain playing the "Last Post" until the bubbles came out of his trumpet.

After being commissioned he was posted to 158 Field Regiment for the advance on Burma, then appointed a camouflage instructor to tour units on the Deccan plain, where he met a village boy who recited Charles Kingsley's poem "O Mary, call the cattle home across the sands of Dee".

As the war ended Charlesworth volunteered to join the unit which disarmed the Germans at Tromsö, in Norway, before returning to Oxford to complete his degree. He then became a history master at Shrewsbury.

In 1953 he took a term off to teach at Geelong Grammar School in Australia, where he introduced fives and developed an admiration for the headmaster, Jim Darling, whom he later thought should have been appointed to head Shrewsbury. After returning to Shropshire, he was appointed head of School House and married the widow of a school contemporary, Joy Broke-Smith, who had three children and with whom he was to have two sons. Soon the family left for Lawrence.

On coming home after five years to find Shrewsbury greatly changed, Charlesworth did every job but that of matron in the succeeding decades. He was acting headmaster twice, Second Master and the head of several houses; he took games, wrote light verse for reviews, lectured on the school's history and edited the *Salopian Record*. He came to be known as "Mr Shrewsbury".

He also wrote a life of the housemaster J. B. Oldham and an account of the school during the Second World War. In his perceptive autobiography, *Behind the Headlines* (1994), he reflected on the changes in the public school system, and embarrassed one former pupil, the left-wing journalist Paul Foot, by recalling Foot's letter to him from Oxford. Declaring that, despite being a socialist, he always supported the public schools, Foot had told Charlesworth: "We may find each other in the last ditch."

On finally retiring Michael Charlesworth settled a couple of hundred yards from the school. He found plenty to do as a parish councillor, editing a book for the Redundant Churches Fund and writing letters to *The Daily Telegraph* defending President Musharraf's government in Pakistan. Military rule might not be perfect, he maintained, but it provided a protective shield in a country which had never really taken to democracy.

~

# CANADA

---

## Jack Pickersgill

JACK PICKERSGILL (who died on November 14 1997, aged 92) enjoyed an unprecedented career at the centre of power in Ottawa for 30 years, which saw his slick transference from civil service to parliamentary arena and back again.

As the trusted adviser of three Prime Ministers he helped to foster the impression that Canada's Liberals were the "party of government", even claiming that their election would benefit not only Canada but mankind in general. More than Lester Pearson, whom he followed from bureaucracy onto the political stage, Pickersgill proved a surprisingly effective debater. However, his reputation as a backroom fixer led the word "pickersgillian" to be coined for any partisan ploy that was too clever by half.

John Whitney Pickersgill was born at Wyecombe, Ontario, on June 23 1905 and brought up at Ahern, Manitoba, where his father farmed. He went to the University of Manitoba and New College, Oxford, before teaching history at Wesley College, Winnipeg. In 1937 he joined the External Affairs Department and soon found himself temporarily transferred to the staff of the Prime Minister, Mackenzie King.

Although his chief was exasperated by the young man's presumption at times, Pickersgill had a close relationship with King, whose speeches, avoiding the word "challenge" but making frequent use of "sober" and "decent", he learnt to draft with great accuracy. When King resigned in 1948, his successor, Louis St Laurent, had comparatively little political experience, and so came to rely even more on Pickersgill, whom he promoted to Clerk to the Privy Council and Cabinet Secretary. But seven months later, Pickersgill resigned to fight a federal seat on Newfoundland which he had been offered by the all-powerful Premier, Joey Smallwood.

Despite Pickersgill's doubts about his suitability to represent the fishermen of Bonavista-Twillingate, Smallwood assured him: "Don't worry. When I'm through with you, you won't recognise yourself." Pickersgill's insistence that he could spend no more than five days wooing his new constituency posed no problem.

His arrival aboard a steamer was greeted by local fishermen with a blast of 30 sealing guns and a Salvation Army band playing *Hold the Fort, I am Coming*. On a platform, Smallwood would point to the candidate saying: "This is Pickersgill. Isn't that an incredible name?" Then, leaning forward, the tiny Premier would confide: "You'd better like him. He's the second most important man in Ottawa and the father of Family Allowances. Some day he will be Prime Minister."

Endorsed by a large majority, and nicknamed "Sailor Jack" after he bought a 110 ft schooner to travel round his constituency, Pickersgill returned to the Cabinet Room as first Secretary of State and then Minister of Immigration. In the latter post he was responsible for a plan to airlift immigrants from Britain, though a chance remark about no immigrant being as good as a Canadian baby dogged him.

Despite his long involvement in political life, Pickersgill still retained traces of the prairie farm boy, demonstrating personal frugality in such ways as alternating an often frayed New College brown and silver stripe tie with another bearing polka dots. His right-wing, conservative sentiments went with a fund of detailed and obscure knowledge, such as that Manitoba's cabinet in 1922 was made up entirely of Presbyterians, and helped to make him an expert parliamentary tactician.

However, Pickersgill made two bad mistakes. He backed a motion of closure in a debate on the Bill to authorise the building of a pipeline, which led to the Liberals' defeat after 22 years in the 1956 general election. He also drafted a resolution for his party's new leader Lester Pearson, which gave John Diefenbaker the excuse to return to the polls for his 1957 landslide victory.

For a time, Pickersgill was not asked for advice, and volunteered none. Gradually the sight of his clumsy, penguin-like figure bobbing up and down in the House and his cackling style of debate rallied the demoralised Liberals. He was duly appointed Secretary of State and Leader of the House when Pearson became Prime Minister in 1963.

Despite the best assumptions, however, a minority Liberal government proved even more chaotic than the administration it replaced. Pickersgill soldiered on loyally, but he could see the writing on the wall. After three years as Transport Minister, he steered through a Bill creating a Canadian Transportation Commission whose president, unusually, could continue in the job until 70. He then resigned both seat and office, and took the $40,000-a-year post himself. He retired from it, aged 67, during Pierre Trudeau's prime ministership.

Pickersgill, who was married twice and had four children, wrote several volumes of reminiscences. But he made a far more valuable contribution as a literary executor of Mackenzie King's papers. King had left instructions that his diaries should be destroyed after an official biography had been written, but Pickersgill found a way round this, and then edited them himself, in four volumes. His old Tory opponent Diefenbaker labelled them "selectivities", a judgment justified by scholars' later discoveries of King's spiritualist and possibly sexual activities, but in saving that remarkable document Pickersgill undoubtedly did an invaluable service.

# Jean Drapeau

JEAN DRAPEAU (who died on August 12 1999, aged 83) drew the world's attention to Montreal by the grandiose municipal schemes he launched during 29 years as the city's mayor.

A small, pious man who rose at 5 a.m. and loved opera, Drapeau was said to keep a copy of Machiavelli's *The Prince* on his desk. He was responsible for the construction of two artificial islands in the St Lawrence, to house the World's Fair Expo of 1967 and a stadium for the 1976 Olympics, which he described as "a poem in concrete". As well as initiating an underground railway modelled on the Paris Metro, he also gave the city Grand Prix racing and a Major League baseball team.

Such attractions added to Montreal's reputation as the most exciting and sophisticated city in North America; but Montrealers had to pay a price in mushrooming civic debt and put up with a lackadaisical approach to public health and housing. Drapeau justified his schemes with the argument that they could be shared by every citizen, without exception. He predicted that they would lead to a new kind of prosperity, ignoring clear evidence that his prejudice against English Montrealers was driving the city's commercial elite, and their financial capital, to Toronto. Yet it was a measure of Drapeau's

*Drapeau declared that Olympic Games could no more have a deficit than a man could have a baby.* (AP/CP, Ryan Remiorz)

standing and reputation for personal honesty that he was able to shrug off a highly critical report on his stewardship of the Olympics by declaring: "Two thousand five hundred years ago Pericles, too, was criticised for building the Acropolis" and go on to win another election.

Jean Drapeau was born on February 18 1916, the son of an insurance broker. He was educated at St Jean de Brebeuf College and Montreal University, where he fell under the influence of the French Canadian nationalist, the Abbé Groulx. His first political speech, when he was 16, was addressed to his mother's bridge circle, warning them against the leering attention their daughters should expect if they lived in apartment blocks.

Strongly opposing involvement in the Second World War, Drapeau unsuccessfully fought a parliamentary by-election as an anti-conscription candidate and also failed to win a seat in a provincial general election. He then settled down to practising criminal law, which led him to become counsel to a corruption inquiry; this in turn enabled him to run for Mayor. Montreal's criminal underworld was sufficiently concerned that it spent (according to papers later captured by the Mounties) $100,000 opposing his candidature; even so he won comfortably.

Drapeau began by appointing a new police chief who energetically closed down brothels, illicit drinking clubs and gambling dens. Pinball machines were outlawed, and the practice of giving money to favoured newspaper reporters ceased. Not all of these measures were universally popular, and together with the enmity of the powerful Premier, Maurice Duplessis, they cost him the next election.

But in 1960 Drapeau regained power at City Hall, and immediately instigated a fresh crackdown on crime by importing senior officers from Scotland Yard and the Paris Prefecture. With a political philosophy of "discipline democracy", which in practice meant that he should be left alone to make the decisions, he formed his own party, concerned only with municipal elections, and summed up his approach: "No problems. Only solutions."

One of his ideas for Expo '67 was to borrow the Eiffel Tower from Paris; the request was turned down. When it was pointed out that his proposed new roads to the fair would pass through some of Montreal's less salubrious districts, Drapeau ordered seven-feet-high wooden walls to be built along them; they were duly daubed *Visitez les Slums* by the local populace.

The most striking gesture made in Canada's centenary year, 1967, however, was by Charles de Gaulle, who arrived in Montreal after making a series of increasingly nationalistic speeches during a progress through Quebec. When the French President arrived at City Hall, an uneasy Drapeau had the microphone on the balcony disconnected; but a member of the presidential entourage turned it on in time for de Gaulle to proclaim: "*Vive Montreal, Vive le Quebec. Vive le Quebec Libre.*"

In the ensuing storm, de Gaulle's visit to Ottawa was cancelled and the following day Drapeau replied in a speech simultaneously translated and broadcast across Canada. Quebeckers had long been their own guardians of French civilisation, he declared, and he hoped that they would continue to be so within the whole of Canada. This turned Drapeau into something of a national hero, and he was appointed a Companion of the Order of Canada. Yet he was received no less warmly at the Elysée Palace on his next visit to Paris.

The ferment of Quebec nationalism and international student unrest led to riots at the traditional St Jean Baptiste Day parade, which saw Drapeau driven from the reviewing stand. The demonstrators' cry "*Drapeau au poteau*" was also taken up by the riot squad who occupied City Hall in pursuit of a pay claim; Drapeau even suspected the police of bombing his home. When the British Trade Commissioner, James Cross, was kidnapped, he supported the activation of the draconian War Measures Act.

After winning another large majority in the next mayoral election, Drapeau punished newspapers for what he saw as their disloyalty by banning vending boxes from the streets, and concentrated on the Olympic stadium designed by the French architect Roger Taillibert. Dismissing suggestions that he might be over-ambitious, Drapeau announced: "The Games can no more have a deficit than a man can have a baby." Although patronage and corruption in connection with the stadium were blatant, and involved some of those close to Drapeau, the Games proceeded without undue mishap: Drapeau was cheered; the Queen was not booed. But the total costs have since been calculated at $3.5 billion, more than five times over budget.

After being allowed to stand for election once more on the understanding that it would be the last time, Drapeau retired on a modest pension in 1986. He then became Canadian Ambassador to UNESCO in Paris for five years.

There were vigorous announcements that he would defend himself against charges of extravagance and mismanagement of the Olympics, and he promised a book on de Gaulle. Nothing happened. By the time of his death the concrete was falling off the stadium, and the Expo site housed a casino. Ironically, considering his crusade against gambling, Drapeau's most valuable innovation was the lottery.

Jean Drapeau married, in 1945, Marie-Claire Boucher; they had three sons.

## The Earl of Egmont

THE 11TH EARL OF EGMONT (who died in Alberta on December 10 2001, aged 87) became one of the peerage's most romantic figures at the age of 15 when he reluctantly moved from a two-room prairie shack to Avon Castle, Hampshire, on his father's inheritance of the earldom.

Members of a junior branch of the Perceval family, which had emigrated to Iowa and then Alberta in the late 19th century, the boy and his widowed father "bached" together on a 600-acre ranch at Priddis, near Calgary. Wearing chaps, boots and stetsons, they contentedly built up a herd of cattle, chopped their own wood and cooked their own meals. Then, on January 12 1929, Lord Beaverbrook, the former owner of a Calgary bowling alley, ordered a *Daily Express* reporter in London to inform the father of his good fortune. "This is the first I have heard of it," replied the 56-year-old 10th Earl when he was brought to a telephone station. "I have been out with a bunch of cattle for the past few days and have just got in."

His son Frederick George Moore Perceval, who was born at Calgary on April 14 1914, now had the courtesy title Viscount Perceval; however, he was unimpressed by the change in the family fortunes. "You taught me to read and write, and you taught me to ride and shoot," he told his father. "We've got a nice home here, and I don't want to leave it." But the shack had pictures of English scenes on the walls, and they had talked of the inheritance that might one day be theirs. After a sale of their effects, in which the boy's two mongrels, Jack and Rummy, made 25 cents each and his saddle pony, Pat, $3.25, they set off.

Already local reporters were so persistent that they decided to depart from a small station outside Calgary. As the pair boarded ship at Montreal, father and son swapped their stetsons for caps. They landed in England to find themselves besieged all day and late at night for weeks. Even apart from their unfamiliarity with metropolitan life, the weatherbeaten "cowboy earl" and his son, with their Western drawls, proved of abiding interest to the press.

An estate agent worked out that around £300,000 went with the Irish Earldom of Egmont, the Viscountcy of Perceval of Kanturk and the Barony of Arden of Arden, Co Cork, as well as the Barony of Lovel and Holland in the United Kingdom. The inheritance came through their descent from Spencer Perceval, the Prime Minister assassinated at Westminster in 1812, who was the seventh son of the 2nd Earl.

The new Earl and his son excited a fresh round of press interest when their claim to both the land and titles were disputed by two other equally colourful claimants: a Hornsey baker, who said he had been born in Australia as the son of the 6th Earl's brother, and a retired Lancastrian optician. Both cases were dismissed in court, but when debts and death duties necessitated the sale of silver and pictures, including a little-known Reynolds and a Beechey, the optician caused a sensation at Christie's by objecting at the top of his voice that they belonged to him. To add to the confusion, the House of Lords did not formally recognise the father's claim until 1939.

But father and son were able to move into Avon Castle, with its private railway halt and 1,300 acres at Ringwood, Hampshire, seven months after their arrival. By then the Earl was thoroughly bemused by the England he had not seen since the age of six, and his son was firmly for returning to Priddis. Instead, they dismissed the servants and moved into the huge kitchen to re-create their Albertan self-sufficiency.

The gates were closed; the house shuttered; overtures from county neighbours were rebuffed. The new Earl got on well enough with the villagers he met in the pub and local shop, though he didn't care for the way they always called him "sir". He talked about sending his son to Oxford, but the boy showed no sign of continuing his schooling and was left largely to his own lonely devices.

The young Lord Perceval occasionally played with other boys at Ringwood but was more often to be seen riding alone on his bicycle; later he bought a motorcycle which he enjoyed riding late at night along deserted roads at up to 85 mph. The Earl continued to be of abiding interest to the press, which dubbed him "the loneliest peer in England". Then fate intervened: he was killed in a motor accident in Southampton.

While the villagers spoke up for their kindly, shy neighbour, the *Sunday Express's* theatre critic, James Agate, excoriated county society: "Doubtless the late earl's accent and manners may, like his boots, have been a shade too thick for the fine carpets of Hampshire. Doubtless he was no master of small talk, because on an Alberta ranch, if you talk at all, the subjects will probably be pretty big. They may be kittle cattle but they certainly won't be tittle tattle."

The local MP wrote in reply that efforts had been made to get to know the lonely peer. But the 18-year-old new Earl did not wait to give Hampshire society a second chance. He put the estate on the market, and set out for Canada. On encountering a Calgary journalist on the train at Winnipeg his first questions were about the present owner of his saddle-pony and the date of the annual Stampede.

After kitting himself out with saddle and chaps, the young Egmont set out for Priddis whose population turned out to greet him. Yes, he had liked the racing but not the crowds at the Derby. London was a tiring place where there were lots of shows, though he couldn't understand why he had to pay sixpence for a programme full of advertisements. "What English people do not realise," he explained, "is that there is a greater spirit of freedom and generosity over here in Canada." That afternoon, he borrowed a horse and set off for a ride.

A few months later, after participating in the Stampede, Egmont married his cousin, Geraldine Moodie, a dental nurse who had been his childhood sweetheart. The honeymoon involved the usual pursuit by newsmen, who remained fascinated by "the only member of the House of Lords who could rope, throw and brand a steer". The couple had to return home from Victoria, British Columbia, after they had been spotted, and then set off again for Florida. However, the new countess was made of stern stuff, and dealt with prying reporters by leading her husband away firmly by the arm before he had time to provide them with any more colourful copy.

Egmont hardly fulfilled normal expectations of a belted earl when encountered on his ranch in bib overalls and a dusty hat, with six days' beard. He liked his neighbours to address him as "Fred"; but they called him "the Earl" behind his back.

Settling down to develop some of the finest stock in the West on the Priddis ranch, Egmont resisted his wife's promptings that they go to England until 1938, after he had rescued their son from a fire which destroyed their ranch-house. He bought a car in London, toured the country and talked about sending the boy to Eton. Instead, he put Avon Castle on the market and returned to Priddis where he built a 26-room ranch-house, complete with solid oak floors that had to be supported by 12-inch steel girders in the basement.

When the farm was sold 21 years later to a property company which came in advance of Calgary's spreading suburbs, he told the ever-interested *Daily Express* that he might consider moving back to Britain, where he still had land at Epsom. However, he used his handsome profit to buy the 5,000-acre Two-Dot Ranch at Nanton, 40 miles south of the city, which had once belonged to the Earl of Minto, Canada's Governor-General from 1898 to 1904. Egmont continued to keep largely to himself, though he was delighted on one occasion to be introduced to a member of his family from Britain, who was staying on a neighbouring ranch.

When Canada's constitution was patriated by the repeal of the Westminster British North America Act in the early 1980s, a Canadian reporter rang Egmont to ask if he would go to London to speak in what was expected to be a controversial Lords debate. The countess answered the phone. "You can't speak to him now. He's out doing his chores," she snapped, before venturing her own opinion that there was no call for the repeal, anyway. Later, Egmont told a neighbour that he rather wished that he had gone over to take his seat in the House.

Egmont was survived by his heir Thomas Frederick Gerald, Viscount Perceval, who was born on August 17 1934, a younger son and two daughters.

~

## Lady Barlow

LADY BARLOW (who died on March 29 2002, in St John's, Newfoundland, aged 73) was a redoubtable defender of the monarchy and an enthusiastic breeder of Labrador dogs.

*Lady Barlow with Sandringham Chive, a personal gift from the Queen.*

A larger than life character in the great tradition of Englishwomen abroad, Jacqueline Barlow founded the Monarchist League of Newfoundland in 1975. She helped to secure Canadian cabinet approval for the designation "Royal" to be conferred on the Newfoundland Constabulary; ran regular dinners to celebrate the birthdays of the Queen and Prince of Wales; and drove cars with a Union pennant flying from the aerial. At the Silver Jubilee in 1977, Lady Barlow organised a Declaration of Loyalty (a pointed contradiction of the

American Declaration of Independence). It was signed by about four-fifths of the 500,000 Newfoundlanders, and presented by Newfoundland veterans of the two world wars to the Queen at Balmoral.

One reason for her success in gathering signatures was that she had toured the island's schools, and asked postmistresses to ensure that a copy of the Declaration was waiting for anyone who visited their premises. She also commissioned what was claimed to be the largest Union flag, 42 feet by 28 feet. It was flown over City Hall in St John's, the capital, and then from a specially constructed flagpole at Cupids, in Conception Bay, where the first official English colony was established in 1610.

As the monarchy came under increasing pressure in the 1990s, Lady Barlow's crisp, confident British tones in support of the institution became a familiar sound on Canadian airwaves. She had clear views about duty, regretting, when Diana Princess of Wales had failed to fulfill "the high hopes we all had for her", that it was no longer possible for her to be lodged in comfortable quarters at the Tower of London. Nevertheless, she had no doubt that the major fault lay with the British tabloids: "Look where this petty, piddling, gawping interest in the private lives of the Royal Family has got us. This must stop!" she thundered in one of her letters to *The Daily Telegraph*. Pointing out that, for many loyal subjects outside the British Isles, the monarchy represented a safeguard unequalled in any other system of government, she declared: "When you insult the Crown, you insult all of us."

The daughter of a cotton broker who, as an RNVR officer during the Second World War, had patrolled the coasts of Scotland with seven trawlers and one gun, she was born Jacqueline Claire de Marigny Audley at Hale, Cheshire, on January 15 1929. Her wartime years were spent on the Isle of Arran and at a convent school in Ayrshire. She went to Canada with her father after the war, but came back to England to join the Wrens as an officer cadet.

Having later decided not to proceed with a naval career, she returned to Montreal, where she found scope for her talents controlling unruly students as a librarian at the McGill University medical school. In 1952, she married the architect Sir Christopher Barlow, 7th Baronet, with whom she had a son and two daughters. When the family moved to Newfoundland, she immediately felt at home on an island where almost every home had a photograph of Her Majesty the Queen. Here she devotedly nurtured her succession of Labradors which, with one exception, were named after British admirals – Blake, Vian, Cochrane, Duckworth, Drake, Nelson and Beatty.

The breed was traditionally associated with Lady Barlow's ancestor the 2nd Earl of Malmesbury, who was said to have imported the first "Little Newfoundland" water dogs in the 1820s; he saw them jump from Newfoundland fishing boats into the sea off Poole to retrieve fish that had been thrown away. Malmesbury's son, the 3rd Earl, decided the name was rather a mouthful, and changed it to Labrador. However, the dogs were said to have originated in various places (particularly Portugal), until Lady Barlow decided to investigate.

Encouraged by Sir Leonard Outerbridge, a former Lieutenant-Governor of Newfoundland, she took a schooner to some southern outports without roads to trace three remaining original water dogs. Later the American expert Richard Wolters retraced her route and paid fulsome tribute to her in his book *The Labrador Retriever*. Lady Barlow edited *Labrador Characters*, a collection of accounts of the almost human characteristics of these dogs. She wrote frequently for *Labrador Quarterly*, showed her dogs, and also judged in Canada and the United States.

On a visit to Britain in 1982 she was invited to Buckingham Palace where, over a gin and tonic, the Queen offered her a puppy from Sandringham. Called Sandringham Chive, he was the son of the field champion Sandringham Sydney, and became Lady Barlow's greatest pride. She reported regularly on his progress via the Queen's private secretaries, and would appear so regularly with the dog whenever a member of the Royal Family came to the island that Princess Anne was heard to mutter: "Not that ruddy dog again."

Lady Barlow could be devastatingly blunt, and she never wavered in her Britishness. Her voice contained few traces of North American intonation, and she showed little interest in an offer of the Order of Canada. Fellow monarchists on the mainland sometimes felt she was as much an embarrassment as an aid to their cause. But on Newfoundland, where the islanders of West Country and Irish origin are still unsure whether they should have joined Canada in 1949, even ambitious politicians proved reluctant to quarrel with Lady Barlow more than once. In return, she repaid the Newfoundlanders with an unstinting love for their island. She would not hesitate to launch a diatribe against the iniquity of the mainlanders' propensity for telling "Newfie" jokes, then suddenly ask, "But, have you heard this one?"

Leaning back in her chair, with a cup of tea to hand and her dogs around her, she would confide: "I say, which is perhaps naughty, that Newfoundland is as nice as England used to be."

## Andrew Macpherson

ANDREW MACPHERSON (who died on April 23 2002, aged 69) first set foot in the Arctic as a 17-year-old schoolboy on an expedition to map the last unexplored land in Canada.

A pupil at Glebe Collegiate in Ottawa, he was a neighbour of the explorer-zoologist Tom Manning, with whom he had gone on several hunting expeditions locally. Manning then invited him to become his cook and zoological assistant on the Canadian Geographical Bureau's summer expedition to a 3,000 square mile island at Foxe Bay in the

*Macpherson, aged 17, when he went on a survey of the newly named Prince Charles Island in the Eastern Arctic.* (Geoffrey Hattersley-Smith)

Eastern Arctic, which had been photographed by the RCAF for the first time the previous year. Using a specially built 45-foot motor vessel, they surveyed the fauna, flora and main geographical and geological features of not only the large island, which was named Prince Charles Island, but two others, which became Air Force and Foley Islands.

When Macpherson returned to school after three months he had decided to become a zoologist.

The son of a businessman, who was descended from the Jacobite chief Cluny Macpherson and edited the Clan Macpherson journal, Andrew Hall Macpherson was born in London on June 2 1932. In 1940, he and his older sister Jay were evacuated with their mother to St John's, Newfoundland, where he went to Bishop Feild School, and then moved to Ottawa. Mrs Macpherson found work with the National Film Board, and so the family made only rare visits to Britain. As a result, the children used to refer to "our father which art in England".

In the summer of 1950, when Andrew Macpherson was at Carleton College, he was Manning's zoological and geographical assistant in James Bay, south-east of Hudson Bay. Since they were the only two members of the expedition, he was restricted to one book, a collection of Browning, whom he delighted in quoting ever afterwards.

They next went on a Canadian Defence Research Board expedition to aid future nuclear operations by making inshore hydrographic and oceanographic observations around the Beaufort Sea. This meant that they had to trap and shoot specimens of mammals and birds. One morning they woke to discover that a huge Barren Ground grizzly bear had passed their tent in the night, leaving tracks 10 inches long; but to Macpherson's disappointment, they spotted the creature too far away to attempt a shot.

In 1952, Manning and Macpherson returned to the western Arctic to circumnavigate Banks Island in a canoe with an outboard motor to survey and sound its bays and harbours. Starting from the south coast, they travelled up the west. But after rounding the north-west cape in mid-August, they were beset by ice in M'Clure Strait, close to where Captain Robert M'Clure's ship *Investigator* had been abandoned in 1853 while seeking the remains of Sir John Franklin's ill-fated expedition.

Like M'Clure, the last white man to visit the spot, they were obliged to retreat overland. This involved a march of more than 200 miles with a small hand-sledge made from barrel staves left by M'Clure. They had only limited rations as they made their way through frequent snow showers and marshy ground; and for part of the journey Macpherson had to lead Manning like a bear because he had gone snow-blind. After 14 days the pair were picked up by an Inuit trading schooner on the south coast.

The following summer, Manning had to complete the trip around the island with another companion because Macpherson had been called back to Britain by his father, who had not seen him since 1940. He was taken to Culloden, where their ancestor had missed the battle which saw the defeat of the Jacobite cause; but Macpherson would have preferred to be on Banks Island.

For several months during each of the next three summers he accompanied Manning on zoological field work for the Canadian National Museum around James Bay, in Ungava and the Belcher Islands. In 1957, Manning extended this work to the central Arctic coast and islands further north, leading a party of three, since Macpherson had married Betty Menzer, who was determined to accompany him. They headed to Yellowknife in the Northwest Territories in Manning's van, thence travelled by light aircraft to Adelaide Peninsula and King William Island for the summer. In 1958, the Macphersons again accompanied Manning further north to Prince of Wales Island.

By now Macpherson had gained his M.Sc. from McGill University, and had worked for a year as assistant curator of birds at the National Museum. However, when he heard that Manning was missing in the north, he immediately took a plane. Knowing that Manning would never go off without telling someone, he made use of his knowledge of the local language to inquire among Eskimos who eventually told him where to find his friend on the ice.

It was while visiting Baker Lake that he overheard an Indian widow visiting her children's school say that she could paint if she had the materials, and bought her paper and pencils; Jessie Oonark produced a set of six drawings, and went on to become a member of the Royal Canadian Academy of Arts.

Macpherson now joined the Canadian Wildlife Service and spent five summers in Keewatin, north-west of Hudson Bay, and at Resolute on Cornwallis Island to produce his definitive report, *The Dynamics of Canadian Arctic Fox Populations* (1969).

For two years he was seconded as scientific adviser to the Privy Council Office in Ottawa before being appointed director of the Western Region in the Canadian Wildlife Service. He then became director-general of the Western and Northern Region in the Environment Department.

After taking early retirement in 1988, Macpherson worked as a private consultant on zoological and administrative problems at Edmonton, Alberta. He was a founding member and secretary of the Sustainable Population Society, and the author of a manual on ice fishing.

Andrew Macpherson's wife died in 2001, and he was survived by two sons and a daughter.

〜

## Yousuf Karsh

YOUSUF KARSH (who died on July 13 2002, aged 93) took the world's most famous portrait photograph when he captured the bulldog spirit of Winston Churchill during the darkest days of the Second World War.

Churchill had just delivered his speech containing the quip "some chicken, some neck" to the Canadian Parliament on December 30 1941. He was walking into the Speaker's Chamber, arm in arm with the Canadian Prime Minister, Mackenzie King, when the photographer flicked on his lights. "Two minutes for one shot, and I mean two minutes for one shot," growled the great man as he lit a cigar. Karsh, however, did not want a photograph with that already familiar prop. He held out an ashtray. Churchill carried on smoking. Muttering "Forgive me, sir", the photographer stepped swiftly forward to remove the cigar from the prime ministerial lips. "By the time I got back to my camera," he recalled, "he looked so belligerent he could have devoured me." In an instant, Karsh had captured the Churchillian defiance on film.

The picture appeared on the cover of *Life* magazine, and was syndicated throughout the world. Later it became the centrepiece of Karsh's portrait books and was used on the postage stamps of at least six Commonwealth countries. Churchill himself sensed that it was a remarkable shot. "You can even make a roaring lion stand still to be photographed," he said with a sudden change of mood, prompting Karsh to take another shot. When this second picture was published a decade later it showed a portly gentleman smiling grimly, as if surprised while taking his ease at his club.

*Karsh examining the transparency of a picture of Her Majesty the Queen Elizabeth in 1988.* (AP/CP/Ron Poling)

From the moment the Churchill picture first appeared, Karsh found royal families, statesmen, scientists, artists, writers and musicians eager to welcome him whenever he arrived with his vast array of equipment. They would be smitten by this small, deferential man who listened to their speeches and read their books, then observed their mannerisms as he engaged them with his constant patter of heavily accented English, while carefully staging their "visual idealisation". "Karsh, you have immortalised me," Lord Beaverbrook told him. "I'm sitting for Karsh," the humorist Art Buchwald typed as his picture was being taken, "and it is for Posterity."

A Karsh portrait concentrated on the face, bathing it in a distinctive light which was balanced by sombre shadow. With the use only of the occasional prop and the always expressive deployment of hands, the photographer showed his subjects as they would have liked to have been remembered in their fields of endeavour. For some critics Karsh pictures, with their careful poses, seemed overlit and predictable, even akin to public relations exercises. His preference for black and white over colour only added to the sense of deliberate mystery. Nevertheless, while Karsh was prepared to take his sitters at their own valuation, such as Earl Mountbatten standing before a gilt mirror, he achieved some surprising perspectives. Clement Attlee was shown smiling and Khrushchev grinning out of a balaclava, while the actress Anita Ekberg appeared to be almost all bosom.

Yousuf Karsh was born on December 23 1908 at Mardin, Armenia, the son of an illiterate merchant, and grew up amid the Turkish genocide during which two of his uncles were killed in jail. The family escaped to Syria in a month-long journey with a Kurdish caravan.

Aged 16, speaking no English and little French, Yousuf was dispatched to join an uncle whom he had never met, at Sherbrooke, Quebec. For a time he went to school, hoping to study medicine, but his course was set when his uncle gave him a Box Brownie. Soon after, one of his landscapes was put into a competition by a fellow pupil and won the $50 first prize.

Karsh joined his uncle's photographic business, then spent three years in Boston, Massachusetts, with John Garo, an Armenian photographer. Garo advised him to study Velasquez and Rembrandt, and taught him how to use natural light and to make bathtub gin for the studio's customers. At the end of his apprenticeship, the pupil returned to Canada, where he established himself in the capital under the grandiloquent title "Karsh of Ottawa".

One of his earliest ventures was to join an amateur drama group, where he met his first wife, Solange Gauthier, and was introduced to the possibilities of artificial lighting. He also encountered Viscount Duncannon, son of the Earl of Bessborough, the Governor-General, who commissioned a portrait. The photographer was so nervous that the pictures were over-exposed and had to be redone.

But Karsh soon won the patronage of Mackenzie King, who invited him to photograph President Roosevelt on a visit to the Quebec Citadel. Karsh did not have his equipment set up in time for the general press conference. But when everyone else had gone, King reappeared on the terrace with Roosevelt and the new Governor-General, Lord

Tweedsmuir (the novelist John Buchan). They obligingly stood self-consciously erect. Karsh pretended to take the picture and thanked the group, at which point they relaxed as Tweedsmuir launched into an anecdote. Then Karsh took his first photograph to attract international attention.

In 1943, the success of the Churchill portrait enabled Karsh to cross the Atlantic to produce a series of highly-acclaimed pictures of the major figures in wartime Britain, among them General Montgomery, who was the first to claim that he had been "Karshed", General Eisenhower, King George VI, Noel Coward, and William Temple, the Archbishop of Canterbury.

With the return of peace, Karsh found that the great and the good were more than willing to welcome him into their houses. They would also visit him at his sixth-floor suite in Ottawa's Château Laurier Hotel, where he plied his trade to visiting businessmen, though his lack of interest in some of them is clear. British and Canadian prime ministers, American presidents, all the Popes (with the exception of the shortlived John Paul I) and many Hollywood stars submitted themselves to Karsh's conspiratorial camera.

He showed the poet Robert Frost sprawled in an armchair; pictured from behind the cellist Pablo Casals playing Bach; showed Jimmy Carter in a worried mood; and captured Ronald Reagan bursting into a smile. A favourite subject, from her childhood onwards, was Her Majesty The Queen, whom he portrayed over the decades, as few other photographers have done, smiling and relaxed. When one of his seven portraits of her appeared on the front of a Canadian $1 bill, a landscape of logs on the River Ottawa by his brother Malak appeared on the back.

There were more sessions with Churchill. Just before he stepped down as Prime Minister, Karsh missed a chance to catch him drinking. "The world knows of my virtue," the old man said as he downed a glass of wine at a gulp while they prepared for a session. But there was a final Karsh photograph taken shortly before Churchill's death showing him frail and holding a cigar, though with still commanding eyes.

Perhaps for reasons of tact, Karsh admitted that one of his greatest failures was Mackenzie King, whose portraits suggested a colourless executive rather than the master of ruthless political intrigue that he was. Although best-known for his portraits, Karsh collaborated with the American Bishop Fulton Sheen on books about the landscapes of

Rome and the Holy Land. He also did some industrial work for large motor car companies, a colour assignment on arctic wild flowers for *Time* magazine and an annual poster for the Muscular Dystrophy Association of America.

An intense, dapper man, Karsh lived for many years in a house outside Ottawa called "Little Wings", so called because it was on a migratory route for birds. It contained many works of art by well-known artists, but only one photograph, showing his beautiful second wife, Estrellita Nachbov, whom he married after his first wife's death in 1961.

Karsh, who was appointed CC in 1990 and moved to Boston on his retirement in 1992, liked to play down claims for his work. "My best," he would say, "could be the picture I take tomorrow."

~

## Father Les Costello

FATHER LES COSTELLO (who died on December 12 2002, aged 74) was the only professional ice-hockey player to quit the game to go into the priesthood. He left the Toronto Maple Leafs after two years while still in his prime, but never entirely severed his connections with the sport; in 1962 he co-founded the Flying Fathers, a team of skating Catholic priests recruited from across Canada, which raised around $4 million for good causes in more than 1,000 exhibition games.

Costello made his debut for the Leafs during the playoffs for the Grey Cup in early 1948 when he scored two goals and three assists. They were leading the Boston Bruins by three games to one in the semi-finals when the 20-year-old rookie. standing 5 ft 3 in and weighing 11 st 4 lb, took a pass from the Leafs' centre, Max Bentley, to score the game's winning goal. The team went on to defeat the Detroit Red Wings in the Stanley Cup that year.

The following season Costello was frustrated by a coach who, he felt, took the fun out of hockey. During one practice, when he was being subjected to a stern lecture, Costello skated over to the coach, handed him his gauntlets and stick, and said: "If you're so good, you do it." The incident earned Costello a ticket to a minor team in Pittsburgh, and it was while there that he began to worry about becoming what he called a "hockey bum". He soon returned to play for the Leafs, but quit in 1950.

The newspapers made much of his drop in pay from $7,200 a year as a National Hockey League player to $50 a month as a parish priest; but Costello had no doubts about the wisdom of his action. "I'd rather teach people to live with God than thrill them occasionally on Saturday nights," he told *Liberty* magazine in 1959 in an article headlined "Priest with a puck". "Days at the movies, nights at the hockey rink: I thought there must be a better way to end my life."

The son of a gold miner, Leslie John Thomas Costello was born on February 16 1928 at South Porcupine, a northern Ontario gold mine named after Noah Timmins, a founder of Hollinger Gold Mines in 1910, which produced more than 20 million ounces over 60 years.

Young Les was an outstanding schoolboy player, a fine skater with the resilience to take the physical buffeting from other players, like his younger brother Murray who also played in the NHL for Boston, Chicago and Detroit. He went to South Porcupine High School before moving south to Toronto, where he played for St Michael's College of the University of Toronto. Valued more for his hockey skills than his scholastic work, he was part of the team that won the Memorial Cup in 1945. Two years later, he turned professional.

In 1950 Costello returned to St Michael's as a student at St Augustine's seminary, and was ordained seven years later when he celebrated his first Mass at St Joachim's Church, South Porcupine. He served for a short time as a priest to Kirkland Lake, where he turned out for a local team, then returned to Timmins as parish priest of St Alphonsus's on the city's outskirts to minister to the miners and Indians.

Costello was a great story-teller, and liked to start and end every sermon with a light joke. When in the company of the tough miners of Timmins, his language could be as salty as theirs. He also enjoyed practical jokes: at more than one game with the Flying Fathers, he would arrange for a woman with a baby to turn up looking for the child's father, as he hid behind the other players.

He organised many local charities. His main mission, named after St Martin de Porres, supplied food, furniture and clothing to the needy. He also had a connection with Timmins's most famous export after gold, the country singer Shania Twain, whose parents he married and buried. When his church needed a new organ Shania Twain sent him $5,000.

Costello remained an active man, who liked cross-country skiing in the bush during the long northern winters. He skated almost every day at an arena a few blocks from his church, and hit his head while stretching for the puck during a warm-up before an exhibition game with the Flying Fathers at Kincardine, Ontario. He died on the ice.

~

## Royce Frith

ROYCE FRITH (who died on March 17 2005, aged 81) was the ebullient Canadian High Commissioner in London whose visit to Cornwall during the Canadian–Spanish row over North Atlantic fishing in 1995 demonstrated the continuing links between Britain and the senior dominion.

*Royce Frith thanking the people of Cornwall at Newlyn for supporting Canadian fishermen in their dispute with Spanish rivals in the North Atlantic.* (AP)

The Canadians were so alarmed over their depleted fish stocks that they warned the Spanish fleet to keep away, and then arrested one vessel caught fishing for Canadian turbot. The Spanish were incandescent with rage; John Major's government tried to steer a neutral path between Canada and the European Union. But the British public erupted in Canada's favour. The High Commission was inundated with hundreds of phone calls in support; thousands of letters poured in; *Daily Telegraph* readers demanded to know why Britain was not supporting fellow subjects of Her Majesty the Queen.

For West Country fishermen, it was not just a matter of supporting those who might well be distant kin on the other side of the Atlantic, but a chance to vent their anger at the Common Fisheries Policy which was enabling the Spanish to plunder British fish stocks.

Frith's superiors in Ottawa wanted to avoid upsetting the Westminster government or exacerbating tension with the EU. But, conscious of nearing the end of his career, he set off on a two-day Cornish tour without formally seeking permission. On arriving at Newlyn, Frith thanked the community for its moral support. As he plunged into the crowd distributing Maple Leaf flags and Canadian buttons, every person and every vessel in the harbour seemed to be festooned with support for the dominion. He eventually had to be extricated on a forklift truck. "It's a pity the fish don't have votes," he quipped.

When the EU eventually brokered an agreement, the Spanish were still outraged; but there was no doubt that Frith had mounted a skilful defence, declaring that the Canadian flag had become "the symbol of conservation" throughout Britain. Such a diplomatic triumph had been unmatched since the days before Canadians set out to become "the boy scouts of the world".

Although Frith was High Commissioner for only two years, he had another notable success when he successfully opposed the Canadian government's plan to give up the lease of Canada House in Trafalgar Square. This was, he declared, a surprising decision which would do enormous damage to Canadian prestige, considering that a new cultural centre was being constructed in Paris. For good measure, he reminded Paul Martin, the Foreign Minister, that his father in the 1970s had been one of the most distinguished High Commissioners in London. The Queen, he let slip afterwards, was not unhappy at the outcome.

Royce Herbert Frith was born at Lachine, Quebec, on November 12 1923 and graduated from the University of Toronto and Osgoode Hall Law School in Toronto, where he began to practise while working for the Liberal Party. With a diploma from Ottawa University, he became a member of the Bilingualism and Biculturalism Commission, which made a case for French to be made the nation's first language with English; he then became legal adviser to the Commissioner of Official Languages.

Although a loyal Liberal, who could deliver the party vote in Ontario, colleagues sometimes found Frith difficult. He would occasionally take on court cases which were directed against party interests, and he became involved in a bitter quarrel with the wife of the Prime Minister, John Turner, during the party's ill-fated general election campaign of 1984.

After being sent to the Senate, he proved himself an able deputy leader while the Liberals were in power, and then an equally energetic opposition leader after Brian Mulroney's Tories regained office. He led a vigorous, if fruitless, struggle against the introduction of a Goods and Services Tax, and claimed to be so appalled by the growth of prime ministerial power that he wrote a colourfully titled denunciation, *Hoods on the Hill* (1991).

There were inevitable complaints about cronyism when Frith was appointed to London in 1994. But he dismissed them genially, claiming that he had once played Henry Higgins in an amateur production of *My Fair Lady* and now looked forward to seeing some of the places in it. After being prematurely recalled home, he spent his last day watching a Test Match at Lord's, and taking tea with the former England captain Colin Cowdrey.

A tall dandy, Frith had a reputation in his younger days for being too smooth for his own good. But he undoubtedly had presence; an American got up after an interview, saying: "Very nice to meet you, Your Majesty."

Royce Frith, who was appointed OC in 2001, married, in 1948, Elizabeth Davison, with whom he had a son and a daughter.

~

## Bob Hunter

BOB HUNTER (who died on May 2 2005, aged 63) was the flamboyant journalist responsible for turning a tiny anti-nuclear protest group into Greenpeace, the best-known environmental lobby group in the world.

A "counter culture" columnist with the *Vancouver Sun* who sported headband, long hair and flared trousers, Hunter joined 11 men setting out in an elderly fishing boat to demonstrate against American testing in the northern Pacific in 1971. The boat was too slow to keep up with the Americans, who threatened to arrest them if they did, and it never reached the test ground on Amchitka, one of the Aleutian islands. But Hunter filed regular reports over its telephone, and a CBC radio reporter sent daily broadcasts.

As a result the public, already stirred by the uninhibited mixture of sex and drugs which was seeping up from San Francisco, became

*Hunter* (left) *with his fellow Greenpeace founder Patrick Moore, on an anti-whaling expedition in 1975.* (AP)

hooked on the issue. Coast Guards wrote a public letter supporting the demonstrators; W. A. C. ("Wacky") Bennett, British Columbia's Social Credit Premier, took part in a march; President Richard Nixon fumed. By the time the boat returned to Vancouver after its 45-day journey, public opinion had changed so much that the island was eventually turned into a wildlife sanctuary. Hunter admitted that he had dropped any attempt to maintain journalistic independence. "In reality, I wound up on the first watch," he recalled.

With his head full of beat poets, French philosophers and Marshall McLuhan's musings on the "global village", he demonstrated a brilliant grasp of the way news media could now be manipulated. After insisting that the group's name be changed from the "Don't Make a Wave Committee" to Greenpeace, which could be easily fitted into a headline, he became the foundation's chairman as member "Number 000".

As the disparate membership of hippies, draft dodgers and middle-aged Quakers mushroomed, there was considerable heart-searching about whether the organisation should take up other causes. But Hunter insisted it must do so, grandly proclaiming: "The media is a courtroom. There is stark justice at work."

He remained in Vancouver to mastermind coverage when Greenpeace's ship was sent down to protest about French nuclear tests in the South Pacific. Later he led the demonstrations against the Newfoundland seal hunt, the dumping of toxic waste in European waters, and whaling expeditions. But he realised that it was possible to take the cause too seriously. To make his point, he took on the job of latrine officer when an old minesweeeper was chosen to stage an anti-whaling demonstration. When the ship placed herself between whales and a fleet of Russian boats, a flight of harpoons was launched, one of which was photographed passing though Hunter's long hair.

The son of a truck driver, Robert Lorne Hunter was born at St Boniface, Manitoba, on October 13 1941. Even as a boy he was obsessed with authorship, ignoring lessons to write books, for which he would make special covers adorned with critics' comments, such as "Hunter's best yet".

On leaving school, he first did odd jobs, then set off on a trip around the world. He got as far as Los Angeles, returned home and then headed for Paris, where he took a room on the Left Bank, to find he had nothing to write about. He had more satisfaction in London, where he became an admirer of Bertrand Russell and the Campaign for Nuclear Disarmament, and met his first wife Zoe, with whom he was to have two children.

Returning home, he found a job on the *Winnipeg Tribune*. But after a year, he felt the lure of the West Coast again and moved to Vancouver, where he found he had been hired by *The Province* as a copyboy, not as a reporter. But when *Erebus*, his grimly comic novel about a boy working in a slaughterhouse, received favourable reviews, and was nominated for a Governor-General's award, he was given his column in *The Vancouver Sun*. Although few readers can initially have agreed with the views of a "hippie-trippy, long-haired freak" on the way ecology would change perceptions of science, politics and philosophy, Hunter proved compulsive reading.

He was temperamentally unsuited for any managerial role, but recognised that the public perception of Greenpeace was changing, so that exasperated governments now considered it politic to show respect. He cut his hair and started to wear suits, though when he married his second wife Bobbi, with whom he was to have two children, it was in a Buddhist ceremony. With self-conscious parody, he described himself as "an apocalypticist", urging audiences to "save the three-legged salamander from southern Saskatoon" and bewailing "My God, the planet is being destroyed while I lie on my waterbed. I must do something."

Although it was a wrench, Hunter resigned his chairmanship after the foundation of Greenpeace International in Amsterdam in 1979 and returned to writing. There were scripts for television programmes and books about the environment, as well as lectures and freelance articles, though some fellow environment journalists felt his partisanship did not always aid the cause.

His later books included *Occupied Canada: A Young White Man Discovers his Unsuspected Past*, which won a Governor-General's Award, and *Zen and the Art of International Freeloading*. The last, *2030: Confronting the Armageddon in our Lifetime*, so impressed a grandmother in her seventies that she drove from Vancouver Island to Ottawa in a low-emission car in order to deliver a copy to every MP along the way.

After moving to Ontario, Hunter was singled out by *Time* magazine in 2000 as one of the eco-heroes of the past century. By the following year he had become so respectable that he stood as a Liberal in a by-election for the Provincial Parliament. When his socialist opponents read out some pornographic passages from a travel book published more than a decade earlier, he protested that it was not an auto-biographical work and threatened to sue his triumphant rival.

Finally, Hunter covered ecological stories for local television stations, and had a programme in which a camera crew filmed him sitting at home in his bathrobe at 5.30 a.m., as he reviewed the morning's newspapers and criticised their news values.

# THE CARIBBEAN

### Michael Manley

MICHAEL MANLEY (who died on March 6 1997, aged 72) was Prime Minister of Jamaica from 1972 to 1980 and then, after a remarkable political *volte face*, swept to power again in 1989.

*Manley with Fidel Castro before his enthusiasm for the Cuban leader mellowed (AP)*

His metamorphosis from rugged socialism to capitalism, symbolised by the exchange of his trademark bush jacket for an elegant suit and tie, brought him a landslide general election victory over his arch-rival Edward Seaga, leader of the Jamaican Labour Party (JLP).

The charisma with which Manley had mesmerised his audiences since his first election was still there, though the emphasis was no longer on radicalism, but on the practical policies needed to tackle Jamaica's appalling problems: 20 per cent unemployment, foreign debts of more than £2 billion (consuming 40 per cent of export earnings) and a rise in violent crime. The man who had frightened old-established Jamaican families, sent British and American investors fleeing from the island during his first two terms in office, while causing 10,000 small businesses to close, had finally shed his left-wing extremism. Although Manley declared that he intended eventually to restore diplomatic relations with Cuba, which had been broken off by Seaga, he ruled out exchange visits with his old friend, Fidel Castro, professing "a terrible sadness" that the Cuban leader had rejected Mikhail Gorbachev's reforms.

A daunting figure more than six feet two inches tall, Manley was well respected by most islanders. Whenever he toured the towns and the slums he carried his "Rod of Joshua", an ivory-handled ebony baton given to him by Emperor Haile Selassie of Ethiopia, which became a symbol of power to the Rastafarian community in Jamaica.

Michael Norman Manley was born at St Andrew, Jamaica, on December 10 1924, the son of Norman Washington Manley, who formed the People's National Party (PNP) in 1938 and led the island to independence in 1962, and a Scots-born sculptress.

Manley was educated at Jamaica College and McGill University, Montreal, which he left early for the RCAF to serve for 18 months without seeing action. After the Second World War, he studied economics at the London School of Economics, and worked as a book reviewer and freelance journalist for the BBC before returning home to become associate editor of the weekly newspaper *Public Opinion*.

Joining the PNP, he became a member of its national executive council within a year, and went on to become a negotiator for the National Workers' Union, which later appointed him its first vice-president. In 1959, he led a crippling sugar industry strike, which prompted a government committee to be set up to investigate malpractices in the plantations. This revealed that the sugar companies had failed to report $4 million in profits between 1945 and 1950.

After entering the Senate in 1962, and becoming an MP in 1967, he succeeded his father as PNP President to lead the opposition to a Labour government which, despite its name, followed closely the policies of the British Conservative Party. Brandishing Selassie's baton with the slogan "Joshua with the rod of correction", he promised to use it to rid Jamaica of the old right-wingers and their "corrupt" colonialism. His platform was based on the use of regionalism to promote trade and strengthen national economies, a policy opposed not only by the ruling Labour government but also by some members of his own party. Domestically, he called for joint private–public ownership of mineral resources and a programme to promote racial awareness.

Accusing the government of Hugh Shearer of ignoring the poor, Manley captured two-thirds of the seats in the House of Representatives. To kick-start a moribund economy and increase employment, he launched a crash programme of public works, promoted the development of local industries, encouraged tourism and cut government spending. He set up a free education system, started a pilot scheme to encourage farmers to extend their lands, and told the island's School of Music to admit more itinerant folk musicians, whose reggae rhythms embodied feelings of protest. "If anybody is going to protest against me, at least I want them to do it with style," he said. Those who did protest were victimised in the courts, exiled or beaten up. He also sent his senior police officers to Cuba for training.

The exodus of rich Jamaicans contributed to another landslide election success for Manley in 1976. But it coincided with an outbreak of violence, in which 100 people were killed by gangs of youths in Kingston's slums. Manley imposed a state of emergency. Land became subject to seizure, mail was censored, workers were sacked on political grounds, and he gained control of the broadcasting corporation.

In the late 1970s the International Monetary Fund laid down stringent conditions for continuing its financial support. It insisted that the Jamaican currency should be devalued by 40 per cent, that public expenditure be slashed and unemployment be allowed to rise.

By now vice-president of the Socialist International and the acknowledged spokesman for the world's poorest countries, Manley flew to Moscow to try to break the IMF stranglehold on his country, which was now reeling under a 47 per cent inflation rate. There was no cash and no new markets for the struggling bauxite and sugar industries. Then oil prices rose dramatically. When the IMF tightened the screw and he had to call a general election, one Jamaican banker claimed that there was only 30 days' credit left for food and medicine.

Eight hundred people died in clashes during the run-up to polling day, and Manley survived two assassination attempts. Edward Seaga, a Harvard-educated free marketeer, and therefore the darling of President Reagan's administration, won a resounding victory. Promising to make Jamaica the model of free enterprise in Reagan's "Caribbean Basin Initiative", in which countries accepting Washington doctrine would benefit from American aid, the new Prime Minister severed diplomatic relations with Cuba and introduced tough austerity measures, which improved growth and attracted millions of tourists back to Jamaica. In 1983, he called a snap election, boycotted by Manley on the grounds that it had been corruptly initiated, and consequently took all 60 seats in the House, leaving it without an opposition. But the promised American aid made little difference to the island's continuing economic plight, and most Jamaicans felt that Manley could have done better. After eight years even American officialdom was disillusioned with Seaga.

Jamaica had the highest per capita foreign debt of any developing country; its agriculture was failing; and investment was absent while social services, housing and roads were deteriorating. Not only was there no sign of a free market, the gap between the rich and the poor was widening. And in the autumn of 1988, Hurricane Gilbert destroyed the island's entire banana crop and flattened tens of thousands of homes. Seaga was incensed that the US Congress had failed to approve important parts of President Reagan's Caribbean Basin Initiative, with the result that promised cash never arrived.

In the meantime, Manley was winning support from American Republicans, who had once damned him, and in the 1989 Jamaican election campaign, he reappeared to captivate the crowds. Sixty per cent of the population was under 24, with little memory of his earlier regime; and they were spellbound by his oratory. On polling day he won 57 per cent of the vote. Contemplating the future at his 40-acre estate of rose and coffee bushes, north of Kingston, he admitted his early naivety, that he had been "locked into trade union thinking", and had allowed his left wing to dominate him. He even promised to retain the best of Seaga's policies in preparing to meet Jamaica's economic challenge. Three years later he retired from office because of ill health.

Michael Manley wrote seven books, including a history of West Indian cricket, which was one of his passions along with classical music. He was five times married, and had two sons and three daughters.

～

## Sir Eric Gairy

SIR ERIC GAIRY (who died on August 23 1997, aged 75) was a highly eccentric Prime Minister of Grenada, responsible for leading his country to independence in 1974 before being ousted from power five years later, while he was in New York to address the United Nations on unidentified flying objects.

A self-proclaimed expert on UFOs, he urged the necessity of keeping watch for such visitors from outer space only to find that the threat to him lay closer to home. Provoked by his strong-arm tactics and his

*Gairy made diplomats wince when he talked of inviting the British and Americans to establish bases.* (PA)

peculiarities, such as leaving Grenada to judge the 1970 Miss World contest in London, his opponents mounted their coup. The new government of Maurice Bishop then filled the island's museum with such choice possessions from his house as a marble bath which had belonged to Josephine Bonaparte, gigantic crucifixes, voodoo fetishes and his favourite book, a thriller entitled *Who Killed Enoch Powell?*

The mood of the island soon turned darker. Gairy opted for exile in California while Bishop's New Jewel Movement took an increasingly Marxist turn. His close ties with Cuba and the building of an airport designed for heavy military jets quickly alarmed the United States. In October 1983, Bishop was arrested, and later murdered by his former colleagues. This prompted the invasion of the island by United States troops (ostensibly to protect American medical students) and the subsequent ousting of the pro-Communist junta. President Reagan's intervention in the affairs of a Commonwealth country caused a temporary rift in his relations with Margaret Thatcher.

When Gairy returned after the invasion to contest the elections in December 1984, he claimed to have changed his approach to politics, although his manifesto retained some eccentric touches, including pledges to exempt church ministers from searches by Customs, to make teachers dress more tidily and to restore the "beautiful sport of horse racing". Diplomats winced when he talked of inviting in British and American bases. Gairy's Grenada United Labour Party (GULP) won only one seat against the 14 taken by his opponent Herbert Blaize; and he failed to persuade this lone victor to resign. Subsequently, GULP failed to regain power in the elections of 1990 and 1995.

Nevertheless Gairy remained the island's best-known politician, though increasingly confined by blindness to his well-guarded villa.

Many in the business community pined for someone as willing as he to arrange deals in return for a suitable consideration. But while Grenada did not remain immune to corruption, its weakness for demagogues had passed.

Eric Matthew Gairy was born into a poor country family at St Andrew's, Grenada, on February 18 1922. After education at the local Roman Catholic school, he joined other young Grenadians toiling in the Dutch oilfields of Aruba, an island off the Venezuelan coast. Next he became a schoolmaster.

By the late 1940s Gairy, still in his late twenties, was already known by the rural poor as "Uncle Gairy" for his championing of their rights. He founded the Manual, Maritime and Menial Workers' Union, from which in 1950 he organised Grenada's first political party, the left-leaning GULP. Loathed by the island's white planters and employers, he promised a better life for the rural black population who produced its valuable exports of bananas, cocoa beans and nutmeg seeds. He caused a particular upset by organising a strike of household servants.

In 1951 Gairy was elected to the Legislative Council, and then began a campaign to increase the workers' pay of 3s 6d a day while threatening to call a general strike. Soon large crowds were coming to hear him, a slight, handsome figure with a resonant voice. While his manner was calm his message was inflammatory, prefiguring the violence that would mark his years in office. A typical speech before the strike went: "Look, good people, Uncle Eric don't like to get mad. But some of the big boys have said they are out to 'get' Gairy. My people, if the day comes when you hear Uncle Gairy has become a ghost, remember to make certain a lot of the big guys are ghosts too. Then Uncle Gairy's ghost won't be mad because he likes company."

Herbert Blaize, the creator of the Grenada National Party, whom Gairy had met at Aruba, was also in the vanguard of the subsequent general strike and, on the orders of the Governor-General, the pair were briefly banished to Carriacou, a tiny dependency 30 miles north of Grenada. When Gairy finally agreed to call off the stike, he captured six of the eight seats in the legislature, and became Chief Minister.

Grenada, which had been discovered by Columbus in 1498, then colonised by the French in 1650 before being ceded to Britain in 1783, was now firmly on the road to change. In 1958 it joined the Federation of the West Indies, but a commission of inquiry two years later criticised Gairy for "financial adventures" and browbeating the public service. He was dismissed while the Grenadian constitution was suspended. Two years later the federation was dissolved.

In the 1967 general election, however, Gairy defeated the moderate Blaize and became Premier. Internal self-government was soon granted, he had the Grenadian-appointed Governor dismissed, and the country achieved independence within the Commonwealth in 1974, with Gairy as Prime Minister.

He proceeded to retain his hold on power with a brutal, autocratic and corrupt regime, taking into his own ministerial portfolio everything from defence to tourism. He awarded government contracts to supporters and responded to dissent with restrictions on the media and unions. Order was maintained by his "Mongoose Gang" of thugs and by fostering his reputation among country people for strong *obeah*, or prowess in voodoo.

Violence escalated as independence approached. In November 1973 members of the New Jewel Movement, including Maurice Bishop, were set upon and beaten up by the Mongoose Gang. A few months later, Bishop's father was murdered by the secret police. When Gairy gave his Independence Day speech from the ramparts of Fort George, he ensured that Bishop heard it by locking him in the dungeon of the fortress, beneath the feet of the visiting dignitaries.

In 1996 Gairy suffered a stroke and announced that he would resign as party leader. But his choice of a successor, Jerry Seales, a young lawyer, irritated older contenders and split the party.

Eric Gairy, who was knighted in 1977, left a widow and two daughters, one of whom, Marcelle, became Grenada's High Commissioner in London.

~

## Sir Lionel Luckhoo

SIR LIONEL LUCKHOO (who died on December 12 1997, aged 83) was a flamboyant Guyanese barrister listed in the *Guinness Book of Records* as the world's most successful advocate, with 245 consecutive successes.

Known as the "Perry Mason of the Caribbean", Luckhoo was also a highly respected High Commissioner in London for both Guyana and Barbados, a candidate for Prime Minister, and later a globe-trotting evangelical preacher who founded the Luckhoo Mission in Dallas, Texas.

Lionel Alfred Luckhoo was born at New Amsterdam, British Guiana, on March 2 1914, the second of three sons. His Indian grandfather, Lokhooa, had been "recruited" to work on a sugar plantation in British Guiana while sightseeing as a boy with his two brothers at Lucknow in 1859. The recruiter painted a bright picture of the prospects in a strange land called "Damra Tapu" (Demerara, a province in British Guiana), where in five years they could make a fortune, before returning home.

Lokhooa and his brothers, aged 13, 11 and 7, crossed the Indian and Pacific Oceans aboard *Victor Emanuel,* and were assigned to a sugar plantation as indentured labour. Lokhooa converted to Christianity, thereafter calling himself Moses Luckhoo. When, after years of hard work, he had saved enough to buy his way out of his indentures, he qualified as an interpreter then went on to open several provision stores, eventually becoming one of New Amsterdam's richest merchants. Lionel's father, Edward Alfred, one of Moses's six sons, became the first East Indian solicitor in the colony in 1899, and later Mayor of New Amsterdam.

Young Lionel was educated at Queen's College, Georgetown, before going to London to study medicine at St Thomas's Hospital. Realising that he could not stand the sight of blood, he switched to law, and was called to the Bar by Middle Temple in 1940. He left for home during the Dunkirk evacuation to set up in legal practice with his brother in Georgetown.

As his record suggests, Lionel Luckhoo was extraordinarily persuasive with juries. He was incisive in cross examination, and got straight to the nub of a case. Between 1940 and 1985, when he finally retired, almost all his clients were acquitted at trial. The few that were not had their convictions overturned on appeal to the Privy Council.

One such case, *Noor Mohamed* v. *R* (1949), remains an authority on "similar fact" evidence. The defendant, a goldsmith, was accused of murdering the woman he lived with by causing her to take cyanide, a substance which he used for his trade. There was no direct evidence that he had done so, and there was some suggestion that she had committed suicide. At the trial, the prosecution advanced evidence that the goldsmith had previously killed his wife with cyanide while pretending that it was a cure for toothache. On appeal, Luckhoo successfully argued that the prejudicial effect of this outweighed its probative value, so it had been wrongly admitted.

After independence, Luckhoo argued for keeping appeals to the Privy Council, feeling that its legitimacy could not be easily replicated in the Caribbean. During the early 1960s, he acted for the maverick cult leader Jim Jones in a child custody case. Jones held sway over a great many Guyanese, duped by his fake healing ceremonies and seduced into adopting his free-love lifestyle. In 1978, he orchestrated the mass suicide of some 900 people in his commune known as Jonestown. Luckhoo later admitted that dissuading the deeply unstable Jones from committing suicide on an earlier occasion was one of his greatest regrets.

In the meantime, Luckhoo had served as a member of the State Council, 1952–3, and as Minister without Portfolio, 1954–7. He was Mayor of Georgetown in 1954, 1955, 1960 and 1961. In the late 1950s, he stood for Prime Minister against the coalition led by Cheddi Jagan and Forbes Burnham. Cheddi Jagan's Progessive People's Party appeared so pro-communist in 1953 that Britain suspended the constitution for four years and dispatched troops. As well as being a staunch Anglophile, Luckhoo was fiercely anti-communist. But his National Labour Front expounded conservative ideas for which the country was not yet ready, and he failed to garner enough grass-roots support.

When Guyana gained independence in 1966, Luckhoo became its first High Commissioner in London. That autumn he also became Barbados's first High Commissioner (through his friendship with the Barbadian Prime Minister, Errol Barrow), thereby pioneering the cost-saving system of joint representation that has since been adopted by many small countries. His motor car carried two flags, and not infrequently two places were laid for him at official banquets.

From 1967 to 1970, Luckhoo also represented Guyana and Barbados as ambassador in Paris, Bonn and The Hague. But he gave up his diplomatic career in 1970 and entered chambers in the Temple, returning to Guyana in 1974, after the failure of his first marriage. Until retiring in 1980, he concentrated on appeal work.

Luckhoo was very attached to the Turf. The first horse that he and his brothers owned was called First Luck; it went on to win 33 races in Guyana and Trinidad, thereby financing a string of 10 horses. He later had several in training in England with Sam Hall, one of which, Philodendrun, won the Liverpool Summer Cup in 1960. He was a regular attender of Royal Ascot, and in 1960 published

"The Fitzluck Theory of Breeding Racehorses" in *The Blood-Horse*, an American magazine.

Luckhoo was always immaculately attired, and had a short, sharp step and gait. Everything was done in a slightly hurried way. He was a brilliant off-the-cuff speaker, and an accomplished magician and member of the Magic Circle. He had always been a Christian; in later years he became, as he put it, "an ambassador for Jesus". He founded his mission in 1980, preached around the world, and wrote pamphlets with such titles as *Dear Atheist* and *God is Love*.

Lionel Luckhoo took Silk in 1954, was appointed CBE in 1962, was knighted in 1966 and appointed KCMG in 1969.

He married, first, Sheila Chamberlin, with whom he had two sons and three daughters; after the marriage was dissolved he married his second wife, Jeannie.

—

## Morris Cargill

MORRIS CARGILL (who died on April 8 2000, aged 85) was for almost half a century the best-known journalist in the Caribbean; his column in Jamaica's national newspaper, *The Daily Gleaner*, was regarded by many as the only accurate account of the state of affairs in the country, and was required reading for politicians and plumbers alike.

Although he delighted, above all, in pricking pomposity, Cargill did not hold back from giving his own authoritative view. "I know it's very trendy to admire reggae," he wrote. "Well, I don't. I am stubbornly of the opinion that it is fit only for semi-literate tone-deaf morons ... I wouldn't dream of using an amplifier to bash people in the street with Beethoven."

Taken with his other much-aired dislikes – tough steaks, computers, bad English – such attitudes might be thought to be those of a world-weary reactionary. Instead, Cargill was in favour of decriminalising marijuana. He distrusted authority, loathed racists and converted to Buddhism. "Jamaica and its politicians", he believed, "are West Indian ramshackle, Mrs Malaprop, Black Mischief and the Mafia all tied up in one parcel." Provocative commentary like this divided even the many who admired his writing and brought charges that he was unpatriotic, which he was not. Together with respect for the family, nothing was dearer to him than Jamaica's future, which he feared would be destroyed by nationalism. He made it his task to confront any such threat with humour, and fearlessness.

Morris Cargill was born in the parish of St Andrew, Jamaica, on June 10 1914. His ancestors were Scottish Covenanters who had settled on the island in 1666 and over the centuries acquired large plantations. His father was a partner in the law firm of Cargill, Cargill and Dunn.

Young Morris grew up in Kingston, where his Jamaican nanny kept colds at bay by liberally dosing him with marijuana. He was sent to school locally at Munro College, although in practice he spent much of his time on his uncles' plantations, and then at 13 was dispatched to Stowe, in Buckinghamshire. From there he would return home only for the summer holidays, making the journey by banana boat.

Cargill decided to follow his father into the law, and in 1937 was admitted a solicitor in Jamaica. But he soon became the manager of the Carib Theatre, a Kingston cinema, instead. In 1941, he and his wife Barbara sailed for Britain to make their contribution to the war effort. Cargill worked first for the Ministry of Information and then as business manager of the Crown Film Unit. He also broadcast occasionally on the BBC.

After the war, he went into business for himself, importing Jamaican rum and a coffee-based liqueur he had had made up to his Aunt Mary's recipe. This latter venture was not at first a success, and so Cargill sold his rights to Tia Maria. He fared better with his interests in steel and plastics.

On returning home in 1949 he once more changed career, buying a 720-acre banana plantation, Charlottenburgh, in St Mary. He gradually modernised the cabins of his plantation workers, and valiantly tried to introduce birth control. He gave hundreds of sponges to young women for use as simple barrier contraception, but then discovered that they were using them instead to wipe clean their slates in school. The local population continued to grow apace. Farming in Jamaica, Cargill claimed, was a mixture of running an institution for delinquents and being both medical orderly and magistrate. His labourers trusted him to settle all their disputes, rather than go to court.

He kept up his interest in journalism and broadcasting, and in 1952 he began to write a daily column in the *Gleaner* under the name "Sam White". Soon his opinions were being read all over the West Indies. Somewhat against his better judgment, he was elected to the short-lived Parliament of the West Indies Federation as the member for St Mary in 1958. This meant moving to Trinidad, where, while serving as Deputy Leader of the Opposition, he also edited the *Port of Spain Gazette*. He felt under-employed, however, and in 1963 resigned to return to Jamaica, where he resumed farming and writing his column.

His friends and neighbours in St Mary included Noel Coward and Ian Fleming, who had James Bond seek information about Jamaica from Cargill in two of his books, *Dr No* and *Octopussy*. Cargill also had a phone call from the British Labour leader Hugh Gaitskell, who had chased Anne Rothermere, Fleming's future wife, to find the local press pursuing him. Hiding in an ironmonger's shop, with reporters outside, he persuaded Cargill to drive to the rear of the building to rescue him.

By the 1970s crime was growing steadily, and Cargill was badly wounded by a man attempting to rob his house. Then, when Michael Manley's socialist government came to power, he was threatened with prosecution three times for criticising the Prime Minister in his column.

A campaign to drive Cargill out of Jamaica now began. The last straw came when the water to his plantation was cut off, and he was forced to sell Charlottenburgh. He took a publishing job in Connecticut, and was allowed to take only $50 with him to America. There he wrote a memoir, *Jamaica Farewell* (1977). A change of government, however, brought him back, and with his half-brother John Pringle, who was Jamaica's Ambassador-at-Large, he bought a large estate near Hope Bay, Portland, called "Paradise Plum". But the plantation was devastated by a hurricane and floods, and in 1982 he moved to Kingston to concentrate on journalism.

Although ill health and near-blindness had latterly confined him to a wheelchair, he still wrote his column three times a week until just before his death.

Cargill was, despite the strength of his opinions, a kind and considerate man. He wrote an introduction to *A Gallery of Nazis* and edited *Ian Fleming's Jamaica*, as well as writing with John Hearne, under the pseudonym John Moris, three thrillers. His *Selection of Writings in the Gleaner, 1952–85* appeared in 1987, and was followed in 1998 by another collection, *Public Disturbances*.

Morris Cargill was appointed a Commander of the Order of Distinction (Jamaica) for services to journalism in 1998. He described it as a "sort of equivalent to the CBE, and only given to extinct volcanoes".

He married first, in 1937, Barbara Margot Samuel. They were divorced in 1972, but remained on friendly terms and took their holidays together. They adopted a daughter, who survived them both. A second marriage was also dissolved.

## Dame Eugenia Charles

DAME EUGENIA CHARLES (who died on September 6 2005, aged 86) was the Prime Minister of Dominica known as the "Iron Lady of the Caribbean" for her steely determination to put her country on the path to stability and prosperity.

She attracted international attention in 1983 when, as chairman of the Organisation of East Caribbean States, she persuaded President Ronald Reagan to send American troops to Grenada, Dominica's neighbour and fellow Commonwealth member, to crush a military coup by Cuban-backed leftists who had seized power after overthrowing and murdering Maurice Bishop, the Prime Minister.

The American invasion caused outrage among Commonwealth members and at the UN. It also embarrassed Margaret Thatcher, who had not been warned about the venture until it was too late. In the longer term, however, the American intervention came to be viewed as an "historic marker", which had reversed the tide of Communist infiltration in the region.

Eugenia Charles remained staunch in her defence of the invasion, regarding it as "a pre-emptive strike" which had removed a "dangerous threat to peace and security". When Labour's foreign affairs spokesman, Denis Healey, accused her of having been virtually kidnapped by the Americans, she retorted that he would never have dared to make such an insulting remark about the Prime Minister of Canada, Pierre Trudeau: "It's only because we're small and black that he's prepared to say that." In response to criticism by sundry African leaders, she drily conceded that Caribbean countries had asked themselves Robert Mugabe's question, "Who will be next?" as they looked at Grenada. That was why they had supported the American rescue operation. "The Grenadians wanted it, and that's all that counts," she said. "I don't care what the rest of the world thinks."

The granddaughter of a former slave, Mary Eugenia Charles was born on May 15 1919 at Pointe Michel, near the Dominican capital of

*Eugenia Charles addressing reporters at the White House after American and Caribbean troops had landed on the island of Grenada.* (AP/Bob Daugherty)

Roseau. Her father, John Baptiste Charles, was a successful planter and investor, though it was her mother, Josephine, who dominated her upbringing and encouraged her in her career.

Eugenia Charles was educated at convents in Dominica and Grenada and, after leaving school, took a secretarial course. To improve her shorthand, she practised taking notes in courtrooms, an experience that aroused her interest in the law. After studying at the University of Toronto and the London School of Economics, she was called to the Bar by Inner Temple. She returned to Dominica to become the island's first woman lawyer, opening a practice in Roseau.

Eugenia Charles became interested in politics and, though not active in any party, gained a reputation as an outspoken critic of official corruption through the acidic letters she sent to newspapers. When, in 1968, the ruling Labour Party passed a law of sedition to silence critics (known as the "Shut Your Mouth Bill"), she joined with others to form an organisation called Freedom Fighters and travelled round the country to address protest rallies. A year later Freedom Fighters developed into the centre-right Dominica Freedom Party, and Eugenia Charles reluctantly agreed to become its leader. In 1970 five party members were elected to the Legislature and, although she was not among them, Eugenia Charles took an appointed seat.

Since 1967 Dominica had been part of the six-member West Indies Associated States, which was dependent on Great Britain but moving towards independence.

When formal independence was declared in 1978, Eugenia Charles led the opposition to the scandal-ridden Labour administration of Patrick John, speaking out against its alleged secret business dealings with South Africa and the economic mismanagement that had brought the country to the verge of bankruptcy.

In an atmosphere of mounting public unrest, the Freedom Party was joined by several government ministers, and, after a general strike, the John government was forced out of office. An interim administration under James Seraphine fared little better, and Dominica's woes were compounded by Hurricane David, which killed 42 people, left 65,000 homeless and devastated the banana crop, which was the island's main source of income. In 1980 Eugenia Charles's party won power with more than 52 per cent of the vote.

From the beginning she made clear her determination to lead from the front, taking over, in addition to her prime ministerial responsibilities, the key portfolios of foreign affairs and development and finance. Corrupt officials were dismissed, tax dodgers were penalised and the nation's 200-strong defence force was ordered to disband and hand over its arms to the police after military officers were found to have been selling weapons to Rastafarian marijuana growers. Within 18 months Eugenia Charles had successfully repulsed three coup attempts, two of them orchestrated by Patrick John, who, with his chief agents, was jailed.

In 1981, with American support, she launched a wide-ranging reform programme in education, health care and economic development. By the following year, inflation had fallen from 30 per cent to four per cent; new light industries were starting up; agricultural production had improved; the tourist industry had substantially increased; and the balance of trade deficit was cut by a half.

Eugenia Charles regarded herself very much as the mother of her people, taking a tough line with drug growers and rejecting overtures from foreign businessmen wanting to establish casinos or night clubs on the island, fearing that such establishments might attract criminal elements. Buoyed by the success of her domestic policies and her reputation for tough and principled leadership, she won two more five-year terms before retiring in 1995.

When asked to define the difference between male and female political leadership, Eugenia Charles observed: "Men tend to make decisions and leave it to others to carry out. Women follow up their actions to see what is happening to their plan." She saw little place for Western-style feminism in Dominica's matriarchal society: "In Dominica, we really live women's lib," she explained. "We don't have to expound it."

After stepping down from politics, she returned to her legal practice, though she continued to speak out on political matters and became spokesman for the Caribbean banana industry, defending the preferential access of Caribbean producers to European markets.

Eugenia Charles, who was appointed DBE in 1992, lived with her father until he died in 1983, aged 107. She never married.

# OUTPOSTS

~

## John Cheek

JOHN CHEEK (who died on September 3 1996, aged 56) was the doughty advocate of the Falkland Islanders on the international stage during the Argentinian invasion of 1982.

*John Cheek* (left) *next to Air Commodore Brian Frow, Director-General, Falkland Islands Office in London.* (PA)

It was pure chance that Cheek, who had been elected a member of the Falklands Legislative Council in 1981, happened to be in London on a training course when General Galtieri launched his attack. In the ensuing weeks he demonstrated on radio and television the rugged self-reliance for which the islanders are known, and his quiet strength made him an ideal communicator. Not only did he broadcast frequent messages of encouragement to the Falklanders on the BBC World

Service; he also appeared on television in America, providing invaluable back-up for Sir Nicholas Henderson at the Washington embassy and Sir Anthony Parsons at the UN. Cheek was able to convince because he was the genuine article: a fifth-generation Falkland Islander, whose family had arrived in the 1850s.

The son of a shepherd, John Cheek was born on November 18 1939 on a remote hill farm in West Falkland. He went to school in Port Stanley and then took a job as a radio officer with the Falkland Islands Dependencies Survey, forerunner of the British Antarctic Survey, serving for three years at Hope Bay and later at Stonington Base from the age of 19. He then paid his way through technical college at Colwyn Bay in North Wales before becoming a radio officer in the Merchant Navy. In 1966 he returned to the Falklands to work in the government radio station, and eight years later became an engineer with Cable & Wireless.

Elected to the islands' legislature in 1981, he was a member of the boards of education and health and also of the committees on scholarship and training, hospital management and housing. He called for higher old age pensions and equality for women. He also helped to increase grants under which islanders could receive education abroad. Cheek's skill in advocacy meant that he was 12 times chosen to argue for the Falklanders at the UN, on one occasion debating with an Argentinian delegation which outnumbered him 20 to one. He resigned from the Legislative Council in 1989 after a dispute about agricultural grants. But he was soon back, and in 1995 became one of the three elected members of the Executive Committee.

As a businessman Cheek was a founder member of the islands' chamber of commerce. He helped to develop the fishing industry, which has become the mainstay of the islanders' new-found prosperity. In 1987 he and another councillor set up Fortuna, the Falklands' first indigenous fishing company.

He was a member of the islands' oil management team, and, in 1995, helped to negotiate an agreement with Argentina. But he was adamant that there should be no compromise over the Falklands' sovereignty. "We must not repeat the mistakes of the 1970s," he declared, "when close contacts led to an unwanted dependence on Argentina for transport links and fuel supplies. We obviously have to be as strong as ever in protecting our right of self-determination and in lobbying to maintain our friends and to gain further support."

In 1988 John Cheek was diagnosed as having prostate cancer, but he never allowed this knowledge to affect his dedication and cheerfulness. The end, when it came, was sudden.

John Cheek was married to Jane Biggs, with whom he had two daughters.

~

## General Sir William Jackson

GENERAL SIR WILLIAM JACKSON (who died on March 12 1999, aged 81) was awarded the MC twice during the Second World War, and from 1978 to 1982 was a highly popular Governor and Commander-in-Chief of Gibraltar.

*Bill Jackson* (left) *with the Gibraltar historian Philip Dennis (Michael Brufal).*

Before he took up the post, Bill Jackson had believed it inevitable that Gibraltar would one day be integrated into Spain. "Not any more," he emphasised in 1981. "You realise how bitter the feeling is, and it's been made far worse by Spain's behaviour over the past 26 years." He proved a doughty defender of the Gibraltarians' interests, invariably referring to the Rock's inhabitants as "we". He was delighted to welcome the Prince and Princess of Wales to Gibraltar on their honeymoon, a plan which had caused King Juan Carlos to boycott the royal wedding.

During the Falklands War, Jackson had the delicate task of misleading the Spanish authorities about British strength and intentions, knowing that the Spaniards were in contact with the Argentine government. Later, in 1982, he stamped firmly on the notion that a Spanish admiral might be allowed to fly his flag in Gibraltar following Spain's admission to NATO.

After retiring from the governorship Jackson continued to defend Gibraltar's cause. He wrote *The Rock of the Gibraltarians* (1988), and 10 years later concluded a letter to *The Daily Telegraph* by warning: "It will take several generations to expunge the depth of anti-Spanish feeling generated over the last half a century."

William Godfrey Fothergill Jackson was born on August 28 1917, the son of Colonel Albert Jackson, RAMC. His mother was descended from one of William the Conqueror's commanders.

Young Bill went from Shrewsbury to Woolwich, where he won the King's Medal, then up to King's College, Cambridge, to read mechanical sciences before being commissioned into the Royal Engineers in 1937. Later he commented that most of his training at Woolwich had been useless. He had learned to charge with lance and sabre, but never fired his rifle; he went on only one pistol practice in the entire 18 months he was there. Military history consisted of studying the Napoleonic Wars. Later still, the prevalence of left-wing opinion at his Cambridge college gave him misgivings about the future. Fortunately, when war came, he noted, "my former anti-military colleagues almost to a man joined one of the three Armed Services".

Jackson first commanded a field section, which included Glasgow dockers whose speech he found almost impossible to understand; some of them had had their teeth filed for biting. Nevertheless, they settled down into an efficient unit. They were first issued with tropical clothing, then told that they were going to Finland. When that operation was cancelled they went to Norway, landing at Andalsnes on April 17 1940.

They pushed inland, but the Germans were already there in too great numbers, and orders were soon given to withdraw, inflicting as much damage as possible to the Germans on the way. Jackson's tasks included the blowing of bridges. By the end of the campaign, his courage and resourcefulness under fire had earned him an immediate Military Cross.

On returning to Britain, he was employed in fortifying the East Anglian coast before being posted to 6th Armoured Division, which was based in Cambridge, prior to being dispatched to Algeria in November 1942. The division fought across Algeria to Tunisia. At El Arousa, Jackson was badly wounded when a truck-load of mines exploded near him. After three months in hospital, he was posted to the intelligence staff of Eisenhower's Allied Headquarters in time to help plan the invasion of Sicily.

He next commanded 8th Field Squadron which, in December 1943, landed at Taranto. He took part in the crossing of the Garigliano, and fought at Monte Cassino – about which he wrote a detailed account. He was awarded a Bar to his MC. The squadron then pushed on to Arezzo, where Jackson's scout car was blown up by a mine, shattering his ear drums. After another spell in hospital, he was posted to GHQ Allied Armies in Italy. He found Field Marshal Alexander (on whom he later wrote a book) "curiously self-effacing and with great charm, but seeming to lack the force of a great commander", though he was just that.

In January 1945, Jackson attended the Staff College, Camberley, (which he found most impressive) and was posted to the Far East as GSO1, Fourteenth Army, and then to Malaya, sorting out the problems left after the Japanese surrender. There he met his future wife, Joan Buesden, an ATS officer, with whom he was to have a son and a daughter.

From 1948 to 1950, Jackson was an instructor at the Staff College, Camberley, after which he became a company commander at Sandhurst. Next came a posting as second-in-command of the Royal Engineers, 7th Armoured Division, in Germany and a spell at the War Office, where he helped plan the Suez invasion.

Jackson commanded the Gurkha Engineers in Malaya for two years before returning to Camberley, as Colonel, General Staff. After spells at the War Office and the Imperial Defence College, he became Director, Chief of the Defence Staff's Unison Planning Staff, then Assistant Chief of General Staff, Operational Requirements, at the Ministry of Defence. In 1970 Jackson was appointed General Officer Commanding, Northern Command, and, from 1973 to 1976, Quartermaster General.

He was a military historian at the Cabinet Office from 1977 to 1978 and from 1982 to 1987, and retained to the end of his life an enormous capacity for work, turning out obituaries and book reviews for *The Times* which were notable for their discernment. His books included *Attack in the West* (1953); *Seven Roads to Moscow* (1957); *The Battle for Italy* (1967); *The Battle for Rome* (1969); *The North African Campaign* (1975); *Overlord Normandy* (1978); *British Defence Dilemmas* (1990); *The Chiefs* and *The Governor's Cat* (1992); *The Pomp of Yesterday* and *Fortress to Democracy* (1995); and *Britain's Triumph and Decline in the Middle East* (1996). He was joint editor and author of Volume VI of the British Official History of World War II in the Mediterranean (1984–8), *Withdrawal from Empire* (1986), and *The Alternative Third World War* (1987). He also gave the Kermit Roosevelt Lectures in America in 1976.

Bill Jackson was appointed OBE in 1958, KCB in 1971 and GBE in 1975. He was ADC (General) to the Queen (1974–6), Colonel Commandant, Royal Engineers (1971–81), Gurkha Engineers (1971–6), and RAOC (1973–8).

Endowed with a dry sense of humour, he enjoyed gardening, walking, and fly fishing as well as writing. Together with his incisive intellect and high standards in everything, he was kind, generous and tolerant. His warmth of feeling was evident in his chairmanship of the Friends of Gibraltar Heritage (1990–4).

— 

## Captain Jim Ellis

CAPTAIN JIM ELLIS (who died on January 12 2000, aged 73) was Britain's last resident adviser to the Hadhrami and Mahra states of the Eastern Aden Protectorate.

In 1951 he became military assistant to the renowned Colonel Hugh Boustead, who had responsibility for a frontier of 1,000 miles, mainly along the edge of the great Empty Quarter. Ellis's duty was to patrol this vast desert with a small escort from the Hadhrami Bedouin Legion, often on camels, in order to deter cross-border raiding by the Abida and Dahm tribes of North Yemen and the Yam of Saudi Arabia. The raiders' success depended on being able to replenish their water supply at well-heads before retreating with their booty, so Boustead's priority was to build forts from which the Hadhrami Bedouin Legion could control the wells; between 1953 and 1957, Ellis oversaw construction of three of these.

*Ellis remained in post until his residency was stormed by a mob, which was repelled by Bedouin sentries who then came under fire from the confused palace guard opposite.*

He once came upon a party drilling for oil with a Saudi military escort which had crossed the border. They withdrew under protest but, after suffering the indignity of being disarmed, their Saudi escort feared the wrath of their king and pleaded to be taken into British custody. Courting the displeasure of his own superiors and at the risk of embarrassing Anglo-Saudi relations, Ellis agreed. Some months later the Saudis were repatriated through Aden.

He had to cope with the Bedouin tribes' resentment against the motor transport which was threatening their monopoly of the carrying trade between the coast and the interior; and, in the western province of Qu'aiti, he was involved in protracted negotiations that followed an uprising by several hundred kilted warriors, stained in indigo and some of them armed with matchlocks. He was appointed MBE.

His next post, on permanent attachment to the Colonial Service, was as political officer for the Northern Deserts. In this area, about the size of England and Wales, Petroleum Concessions, a subsidiary of the Iraq Petroleum Company, had started to search for oil. Ellis's brief was "to protect the oil company from the Bedu and to protect the Bedu from the oil company". This he was admirably equipped to do, thanks to his fluent Arabic and seasoned political skills.

In 1957 Petroleum Concessions withdrew, and he spent the next two years in Wahidi State, on the south-western border of the protectorate, before returning to Aden as Permanent Secretary to the Federal Minister for Internal Security, Sultan Saleh bin Hussain al-Audhali, with whom he formed a close friendship.

In the critical run-up to independence, Ellis was sent back to the Eastern Aden Protectorate as Deputy Adviser at Mukalla (capital of the Qu'aiti State), where he became Resident Adviser. He was advanced to OBE in 1968.

The situation was calm on the surface, but remained hostage to events in Aden itself where, amid increasing terrorist violence, the National Liberation Front was emerging as the dominant force. With virtually no cards to play, Ellis strove hard to maintain an atmosphere of "business as usual". He gave as much moral support as possible to the young Qu'aiti Sultan who, fresh from Millfield, with a maturity beyond his 18 years, had just succeeded his father as ruler of the largest and most developed state in the hinterland of Aden.

In May 1967 a bazooka attack on the Residency indicated that National Liberation Front cells were active locally, and fears for the safety of British personnel led to the dispatch of an SAS team to Mukalla, commanded by Charles Guthrie (later Chief of the Defence Staff). During the Arab–Israeli War local nationalist sentiment, fanned by Egyptian propaganda, reached fever pitch. A mob of demonstrators attempted to storm the Residency, directly opposite the Sultan's palace, and Hadhrami Bedouin Legion sentries fired a warning shot over their heads. This deterred the mob, but confused the palace guard, who opened fire on the Residency.

Ellis and his wife, by now the only European woman left in the protectorate, took refuge upstairs as bullets ripped through the shuttered windows. In the bedroom they found their one and only air-conditioner holed beyond repair. Finally the High Commissioner, Sir Humphrey Trevelyan, ordered the withdrawal of all British staff. Ellis was not to see Mukalla again for almost 30 years.

The son of a tenant farmer, James Norrie Ellis was born on August 22 1926 near Berwick-on-Tweed, and never lost his Border accent. He won a scholarship to Fettes, where he was in the first XV, then volunteered for the Army in April 1944 to avoid being called up and sent down a coal mine, which had happened to a cousin.

Enlisting in the ranks of the Queen's Regiment, Ellis was sent to the officer cadet training unit in Bangalore, where he learned Urdu. After being commissioned into the 10th Baluch Regiment, he was under-going jungle warfare training when the war ended, then was posted with the 6th Battalion of the Baluch Regiment to the North West Frontier Province, based in the Khyber Pass. A year later he was posted to Razmak, in South Waziristan, on a barren plateau near the Afghan border, 6,500 feet above sea level, where the British had built a garrison town behind a triple circle of barbed wire and arc lights that was deep in largely hostile tribal territory.

Here, in 1946, Pandit Nehru received his most hostile reception from Pathan tribesmen, during a tour to drum up support for the Congress Party. After Partition the following year, the North West Frontier Province became part of Pakistan. When the Maharajah of Kashmir, a Hindu, decided to take his predominantly Muslim state into India, the Pathan tribes, including the wild, refractory Mahsuds and Wazirs, declared a *jihad* to liberate Kashmir. The enterprise foundered on their lust for booty.

As brigade intelligence officer, aged 21, Ellis's now fluent Pushtu served him well in a region where personality often counted for as much as firepower. He had a clear mind, an equable temperament, a towering physical presence and, above all, an ability to appeal to the Pathans' sense of humour.

In December 1947, when the Pakistan Army withdrew from Waziristan, and handed over its responsibilities to the Corps of Scouts, Ellis accepted a three-year contract as a captain in the Pakistani Army and, in 1948, returned to Waziristan to serve with the Tochi Scouts. He was to become adjutant to the commandant of the Scouts, Colonel Sadiqullah Khan, an Orakzai Pathan whom he greatly respected. When his contract expired Ellis returned to Britain before going out to Aden.

After his retirement from the Colonial Service in 1968, Ellis joined Mobil and later became a stockbroker. He retained a lifelong affection for both Yemen and Pakistan, becoming a founder member of the British–Yemeni Society. On a return visit to Yemen with fellow members in 1995, he was received by both the President and the Prime Minister. Two years later he gladly accepted an invitation to become co-patron, with Leila Ingrams, of Friends of Hadhramaut, a charity formed to support medical and educational projects in south-east Yemen.

Ellis developed a good knowledge of the history of the Surrey countryside where he settled. He and his wife, the former Joanna Rice with whom he adopted a son, were devout Christians, and took an active part in parish life. A man of unassuming modesty and great integrity, he had remarkable powers of recall and was an enthralling raconteur, attributes honed in the company of Pathan and Yemeni tribesmen. Shortly before his death, he recorded recollections of his service overseas for the oral archive of the Museum of Empire and Commonwealth in Bristol.

—

## Nigel Wace

NIGEL WACE (who died on February 4 2005, aged 76) was the leading authority on the plant life of the four Tristan da Cunha Islands, which lie midway between South Africa and South America.

Wace made his first visit to Tristan da Cunha and its neighbour, Gough Island, in 1955 as a member of the expedition, led by John Heaney and Martin Holdgate, which carried out a study of the islands' geography, geology, biology and meteorology. During their six-month stay on uninhabited Gough, he identified some 12 plant species found nowhere else in the world, and the team built a base which was subsequently handed over to the South Africans, who maintain a weather station there.

Wace was primarily concerned with vegetation, but, like his seven colleagues, he became very aware of the huge number of wild house mice, an introduced species, all over the island. It was later confirmed that these were the largest house mice in the world. Although the expedition did not catch any of the creatures in the act of killing baby albatrosses, as they were later reported to do, members noticed that the rodents would nibble people's hair when they were asleep in camp on the mountains.

Wace produced the first detailed description of Gough's vegetation, which later earned him a PhD from Queen's University, Belfast. After the volcanic eruption on Tristan da Cunha in 1961, he collaborated with Jim Dickson to prepare the most authoritative overview of the islands' flora.

For six weeks in 1968 Wace returned with Holdgate to Gough and to Tristan da Cunha to produce a monograph on the interaction of man and nature since the islands' discovery by Portuguese navigators in the early 16th century. Wace was indignant that Gough's discoverer, Gonçalo Álvarez, was nowhere commemorated on the map, and campaigned successfully to have the second highest summit renamed Gonçalo Álvarez Peak. On further visits in 1976, 1984 and 1995, he drew up proposals for the prevention and elimination of invasive plants, and urged that action be taken against the house mice. He also vigorously campaigned for Gough Island to be declared a World Heritage Site.

Nigel Morritt Wace was born in India on January 10 1929, the only son of Sir Blyth Wace, Commissioner and Secretary to the Government of the Punjab. The family claims descent from Wace, the 12th-century Jerseyman and chronicler of the House of Normandy.

Young Nigel attended Brambletye School in Sussex before going to Sheikh Bagh preparatory school in Kashmir, where a strong emphasis on outdoor activities left him, he said, with "a continuing delight and inquisitive interest in different sorts of landscape and people". Having completed his schooling at Cheltenham, Wace was commissioned in the Royal Marines in 1947, but two years later was invalided out with tuberculosis. He then went up to Brasenose College, Oxford, to read agricultural economics, before switching to botany.

His first visit to Gough was the result of meeting John Heaney, who also went to Sheikh Bagh, on a skiing holiday in Switzerland. After returning from the island in 1955, Wace became an assistant lecturer at Belfast University, and then worked for the British Council in London (where he loathed the bureaucracy).

Following his marriage to Margaret White, a secretary at the British embassy in Athens with whom he was to have a son and two daughters, he joined the geography department of Adelaide University, South Australia. Two years later he moved to the National University at Canberra. He served there for many years as lecturer and head of the university's Department of Biogeography and Geomorphology. He contributed greatly to knowledge of the Australian flora, both in settled parts and in the Outback, recalling how a grazier at one station had greeted him as his first visitor in six months.

In later life, Wace acted as a guide and lecturer on cruise ships to the Antarctic. Like Darwin, he had always been interested in the distribution of seeds around the world, and he liked to encourage passengers to drop bottles with messages inside them into the sea. After one "bottle throwing party" in Drake Passage, where passengers inserted 80 messages with a return address at Canberra, he was delighted when one was recovered in New Zealand and another on Easter Island, thus confirming the pattern of circumpolar drift first demonstrated by Sir James Clark Ross in 1842.

Ever the expatriate "Pom", Wace was a man of boyish charm, always devising new ploys to entertain; he never failed to fascinate friends with his "rolling rabbit run", in which rabbits in a cage moved it along so they could eat fresh grass. He also devised "Operation Weed", which involved asking anyone he met for the definition of weeds, often beginning with "D'you think there were weeds in the Garden of Eden?" then going on to discuss whether they could be classified as weeds before the Fall.

Wace enjoyed investigating the mud collected on car tyres or in trouser turn-ups, to demonstrate their role in transporting seeds around Australia. But he failed to gain tax exemption for the trousers used in his research.

## Sir George Sinclair

SIR GEORGE SINCLAIR (who died on September 21 2005, aged 92) was Deputy Governor of Cyprus during the EOKA troubles in the late 1950s, and later a Conservative MP for Dorking.

*Sinclair inspecting British women police officers in Nicosia when he was Deputy Governor in 1957.*

The responsibilities of the Cyprus appointment did not normally include security. But, as right-hand man to Field Marshal Sir John Harding at a time when dithering in London was making a combustible situation ever more dangerous, Sinclair found himself the acting governor during Harding's absences. Both men survived bomb attempts, and shared the distinction of finding themselves in wanted notices, with their pictures, on telephone poles.

After Sir Hugh Foot replaced Harding, and found himself called away to talks in London, Ankara and Athens even more, Sinclair had to cope with the fissuring exasperation on all sides as news of supposedly closed discussions leaked out. When five Turks were killed in rioting in January 1958, he took a successful gamble by withdrawing troops to the perimeter of the Turkish quarter of Nicosia. As independence grew closer, Sinclair found himself in charge again the following year, when he had to call a late night security conference. He took a cautious line, halting arms searches, but issued a forthright warning that the full rigour of the law would be enforced against those who failed to hand in weapons. It was speculated that, after almost five years in the job, he might go on to a more important posting. But he now had other goals.

On retiring from the service Sinclair became a member of Wimbledon Borough Council for three years before winning the safe parliamentary seat of Dorking in 1974. A quiet, kindly man, he was a good constituency member and, unlike some MPs, always seemed to know what he was talking about. He was a strong critic of increasing aircraft noise levels and of proposals to locate a third London airport close to his constituents' backyards.

With his distinguished colonial service, many Dorking electors assumed that they had chosen a vigorous upholder of Britain's continuing imperial role. But he inclined to the left in the party, supporting sanctions against the illegal regime in Rhodesia and opposing attempts to stir up unease about the number of immigrants entering the country.

He blocked a proposal for Enoch Powell to speak at his constituency, though he sat next to Powell on the platform when he came to speak to his constituents a few years later. He also joined Powell in inflicting a defeat on the Conservative government during the committee stage of the Immigration Bill of 1971, in order to protect the rights of people from the dominions to come to Britain.

Sinclair was closely involved in David Steel's campaign to get his Abortion Act on to the statue book, vigorously resisting repeated attempts to modify it. He sponsored an amendment to family planning law to allow vasectomy services on the NHS and was a supporter of free contraception.

While there were rumbles of disagreement in Dorking with some of the causes he supported, Sinclair remained a popular MP, not least for the cricket matches he organised in the constituency. Opponents within his local party used to complain about the number of pictures of him in his campaign literature.

George Evelyn Sinclair was born on November 6 1912 and educated at Abingdon School. He read Greats at Pembroke, Oxford, before entering the Colonial Service in 1936. He became assistant district commissioner in the Gold Coast, then served in the Royal West African Frontier Force for three years during the war. Next, he became secretary to Sir Walter Elliott's Commission on Higher Education in West Africa, which laid the plans for the universities built in the 1950s and 1960s; Sinclair's wife typed the entire report for him. After being posted to Togoland as an energetic senior district commissioner in 1945, he set about preparing Togolanders to join the newly independent state of Ghana, which they did after a UN plebiscite.

Among the voluntary bodies on which he served, Sinclair was chairman of the Governing Bodies of Independent Schools, a consultant of the UN Fund for Population and Development and, lastly, secretary-general of the Global Forum of Spiritual and Parliamentary Leaders on Human Survival at Oxford, which was attended by Mother Teresa and the Dalai Lama in 1998.

When a trade union was threatening to strike over the appointment of a woman bus driver, Sinclair said that he had just been in Uzbekistan, where all the trams and buses were driven by women.

On his return to Ghana in 1998, President Jerry Rawlings organised a reception, where Sinclair astonished the company with a speech in fluent Ashanti.

George Sinclair was appointed OBE in 1950, CMG in 1956 and knighted in 1960. He married, in 1941, Jane Burdekin. After her death in 1971, he married Mollie Sawday, who survived him with one son and three daughters of the first marriage.

# NORTH AFRICA

～

## Sir Michael Weir

SIR MICHAEL WEIR (who died on June 22 2006, aged 81) was a Foreign Office Arabist, whose career began in exercising imperial supervision of medieval societies in the Gulf and ended as ambassador in Egypt, with the priority of aiding Britain's commercial interests.

Weir began in the early 1950s with several temporary but independent postings. One was to the political residency at Qatar, a position of sole responsibility in which he was charged with pushing the ruler to complete the outlawing of slavery and had to preside over the agency court, with no legal training and only Indian legal codes for guidance. It was a time when the region's vague boundaries were growing in importance because of the presence of oil companies, though the explorer Wilfred Thesiger was around, warning Arabs against the evils of the internal combustion engine.

Weir was also sent to Sharjah, where he was woken early one morning by news that the Saudis had invaded two villages near Buraimi oasis, in keeping with a long-standing dispute. This became an "incursion", in Foreign Office language, and he found that he was not permitted to enter the disputed area while the British protest was being made. When some invaders were arrested at the border, he had to release them because they had entered before a ban on their presence had been imposed.

Later, on reporting to Bahrain for instructions before setting off with a military force raised by the Sultan of Muscat, he was astonished to receive a message in the name of Anthony Eden, the Foreign Secretary, saying that he could risk no bloodshed; Weir, who became a fine judge of official humiliations, believed that conveying this to the sheikh who had been wronged was the most distasteful moment of his career.

But Britain was still shedding responsibilities slowly, and Weir was made a "gentleman in attendance" on the ruler of Bahrain at Her

Majesty the Queen's Coronation. This involved being present at every event as an interpreter, kitted out in high-collared, gold-braided frock coat. The small Sheikh Salman proved a firm favourite, not least for his total lack of inhibition. On seeing the bare-legged representative of Fiji, he asked Prince George of Greece why slaves were present. He questioned Her Majesty about whether the crown felt too heavy in the Coronation coach (it was heavy but bearable). When he told her that the thousands of loyal subjects who had lined the streets in the rain reminded him of Palestinian refugees, Weir did not offer a literal translation.

*Weir* (right) *listening in Cairo to Francis Pym, the Foreign Secretary, with the air of a man who had translated judiciously for Winston Churchill after a Coronation dinner.*

Later, when Sir Winston Churchill was sitting on the bottom of some stairs after a banquet, the sheikh insisted on making his acquaintance in order to say that he hoped Britain would support Bahrain's ancestral claim to land opposite Qatar. "Tell him," Churchill replied, "tell him that we try never to desert our friends." The great man paused, then added "unless we have to". Weir forebore to translate this at all.

The son of a primary school headmaster, Michael Scott Weir was born on January 28 1925 and educated at Dunfermline High School, before leaving early to study Turkish at the School of Oriental and

African Studies in London, with a view to wartime intelligence work. This led to a posting to a flying boat squadron in South Wales.

He then joined a fighter squadron in Burma before persuading the Air Ministry to send him to Combined Intelligence in Baghdad. On being demobbed Weir read Classics at Balliol before entering the Foreign Office, which sent him to the Middle East Centre for Arab Studies at Jerusalem, where the future Israeli foreign minister, Abba Eban, was a lecturer.

After the Coronation, Weir returned to his post then joined the South-East Asia department in London, where tedious desk work was broken by attendance at the negotiations over Indo-China after the French had left. He was involved in devising a viable justification for the flimsy South-East Asia Treaty Organisation, but was exasperated to witness the far greater folly of the Suez adventure in the department across the corridor from his. When the operation slid into fiasco, he was heard to shout: "Eden must be mad."

Weir next had what he regarded as a rest cure in San Francisco before going to Washington, where he saw how the United States could make a fist of Middle East policy; one colleague told him how President Eisenhower had promised to make Nasser "the great gookety-gook of the Arab world". When plans were drawn up for the US to go into Lebanon and Britain into Jordan to check the effects of the overthrow of the Iraq government spreading, Weir had to call on John Foster Dulles at home where, in pyjamas and dressing gown, the Secretary of State showed his lack of enthusiasm for foreign adventures.

After a posting as press officer in Cairo, Weir returned to the Foreign Office in London. His role involved overseeing the mutually suspicious British Council, Central Office of Information and BBC Overseas Service. He witnessed another cause for shame when Britain assured the Gulf States that she would not depart precipitately, and then reneged on them over Christmas. A spell as resident at Bahrain, preparing the British withdrawal, was followed by a stint at the UN, where he was kept busy by Rhodesia and the Middle East. When the Egyptians invaded Israel in 1973 Weir received several calls from Henry Kissinger demanding that Britain call for a ceasefire and withdrawal.

As Assistant Under-Secretary for Middle East and UN affairs in London, Weir went out to Rhodesia in one of the futile efforts to resolve the Smith rebellion. His prescient view of the future for the

Shah of Persia, whose situation was declining as he tried to liberalise his rule, led to a posting as ambassador in Cairo instead of Teheran.

His arrival coincided with Egypt forfeiting its key role in the Arab world, when President Sadat signed a treaty with Israel, embarking on a policy of "democratic experiment" and open-door economics, which Weir saw could prove highly combustible if mixed with religious fundamentalism. However, Weir's time was lightened by visits from members of the Royal Family. Sadat insisted on attending a dinner for Prince Philip (as "a mark of respect" for Weir) at which he renounced his early anti-British sentiments, and was no less delighted by the arrival of Prince Andrew, for whom Weir threw a party which ended with the Prince plunging into the pool and pushing in his hostess. However, the light-hearted period ended with the assassination of Sadat when Weir, who was sitting two rows behind the president, dived to the ground, and found himself clutching the American ambassador's foot.

On retiring from the Foreign Service in 1985, he became director of the 21st Century Think-Tank; president of the Egyptian Exploration Society; and of the British Egyptian Society.

Michael Weir was appointed CMG in 1974 and KCMG in 1980. He married, in 1953, Alison Walker with whom he had two sons and two daughters. After a divorce, he married, in 1976, Hilary Reid, a Foreign Office colleague whom he met in New York; they had two sons.

# WEST AFRICA

## Sir Rex Niven

SIR REX NIVEN (who died on February 22 1993, aged 94) was, for nearly 40 years, an exceptionally able and articulate colonial administrator in Nigeria.

*Niven liked to recall the Governor who, after reading the proofs of his* How Nigeria is Governed, *minuted: "Thank God I know at last."*

The country was essentially a British invention, its name having been coined by a *Times* journalist, and British rulers became, as Niven put it, "more Nigerian than the Africans themselves". It was a diverse amalgam of the Muslim, feudal and largely Hausa-speaking northerners and the various peoples of the coastal belt, who include Muslim or pagan Yorubas of the west and mainly Catholic Ibos of the east. In 1966, six years after independence, enmities between these groups erupted in a massacre of the Ibos and the establishment of the separatist eastern state of Biafra.

Niven's career in Nigeria had ended four years earlier. The old colonial administrators tended to retain their loyalty to the regions with which they had been associated; and Niven was a Northerner. But he deprecated the prejudice which some of his fellow officers manifested towards the

Ibos. Nevertheless the title of his book, *The War of Nigerian Unity* (1970), indicated his lack of sympathy for the Biafran struggle for independence. Although the war showed that the British had failed to create a cohesive Nigeria, Niven's career was a model of the diligent and just fashion in which individual colonial administrators had carried out their duties.

When he arrived in the Northern provinces shortly after the First World War, the country was extremely primitive. A young officer could expect his share of adventures with elephants, leopards and snakes. Much of Niven's time was spent mapping the country and building roads, bridges and even his own home. He was obliged to learn by trial and error the niceties of bush finance and justice. He had to officiate at hangings, a punishment which the Africans preferred to long terms of imprisonment, and to put minor offenders in the stocks until a Labour government forbade the practice. So genial were the Africans that Niven once overheard a warder tell a prisoner to hold his gun while he demonstrated how to perform a task. And so dedicated were the colonial officers that during the 1930s' slump they voluntarily renounced a tenth of their salaries and allowances.

Niven never reached the summit of the service, as his quick mind and caustic wit did not always appeal to superiors, so that when a Governor of Northern Nigeria was chosen in 1954, the Colonial Office passed him over in favour of the safer option of Bryan Sharwood-Smith.

A clergyman's son, Cecil Rex Niven was born at Torquay on November 20 1898, and educated at Blundell's and Balliol College, Oxford, until the First World War overtook his university career, and he spent two years with a Royal Field Artillery battery in France and Italy; at barely 20 he won the MC.

After finishing his degree Niven joined the Nigerian Service in 1921. At that date, he would explain, no one in Britain would employ him at more than £200 a year, whereas his starting salary in the Colonial Service was a princely £500, with £60 for equipment. His name came to be especially associated with his long spells in the residencies of Plateau and Bornu Provinces, where it was said that the million nim trees in Maiduguri were so called from a corruption of the name "Niven". In addition to gaining wide experience of provincial administration, he worked in the Finance and Native Affairs branch of the Kaduna Secretariat, and created a public relations department in war-time Lagos.

After leaving the Colonial Service in 1954, Niven became President and, subsequently, the first Speaker of the Northern House of Assembly. His last post in Nigeria was as Commissioner for Special Duties in Northern Nigeria, from 1959 to 1962.

On retirement he became deputy secretary of the Southwark Diocesan Board of Finance and, from 1975 to 1980, a member of the General Synod of the Church of England. A notably loyal alumnus of Balliol, Niven was enterprising enough to put his name forward when the Mastership became vacant in 1989. The College replied courteously that the retiring age for the post was 65 and that he, the prospective candidate, was 90.

Niven was an active supporter of the British–Nigerian Association, and to the end was planning a new series of books on his Nigerian experiences. His memoirs, *A Nigerian Kaleidoscope* (1982) were particularly well received. Other publications included *A Short History of Nigeria* (1937, 12th edition 1971), *West Africa* (1958), *A Short History of the Yoruba Peoples* (1958), *Nine Great Africans* (1964) and *Nigeria* (in "Benn's Nations of the Modern World", 1967). He liked to recall how, after reading the proofs of his *How Nigeria is Governed* (1950), the Governor minuted: "Thank God I know at last."

Niven was appointed CMG in 1953 and appointed KB in 1960.

He married, in 1925, Dorothy Mason, with whom he had two daughters. After her death in 1977, he married, three years later, Pamela Beerbohm, née Leach.

## Victoria Opoku-Ware

VICTORIA OPOKU-WARE (who died on March 6 1996, aged 66) was the senior wife of the Asantehene, Otumfuo Opoku-Ware, the King of the Ashanti.

In the modern republic of Ghana, the Asantehene wields no official executive power, but he is the traditional leader of an important constituency within the country, and he continues to maintain a court. Victoria Opoku-Ware, "Lady Victoria" to the Ashanti people, was an influential figure at court, and used her considerable force of personality to defend the kingdom's interests.

Her nephew, Kwame Anthony Appiah, described her as the most powerful person in the kingdom. "Auntie Vic", he said, "made her weight felt around town, driven around in one of her fleet of Mercedes-

Benzes, cultivating a faintly plutocratic aura."

The daughter of a Christian schoolmaster, Victoria Nana Akua Afiiriyie Bando was born in Kumasi, the Ashanti capital, on April 22 1929, and educated in Ghana at the Wesley Girls' School, Cape Coast. Her family had substantial commercial interests in the region. Aged 13, she was betrothed to Matthew Poku, a member of Lincoln's Inn; they were married in 1945.

In 1970, shortly before he was due to become Ghana's ambassador to Italy, Poku was told of the death of his uncle, the Asantehene Sir Osei Agyeman-Prempeh II. Called back to Kumasi, he emerged as the chosen successor to the

*The Ashanti people's "Lady Victoria" showed that women can exercise power in a patriarchy.*

golden stool of the Ashanti, thanks largely to his wife's adroit advocacy. Although the Asantehene is obliged by tradition to contract a number of dynastic marriages, Victoria established herself as the "First Lady" of the Ashanti. She accompanied her husband on foreign trips, including one to London in 1971, when they were received at Buckingham Palace.

Much of the history of modern Ghana has been dominated by tension between the traditional Ashanti polity and the modern state, based in Accra. Even before Ghana became a republic in 1957, the Prime Minister, Kwame Nkrumah, was pelted in the streets of Kumasi; and since independence no Ghanaian government has ever willingly offended the Ashanti king and his people.

The Asantehene, for his part, is required to strike a careful balance between visible allegiance to the Ghanaian state and responsibility to the Ashanti people. His wife helped him to achieve this. In the process the Ashanti kingdom gained in international status, and the Asantehene came increasingly to resemble a head of state. Widespread popular interest in African culture in recent years has increased interest in the Asantehene still further. Decked out in Ashanti gold and surrounded by courtiers, the Asantehene looks the epitome of an African king, and Victoria promoted that image. But she understood the need to combine the preservation of tradition with the opening up of the monarchy to the modern world.

In 1981, she was active in arrangements for the spectacular Ashanti exhibition at the Museum of Mankind in London, at the opening of which Ashanti drummers performed in nearby New Bond Street. When the exhibition transferred to New York, it was widely reported on television, and the Black American community thronged the streets to see the Asantehene himself. In 1995, Victoria played a prominent role in extensive arrangements for the celebration of her husband's silver jubilee, and she continued to exert her influence on his behalf, seductive or bullying as necessary. "Never assume," Kwame Anthony Appiah wrote, "that individual women cannot gain power under patriarchy".

In her last months she was delighted when the eldest of her second daughter's children entered Eton in the same class as Prince William.

Victoria Opoku-Ware was survived by her husband, the Asantehene, a son and two daughters.

~

## "Prince" Nico Mbarga

"PRINCE" NICO MBARGA (who died in a motorcycle accident on June 24 1997, aged 47) was a one-hit wonder, whose song "Sweet Mother" (1976) sold more than 13 million copies worldwide.

Sung in pidgin English to the light, sweet, lyrical sound of Nico's acoustic guitar, it is an apologetic tribute to a mother for the suffering her son has caused her: "If I no sleep, my mother no go sleep / If I no chop, my mother no go chop / She no dry tire ooo."

The catchy tune, which is accompanied by beautiful guitar breaks, is said to have been turned down by EMI on the ground that it was childish. But when it came out two years later it spread from Nigeria into Central Africa, the Caribbean and Brazil; and with the growing popularity of World Music it was taken up in Canada, the United States and Europe. It has been called Africa's anthem, and in 2004 it topped a BBC poll.

Nico Mbarga was born on January 1 1950 at Abakaliki, in south-eastern Nigeria. His mother was Nigerian, his father from Cameroon.

He became known as "Prince" Nico, due, he said, to royal connections, but also, no doubt, because of the vogue among Nigerian pop musicians to adopt regal titles.

During the Nigerian Civil War in the late 1960s, his family moved to Cameroon, where they stayed until 1972. Mbarga played xylophone, conga, drums and electric guitar in a school band, and started his professional career in a Cameroon hotel band, called the Melody Orchestra. His time away from Nigeria and his family background made him something of an outsider on the Nigerian music scene, which tended to be dominated by Yoruba musicians. Many people assumed that he was a Cameroonian, but, when travelling abroad, he always insisted that he represented Nigeria as a whole.

In 1972, he formed Rocafil Jazz, and settled into the Plaza Hotel in the eastern Nigerian

*Mbarga claimed he had been cheated and duped by the music business and later opened a Sweet Mother hotel.* (Graeme Ewens)

town of Onitsha. The band released an unsuccessful single on EMI in 1973; but its follow-up, "I No Go Marry my Papa", was a local success for his new sound, which he called Panko and was created with a heavy bass, in the Cameroonian style. This he grafted onto a hybrid of eastern (Ibo) guitar, "highlife" (replacing horns with guitars) and Zairean guitar pop. He said that through his music, he was attempting to unite African cultures; and his work is considered closer to the Central African *soukous* guitarists than the Afro-funk of his contemporary, Fela Kuti, or the repetitive layered guitars of Juju musicians like King Sunny Ade.

After EMI dropped him because he was not selling many records, Mbarga was picked up by the owner of the Rogers label in Onitsha, who brought out "Sweet Mother". Between 1975 and 1981, Rocafil Jazz released nine albums on the Rogers label. Then Mbarga came to England to appear in the first Womad festival at Shepton Mallet. Dressed like a throwback to 1970s' glam rock, he leapt on stage in bright yellow knee-length high-heeled boots, red trousers with ruffles up the sides and a bright purple satin shirt. With the Ivory Coasters (a highlife band from London) and a Cameroonian singer, Louisiana Tilda, he offered British audiences their first taste of African guitar band music.

On returning to Nigeria, Nico set up his own label, releasing an album through Polydor in 1983. But he never repeated the success of "Sweet Mother", and complained that he had been "cheated and duped by the music business".

Rocafil Jazz broke up when several of its Cameroonian musicians were sent home, and Mbarga never recovered. He tried to recreate his success with an album by the New Rocafil Jazz band, but it was not a success. He bought the Hotel Calabar, and later opened the Sweet Mother Hotel.

# EAST AFRICA

~

## Sir Michael Blundell

SIR MICHAEL BLUNDELL (who died on February 1 1993, aged 85)
was the politician, farmer and botanist largely responsible, along with
Jomo Kenyatta, for Kenya's peaceful transition from colonial rule to
independence.

*Blundell once challenged Kenya's first black head of government to a bout
of fisticuffs outside Lancaster House for the benefit of the cameras.*

Blundell spent his early political life promoting the interests of white
settlers, but when the British government made known its determination to grant majority rule he saw that whites could survive in
Kenya only if they embraced the new order. This acceptance of the
inevitable earned him the execration of many, but by splitting the white
community he did much to prevent the violence and economic
dislocation that would have accompanied a last-ditch stand.

On entering politics in 1948, as a white farmers' representative in the Rift Valley, he was as keen as any of his constituents to keep the "White Highlands" white, and to defend the privileges of the settler community. But, having commanded Kenyan troops in the Second World War, Blundell also sympathised with African demands for a greater say in the running of their affairs.

Simple racial arithmetic, and the rapid increase in black nationalist agitation during the 1950s, convinced him that the status of Europeans in Kenya could best be upheld by power-sharing between Africans, Asians and Europeans. Such extreme moderation attracted little enthusiasm among white voters, still less among the unenfranchised black masses and their leaders. But it was the Conservative Colonial Secretary, Iain Macleod ("hatchet in hand", as Blundell put it), who administered the *coup de grâce* at talks at Lancaster House in 1960, when he disclosed the British government's commitment to majority rule followed by independence. Blundell feared that such a sudden transition would cause chaos for everyone, but he realised that whites simply had to adapt or leave.

His own first loyalty was to the country and all its peoples; with colleagues in the multiracial New Kenya Group, he tried to convince other whites that their best hope was to accept the coming changes and to co-operate with sympathetic blacks. For this he was ostracised, abused as a traitor, spat upon, pelted with eggs and tomatoes, and had 30 pieces of silver thrown at him with cries of "Judas". He was hurt and angered by what he saw as the stupidity of his critics, but reflected that he would still be farming in Kenya long after they had gone.

The son of a London solicitor, Michael Blundell was born on April 7 1907 and educated at Wellington. He was expected to read law at Oxford, but preferred to go out to Kenya to try his luck on the land.

A hardnosed romantic, who saw the true farmer as an artist who "paints the earth with the varying crops every year", Blundell made sure that his art paid the bills. He started off in a mud hut on a farm still being cut out of the bush, but within 18 months had become manager of a well-established property in the Solai valley. An astute move into pigs and Guernsey cattle helped him through the agricultural depression of the 1930s, and, in the course of a decade in which many Kenya settlers went bust, he was able to buy up the farm he managed.

Blundell later moved to Subukia on the Bahati ("Lucky") escarpment of the Rift Valley, where he farmed with great success.

During the Second World War he served with the Royal Engineers. In 1940 he was given command of an African pioneer battalion which had recently mutinied. The main reason, he discovered, was that they had joined up expecting to fight, not to build roads and dig latrines. Blundell restored their morale by issuing them with slouch hats, like front-line troops, and led them on a lightning advance against the Italians, 2,800 miles in 42 days, through British and Italian Somaliland and Abyssinia. The advance culminated in the fall of Addis Ababa and Gondar. He finished the war as a colonel in South-East Asia.

Afterwards Blundell became Commissioner for European Settlement, administering schemes set up by the British and Kenyan governments to encourage ex-soldiers and their families to start farms in the White Highlands. The settlers were obliged to invest what capital they possessed in their farms, and were repeatedly assured that the British government would continue to protect them and their interests. When this protection was suddenly withdrawn Blundell and the settlers he had encouraged felt equally betrayed.

In 1952 he became leader of the European Elected Members, in effect Leader of the Opposition. He played an important role in the defeat of the Mau Mau campaign (when he was No. 1 on the terrorists' hit list for a time) and was a member of "Sitrep", the Governor's Emergency Committee. Later he crossed the floor to become a minister on the War Council. He saw the importance of wooing "loyal" Kikuyu, and mocked farmers who, in effect, demanded, "Kill all the Kikuyu, but don't kill mine."

Unlike many colonial politicians, Blundell had the self-confidence to treat British politicians, civil servants and journalists as equals. He liked dealing with Labour politicians, whom he generally found warm-hearted if wrong-headed, and enjoyed the sound of Tory MPs in committee. They reminded him of "hippos coming up from the river"; but he regarded them as cold fish, ruthless in pursuit of their own interests. To all he liked to be the no-nonsense, plain-speaking colonial boy. A master of several African languages, he had an easy rapport with Africans of every class but was not afraid to ruffle their sensitivities. He once challenged Ronald Ngala, Kenya's first black head of government, to a bout of fisticuffs outside Lancaster House for the benefit of the cameras.

Although Blundell was best known for his political views, his greatest contribution to Kenya's prosperity was in agriculture. He developed new markets with luxury produce from his own farm; encouraged the production of an environmentally safe insecticide as chairman of the Pyrethrum Board; and disseminated modern agricultural practices through his chairmanship of Egerton Agricultural College.

During his five years as Kenya's Minister of Agriculture in the late 1950s he gave a boost to African agriculture by promoting the reform of land tenure and the consolidation of holdings, establishing settlement schemes and encouraging the move into cash crops. He also tried to reassure white farmers, on the eve of independence, that there was a future for them in Kenya.

Blundell retired from politics in 1962 and returned to his farm. Becoming a Kenyan citizen, he started a new career as a businessman, turning East African Breweries into one of Kenya's most successful companies. He wrote a lively autobiography, *So Rough a Wind* (1964), as well as two authoritative works which reflected his passion for botany: *The Wild Flowers of Kenya* (1982) and *The Collins Guide to the Wild Flowers of East Africa* (1987). In his latter years, when he became immobilised, his garden became an endless source of pleasure.

Michael Blundell was a big, bouncy, energetic man, with the bubbling enthusiasm and quick passions of a schoolboy. He was witty and charming, a natural performer (he had once considered becoming a professional singer) and a great talker.

Appointed MBE in 1943 and KBE in 1962, he married, in 1946, Geraldine Robarts, who died in 1983; they had a daughter.

~

# John Owen

JOHN OWEN (who died on March 1 1995, aged 82) was director of Tanzania's National Parks from 1960 to 1971.

A public servant with a lively distrust of authority, Owen was tall, with a humorous expression, piercing blue eyes and a fierce intelligence; his outstanding personal modesty impressed many of those who worked with him. When he arrived in Arusha, in what was then Tanganyika, there were three national parks; by the time he left 11 years later there were nine. An innovator, who had the energy and imagination to raise funds around the world, Owen was also careful to explain his work to the Tanzanians.

He built hostels in the game reserves where local schoolchildren could stay, introduced training in wildlife management for his African staff, and had a film made with a Swahili soundtrack which was widely distributed. Perhaps his most lasting achievement was to transform a small laboratory into the Serengeti Scientific Research Institute.

Of his African years, Owen liked to recall sitting on a river-bank at dusk, deep inside one of the largest game reserves, and watching a bat hawk striking at its prey in the wind overhead. "The Garden of Eden", he reflected, "must have been much like this."

As well as being a key figure in the African wildlife movement, after his retirement Owen fought and won several quixotic campaigns against the planning authorities of England, battles in which he enjoyed the inestimable advantage of knowing just how the Civil Service operated. He lost the last of his fights, a gallant attempt to halt the construction of the Channel Tunnel, but other campaigns were more successful.

The son of Anglican missionaries, John Simpson Owen was born near the Mountains of the Moon in western Uganda on December 31 1912. His father, Archdeacon Owen, was a notable figure in Ugandan and Kenyan colonial history, whose work as a friend of the Africans, challenging the interests of the white settlers, earned him the sobriquet "Archdemon".

Young John was sent to England to be educated at Christ's Hospital (where he was head boy) and Brasenose College, Oxford, where he read natural sciences. On coming down in 1936 he was selected for the Sudan Political Service.

When he arrived in Khartoum the Governor said to him: "I don't want to see you again, Owen, until you can play polo." Having acquired the requisite skills, Owen was posted as political officer to the Zalengi district. He went on to serve in Omdurman (then the largest town in Africa), and as District Commissioner in Torit, in the far south. In Omdurman he achieved one of the first censuses of an African township, a complicated task at the best of times, and much more so when dealing with a large and illiterate population strongly disinclined to pay taxes. Owen also campaigned with Lady Huddleston, the Governor's wife, against the practice of female circumcision.

It was at Torit, too, that Owen first became involved in conservation. Over the years he was to take an increasing interest in the animals and reptiles of the region, which is on the banks of the Nile by the northern Ugandan border. He was the first to collect a number of snakes, small mammals and bats, and was visited by curators from

North America and Europe. In 1948 he founded Nimule National Park, largely to protect the stamping ground of the local white rhinoceros, which he already believed to be under threat.

Seven years later the Sudan Political Service was dissolved, and Owen was pensioned off. He was appointed OBE for his work in ensuring that the pensions eventually paid by the British government were adequate, a rare case of a public servant honoured for arguing with his superiors. He then took a job with a British multi-national. He hated it, and resigned after four years to go to Tanzania, where he had the personal support of President Nyerere.

On his second retirement in 1971, Owen was awarded an honorary doctorate by Oxford and received the World Wildlife Fund's second Gold Medal; Peter Scott and Bernard Grzimek had shared the first. But once again Owen refused a life of inactivity.

In 1973, when Idi Amin was at the height of his power, he was one of the few Westerners to visit Kampala, ostensibly to inspect the country's game parks. On arrival he was greeted with deep respect by several members of Amin's much-feared bodyguard who (like their leader) were from the Torit region and recognised the man who had administered their childhood villages.

Owen eventually retired to Royal Tunbridge Wells, where he warned about the potential safety hazards of the Channel Tunnel, illustrating his concern in videos, and was subsequently proved to have been right by several fires. He also campaigned against the destruction of High Wood, a stretch of medieval woodland threatened by development. Inspired by China's "Gang of Four", he published a "newspaper", which was posted on the wall of his Regency terraced house, with details of his arguments against the local planning committee. The newspaper was ruled to be illegal, as it was posted on a listed building, but the local citizens paid Owen's fine out of admiration for his determination.

John Owen married, in 1946, Patricia Burns, an education officer working in the Sudan; they had three daughters.

~

# Desmond O'Hagan

DESMOND O'HAGAN (who died on December 12 2001, aged 92) adopted a baby elephant which insisted on sleeping in his bedroom, when he was a young district officer in Kenya.

Tembo, which means elephant in Swahili, was brought into O'Hagan's tent in the bush at the age of two months after his mother had been shot, and from then on declined to leave O'Hagan's side. At first only the size of a large Labrador, he spurned the spare bedroom in the mud hut with a thatched roof, to lie down every night beside O'Hagan's bed. During the day he went to the office, where he quietly watched O'Hagan conducting business and holding court. If there was a dinner in the evening he insisted on coming too, screeching loudly until allowed into the dining room. Feeding the baby elephant was difficult. No elephant's milk was available. Offers of grass were spurned. O'Hagan's friends had to club together to help him find the necessary quantity of undiluted cows' milk.

Then, when O'Hagan went on safari, leaving Tembo in the care of a nurse who was fond of him, the elephant pined for his missing friend and died at the age of nine months.

Desmond O'Hagan was born at Devlin, County Westmeath, on March 3 1909. His

*O'Hagan and Tembo, who screeched until allowed into the dining room.*

parents went out to Kenya to start a coffee estate at Nyeri, but before the trees produced their first crop his father was recalled to the Army for the First World War, and his mother started a field hospital in

Nairobi. For four years the family lived in a tent beside the polo ground.

They returned to a now prosperous estate, where Desmond and his brother learned to ride, shoot and fish, developing a keen interest in the wild life. Desmond was sent to Wellington, which he left at 17 to return to Kenya, where his father had found the profits from a cattle ranch he had started too small, and had decided to grow wheat. While his father ploughed hundreds of acres of virgin black soil during the day, Desmond continued the task into the night.

After two years O'Hagan went to Clare College, Cambridge, where he achieved half-Blues for polo and tennis while reading law and colonial jurisprudence. In 1931, he entered the Colonial Service and was posted to Kisii, an outpost in hilly, wet countryside.

District officers spent much of their time on safari, collecting poll and hut taxes. They were expected to walk everywhere for their salary of £1 a day, but O'Hagan bought a second-hand bicycle to ride ahead of the bearers on his rounds; when he reached a hill he would dismount and leave it to be collected by a tribal policeman. His tasks included hearing appeals with clan elders. Cases often involved the return of the bride price paid for women who had deserted their husbands; he also persuaded the natives to drive young locusts into trenches for burial.

On being transferred to Kakamega, he had a one-legged district commissioner who expected him to inspect detainees at 6.00 a.m. six days a week and also to play tennis with him. O'Hagan was then posted to the Northern Frontier District, where he had to cope with the Somalis and Boran fighting over grazing rights. Safari travel was by camel, but the beasts could be troublesome. Once, they ran off with most of his food when a couple of hippos charged into camp. His tent was also knocked down by elephants in the middle of the night. Following his first home leave, when he was called to the Bar by Inner Temple, O'Hagan became private secretary to the British Resident in Zanzibar for a time.

As the Mau Mau insurgency began in the 1950s, he was noted for his firmness as a provincial commissioner in Central Province. After moving there he also warded off a general strike by appealing to Tom Mboya, a union leader whom he had known as a young man, and organised a visit by Princess Margaret.

Unlike most other colonial officers, O'Hagan did not retire to England. He first served as chairman of the transport licensing authority in Tanganyika, then returned to run the family coffee farm. Proud of the colonial administration's honesty and success in bringing the country to peaceful independence, he stayed on. As a stalwart member of the Muthaiga Club, he won many bridge tournaments and captained the Kenya Seniors at golf.

Desmond O'Hagan, who was appointed CMG in 1957, married, in 1942, Pamela Symes-Thompson; she survived him with a son and two daughters.

~

## "Bunny" Allen

"BUNNY" ALLEN (who died on January 14 2002, aged 95) was the last of the Great White Hunters; he was known across East Africa for his prowess with a rifle and for his romantic appeal to women, notably the film actresses Ava Gardner and Grace Kelly.

Allen's reputation was at its height in the 1950s, when he ran the best, and the most expensive, safaris in Kenya. Clients such as Prince Aly Khan paid handsomely to shoot the big game, elephant, buffalo, lion and leopard, for whose whereabouts Allen seemed to have a sixth sense. This ability came to the attention of Hollywood's studios, and he was regularly employed to find the wildlife needed as a backdrop to such lush epics as *King Solomon's Mines* (1950), *The African Queen* and *Where No Vultures Fly* (1951). In 1953 he was put in charge of the largest safari seen in East Africa, when John Ford came to Kenya to make *Mogambo*.

Allen, who had 20 white hunters under his command, stood in for Clark Gable, the film's star, when there were dangerous scenes of charging animals to be shot, and also found time to conduct love affairs with two other stars, Grace Kelly and Ava Gardner, the latter then married to Frank Sinatra. When the film was released, Allen was deemed so integral to its success that he accompanied the three stars on the publicity tour, and appeared in *What's My Line?* on American television.

Yet he remained a brave and energetic hunter, who loved the outdoor life, even when it imperilled his own. He was mauled by leopards several times and once found himself in the path of a charging Cape buffalo while holding an empty rifle. Flinging it aside, he vaulted nimbly over the animal's horns and landed on its back. Bellowing loudly, the enraged creature cantered some 50 yards with

Allen up top before his son shot the beast dead. Its agile jockey was then in his fifties.

He was born Frank Maurice Allen on April 17 1906 and grew up near Maidenhead, Berkshire. His character was derived less from his father, a timid man who worked for an insurance company, than from his masterful mother. Her father, who built carriages for the Royal Family at Windsor, had Romany blood, and as a young boy Frank made friends with gypsies who lived in Windsor Great Park. From one of them, Piramus Berners, he learned the ways of the woods, and the skill he acquired of snaring rabbits earned him the nickname "Bunny".

He was educated at Sir William Borlase's Grammar School, Marlow, where he was a fine oarsman and an outstanding boxer. Then, in 1927, having formed a taste for travel as a boy when he had followed his mother and her lover to Canada during the Great War, he set out for Kenya, where his two older brothers were already working. One of these, "Ba" Allen, later became Haile Selassie's chief of police in Addis Ababa.

"Bunny" soon found a job managing a farm for Mervyn Soames, whose brother Jack was a central figure in the colony's Happy Valley set. Soames soon began to entrust Allen with taking his guests out shooting, and the new arrival's natural affinity with the bush and instinctive shooting ability brought him to the attention of two of the most respected white hunters, Baron Bror von Blixen and Denys Finch Hatton, whose love affair with Blixen's wife Karen later formed the basis of the film *Out of Africa* (1985).

Allen soon became Finch Hatton's partner on shoots, and was one of the guns on the Prince of Wales's safari in 1928. In time, he took part in three royal safaris, and during the early 1930s helped the future Princess Alice, Duchess of Gloucester, to catch cheetah which were wanted to race against greyhounds at White City. Allen's party captured them by the simple expedient of galloping alongside and diving on their backs.

Despite his middle-class background, Allen's considerable charm and professionalism in the field won him admittance to the more upper-class and slightly older coterie that dominated Kenyan society. He was helped by his strong, dark good looks which allowed him to take full advantage of the looseness of morals that gave rise to the joke "Are you married, or do you live in Kenya?" Allen would eventually work his way through three long-suffering wives.

He came to know well the aviatrix Beryl Markham, the naturalist Joy Adamson and Philip Percival, the hunter personified as "Pop" in Ernest Hemingway's *The Green Hills of Africa*. After learning Swahili, he also enjoyed an excellent rapport with the natives, on whose skills as gunbearers his life often depended.

Following Finch Hatton's death in the early 1930s, Allen continued to work with Blixen, and gained a reputation as one of the finest hunters in the colony. When war came, he enlisted as a private in the 6th King's African Rifles, and was due to receive his commission from the Earl of Erroll, Kenya's Military Secretary, when Erroll was murdered the night before their appointment. The crime was later the subject of James Fox's *White Mischief.*

Allen served in Madagascar and on Kenya's northern frontier, where his skills were put to good use when two lions began to prey on both British and Italian troops, once eating a soldier in his sleeping bag. Allen used the corpses of two Italians to lure the man-eaters into an ambush, and received a congratulatory telegram from the enemy afterwards. He finished the war as a captain.

Over the next decade his safari business flourished. Its success was due to Allen's ability to ensure that all his clients enjoyed themselves, both in the bush and around the fire at night. Few of his rivals were so concerned that their customers had fun, and few, too, had Allen's attractiveness of manner. With his gypsy earring and native wrap-around skirt, he was like catnip to many of his female clients; one came to his tent at night only to find her daughter already in possession.

Although hunting was banned in Kenya from the mid-1970s, Allen adapted well to the changing times, having had enough of shooting. He continued to take guests out to see game until his eighties, when he had retired to the island of Lamu. There he built somewhat unreliable houses in the Arabic style, and taught himself to paint, read the poetry of Rupert Brooke, made marmalade and polished his stories.

Both animals and people instinctively trusted him, and he was much respected locally for his ability to solve problems; in Swahili his nickname was "He Who Finds the Road". He was also admired for his friendliness, although sometimes he liked to retreat to a dark corner to brood.

He wrote three dashing volumes of autobiography, anthologised as *The Wheel of Life* (2002), and after a documentary film of his life, *A Gypsy in Africa*, was released in 1996, he received fan mail from all over the world.

"Bunny" Allen married first, in 1930, Babs Borrius. The marriage was dissolved, and in 1950 he married Murielle Joffe. Following her death in 1996, he married his companion of 40 years, Jeri Warden, who survived him together with the daughter and two sons of his first marriage.

—

## Idi Amin

IDI AMIN, the former Ugandan dictator and self-styled "Conqueror of the British Empire" (who died on August 16 2003, aged around 78) was one of the most reviled individuals in recent history.

Six foot four inches tall and weighing 20 stone, the former heavyweight boxing champion of Uganda appeared to relish his monstrous reputation. Subject to "visitations from God", and reputedly boasting a collection of human heads extensive enough to require its own deep-freeze, Amin was popularly considered to be deranged.

This impression was reinforced by claims from one of his physicians that they he had at various times treated him for hypomania, schizophrenia, tertiary syphilis and general paralysis of the insane. Amin, however, survived too long, exhibiting too shrewd an instinct for manipulation and too ruthless a capacity for cruelty to be dismissed as a mere madman.

Throughout his disastrous rule, he encouraged the West to cultivate a dangerous ambivalence towards him. His genial grin, penchant for grandiose self-publicity and ludicrous public statements on international affairs led to his adoption as a comic figure. He was easily parodied, and was granted his own fictional weekly commentary in *Punch*. However, this fascination, verging on affection, for the grotesqueness of the individual occluded the singular plight of his nation. As many as half a million Ugandans died under his regime in well-documented ways, ranging from mass executions to enforced self-cannibalism.

In one incident, the majority of Uganda's Asian population was expelled. Uganda, the "Pearl of Africa", a "fairytale world" to the young Winston Churchill, was pillaged and bankrupted. Amin summed up his attitude to opponents: "I ate them before they ate me." His exiled Health Minister, Henry Kyemba, confessed that "on several occasions he told me quite proudly that he had eaten the organs or flesh of his human victims".

*Idi Amin said Britain's economic crisis was a disgrace to the rest of the Commonwealth and offered to send vegetables to relieve the suffering.* (AP)

Once, as a lance-corporal in the King's African Rifles, he had embodied the British notion of the reliable native, fulfilling his superiors' prejudiced expectations. "Not much grey matter, but a splendid chap to have about," said one British officer. His willingness to obey without question, his sporting skill and spotless boots won him promotion. Later the stereotype mercilessly mocked its former masters. Although he inspired laughter in the West, the joke was a savage one, and it was not at Amin's expense but at the expense of those who laughed.

Idi Amin Dada Oumee was born around 1925 at Koboko, in the impoverished north-western part of Uganda, into a poor farming family of the small Kakwa tribe. A large child with a reputation as a playground bully, he received little formal education and, attracted by the mystique and power of the British military, joined the King's African Rifles at 18.

He was attached first to the 11th East Africa Division, in which he fought as a rifleman in Burma during the closing days of the Second World War, and then to the 4th Uganda Battalion, in which he was dispatched to quell tribal marauders in northern Uganda. Subsequently, he was involved in operations against Mau Mau in Kenya.

Amin was a sergeant-major by 1957, which represented solid progress within a regiment where intelligence was not necessarily considered a virtue. He was popular with his British officers, who appreciated his skill on the rugby field, unquestioning obedience and touching devotion to all things British.

Furthermore, he made them laugh. Once, persuaded by his commanding officer to open a bank account in which he deposited £10, he had within a few hours written nearly £2,000 worth of cheques, a prophetic indication of his future skill with figures.

Faced with the problem of finding potential officers among the African troops, in 1959 the British Army established the rank of *effendi* for non-commissioned African officers who were potential officer material. Amin was one of the first. Despite failing to complete training courses in both Britain and Israel, he was a major by 1963, and next year a colonel and deputy commander of Uganda's army and air force.

Amin's rise was greatly assisted by the patronage of Milton Obote, a leader in the struggle for independence who became Prime Minister in 1962. Obote had consolidated his position by forming an allegiance with the royalist party of the Baganda tribe, the largest and most influential of Uganda's many, semi-autonomous, tribal kingdoms. The Baganda king, Sir Edward Frederick William Walugembe Luwangula Mutesa II, otherwise known as King Freddie, was made President.

But Uganda's constitution came under strain when it was alleged that Obote and Amin had misappropriated large sums intended to support Congolese rebels. The National Assembly demanded Amin's resignation and Obote, facing parliamentary defeat, used force to suppress the opposition. Amin was rewarded for his steely support by being promoted to full command of the army and air force.

In 1966, Obote sought to secure his authority by abolishing the old tribal kingdoms. The Baganda rebelled, and Amin again proved his loyalty by personally assaulting King Freddie's palace with a heavy gun mounted on his Jeep. The uprising was brutally curtailed, and King Freddie fled to England, where he died three years later.

In an atmosphere of growing corruption and discontent, Obote came increasingly to rely on Amin's forthright attitude towards political problem solving. But inevitably, he grew uneasy and, when Amin was attending President Nasser's funeral in Egypt, purged the army leadership of Amin supporters.

Amin's chance to hit back came when Obote was attending a Commonwealth conference. Key units of the army and police staged a traditional coup, with Amin presiding over affairs from his heavily fortified residence on Prince Charles Drive, overlooking Kampala.

In the aftermath, he declared himself devoid of personal ambition. He would provide free and fair elections and then return the army to barracks. He took to the streets and countryside, stopping looting and dispensing personal cheques to the people, propagating an eccentric but paternal public image. The corrupt Obote regime had been particularly unpopular among the larger tribes, and crowds chanting their approval of Amin thronged Kampala.

Obote's political prisoners were freed, the body of King Freddie returned for burial. One British observer wrote: "I have never encountered a more benevolent and apparently popular leader than General Amin." However, Amin said that it would be at least five years before the population were ready for free elections and that a military government would be necessary. Abolishing Parliament, he announced that he would rule by decree.

Obote's fall was greeted with delight by many outside Uganda. The country had a huge budget deficit, and the interminable tribal disputes were a constant threat to stability. Britain recognised the Amin government, though neighbouring Tanzania was one of several countries which were openly critical or hostile. Many international commentators were prepared to give the new leader the benefit of the doubt. *The New York Times* commented on his "gentle political deftness" and talked sympathetically of the problems now facing him. He was taken seriously.

But while the West believed that Amin's priority would be to tackle the country's sinking economy, he devoted his energies exclusively to consolidating his grasp on power. His first objective was to ensure loyalty within the army. In secrecy, large-scale purges began. The initial targets were members of the Acholi and Langi tribes, from which

Obote and other potential rivals sprang. Killer squads and a range of security departments with names of a chilling ambiguity sprang up: "The Public Safety Unit"; "The State Research Bureau".

When in doubt about whom to arrest, Amin's supporters picked up those whose names began with "O", a common feature of Acholi and Langi surnames. Thousands were massacred. There were stories of soldiers being herded into rooms into which hand-grenades were hurled, of senior officers locked in cells and bayoneted at leisure, of a whole officer corps at Mbarara and Jinja barracks being summoned to parade and then being crushed by tanks. In the prison cells of Mackindye, Naguru and Nakasero, prisoners were compelled to kill each other with 16-pound sledgehammers in the vain hope that they would be spared. Then the hammers were given to other prisoners, who were told the same.

By early 1972, some 5,000 Acholi and Langi soldiers, and at least twice that number of civilians, had disappeared. Two American journalists, Nicholas Stroh and Robert Siedle, vanished while attempting to investigate the massacres. The rivers, lakes and forest around Kampala overflowed with human debris. From time to time the Owen Falls hydro-electric dam on Lake Victoria became clogged with bodies, precipitating power-cuts in Kampala.

Amin launched himself upon the international circuit with the charming naivety of a debutante. In Britain, he was received by Edward Heath and Her Majesty the Queen. He made a visit to Scotland, which made a lasting impression on him. Some years later, he declared that he would be happy to accept the Scots' secret wish to have him as their monarch.

One of his long-standing projects became the creation of a personal bodyguard of six feet four inches tall Scotsmen, all able to play the bagpipes. He also requested Harrier jets to bomb South Africa, Tanzania and the Sudan, all of which he thought were about to invade Uganda. While relations with the Mother Country disintegrated, Israel, where Amin had once received training, was delighted to find an approachable Muslim leader of an African nation, and provided several hundred technicians, military instructors and engineers. Amin, however, doggedly pursued his demands for aircraft to bomb Tanzania.

When the hardware was not forthcoming, he switched allegiance to Libya, which offered extensive economic and military aid. Colonel Gaddafi was apparently under the mistaken impression, encouraged by Amin, that Uganda was a wholly Muslim nation, when only around a fifth were followers of Islam.

In return, Amin expelled Israeli workers, and after terrorists murdered Israeli athletes at the 1972 Munich Olympics, he sent a telegram to Golda Meir, the Israeli Prime Minister. "Germany is the right place," it read, "where, when Hitler was Prime Minister and Supreme Commander, he burnt over six million Jews. This is because Hitler and all the German people know that the Israelis are not people working in the interest of the people of the world."

It was just one of an increasing number of erratic and shocking communications issuing from Kampala. Sometimes Amin gave world leaders advice on personal and political problems, sometimes he simply taunted them. Naturally, Britain was the favourite butt of his humour.

Among his more reasonable jibes was one in which he told Edward Heath that Britain's economic crisis was a disgrace to the rest of the Commonwealth. He started a "Save Britain Fund", offering to send cargoes of vegetables to relieve suffering, and said that he would organise a whip-round of Uganda's friends, "if you will let me know the exact position of the mess". In 1975, he had himself inaugurated President for Life, and was borne aloft by 14 indigent whites, to symbolise the "white man's burden".

President Julius Nyerere of Tanzania was another unlucky object of his attentions. "I love you very much," Amin wrote to him, "and if you were a woman, I would consider marrying you." Later, when a Tanzanian invasion brought him down, he urged Nyerere to settle the matter with a boxing match, to be refereed by the boxer Mohammed Ali.

Economically, Amin's shameless incompetence was soon evident. He had no policies, bar extortion. Whilst he raised military spending by about 500 per cent, inflation rose to 700 per cent, fuelled by his demand that more money should be printed.

The cabinet was subject to violent fluctuations in its size, often presaged by radio announcements publicising the latest unfortunate motor accident involving a civil servant. Such frantic activity led to the occasional hiccup. One former Amin employee, Frank Kalimazo, was attending his daughter's wedding when he was informed that his demise had been announced on the radio. He was part of an administrative backlog.

On another occasion, Amin telephoned the wife of Robert Astles, an English emigré who had been an intimate of the dictator, to offer his regret for the accidental death of her husband and to tell her that she could collect the body from the city morgue. In fact, Astles had evaded the intended assassination. It was one of four occasions when, bored of his company, Amin ordered his death. Years later, when he had finally returned alive to Wimbledon, the unlovely Astles said survival under Amin largely involved staying out of sight until he was in a better mood.

The country's predicament was not assisted by Amin's revelation that he was taking his economic advice from God who, on August 5 1972, ordered him to expel the Asians. There were some 80,000 Asians in Uganda, who were responsible for up to 90 per cent of commerce and 50 per cent of industry. Some 55,000 of them had maintained their British citizenship, and it was on these that Amin turned, charging that they were "sabotaging the economy of the country, and do not have the welfare of Uganda at heart".

Initially he ordered the expulsion of the other 25,000 Asians who had Ugandan citizenship, but later relented. The Asians were told they could take their possessions but were habitually stripped of everything, even their bedding. Most were admitted to Britain, though some went to Canada and the United States.

Irrational though it seemed, Amin's move was in fact a calculated piece of populism, channelling the stored-up resentment of Ugandans at a time when his position was precarious. Furthermore, it made available property valued at £570 million as well as innumerable businesses, which could be dispensed to loyal cronies.

Despite periodic attempts at insurgency from pro-Obote rebels and the increasingly dire predicament of the economy, Amin survived, shored up by what *The New York Times Magazine* described as a "state sinister that would startle fiction writers". African nations were reluctant to intervene openly and precipitate a bloody internecine conflict, not least because some perceived him as a public champion against the former colonial powers. For a time he was President of the Organisation of African States, though there was said to have been opposition to this.

By the late 1970s Amin had outlived his novelty value. The event he intended as the re-launching of his international career ended in humiliation. In 1977, an Air France flight carrying 300 passengers from Tel Aviv to Paris was hijacked by Palestinian terrorists. Amin allowed the aircraft to land at Entebbe, from where the hijackers demanded the release of 53 imprisoned terrorists.

All non-Jewish passengers were released, and the remaining hostages taken to the airport terminal, where Amin mingled benignly with them while Ugandan troops stood guard. Dora Bloch, an elderly woman of joint British and Israeli nationality, fell ill and had to be taken to hospital. While she was away, Israeli commandos landed at the airport, routed Amin's troops, destroyed a flight of MiG aircraft, and flew out one hour and 16 minutes later, taking all the hostages except Dora Bloch after killing all seven hijackers.

Her body turned up on waste ground outside Kampala. It became a capital offence to joke about the affair. Amin was particularly upset about the destruction of the MiG aircraft, and dispatched a telegram to Israel threatening an immediate attack unless compensation was paid, as well as expenses he had incurred "entertaining" the hostages.

In October the following year, 3,000 Ugandan troops entered Tanzania, where they raped and massacred their way through the border countryside. Amin promptly announced he had conquered his neighbour. However, by spring, retaliating Tanzanian forces were in Kampala, Obote was back in power and Amin was hiding in Libya. He remained there until it was rumoured that even Gaddafi could stomach him no longer. From Libya he went to Saudi Arabia, which became his principal home. He was often to be seen in Safeway or Pizza Hut in Jeddah.

Periodically, he made attempts to return to Africa, once turning up in Zaire under a false name. He was sighted briefly in various African states, all of which spat him out. Twice he applied for an American visa, first to visit Disneyland, and subsequently to enable him to pursue a new career as a professional 10-pin bowler. He was refused on both occasions.

After a coup in 1985 by Major-General Tito Okello removed Obote from power, Amin amused himself by telephoning journalists with the glad news that he was on his way back to Kampala. But it was not to be.

At various times the Ugandan authorities considered extraditing him to face charges of murder, but their efforts were half-hearted. Astles's telephone in Wimbledon became Amin's favoured means of communication until, incensed by the size of his telephone bill, the Saudi Arabians finally removed his international dialling facility.

Idi Amin was married at least five times, and acknowledged at least 43 children. His second wife, Kay, died during a failed abortion she undertook to conceal an illicit affair. He reputedly ordered her body to be dismembered and re-assembled with the limbs reversed as a warning to his other wives.

His fifth wife, Sarah, was a member of the Ugandan Army's "suicide" squad. Amin is said to have ordered the murder of her fiancé, Jesse Gitta. His head was one of a number that Amin's former housekeeper recounted seeing stored in the refrigerator of his "Botanical Room". Sarah went into exile with Amin, but he later banished her. In 1987, living penniless in a council flat in Germany, she publicly sought a divorce.

~

## Paul Ngei

PAUL NGEI (who died on August 15 2004, aged 81) became one of the more colourful early members of the independent Kenyan government on the strength of his imprisonment with Jomo Kenyatta, Kenya's first president, under colonial rule.

He served seven years' hard labour at Kapenguria jail, in north-west Kenya, for being a manager of the terrorist organisation Mau Mau. This mysterious movement was rooted in the blood-oath ceremonies of the Kikuyu people, whose fighters used spears and axes to terrorise farmers, farmsteads and blacks deemed to be collaborators. Only 95 whites were killed, while 14,000 Africans and Asians died during the uprising. It was subdued by the deployment of British troops, although modern Kenyan history holds that the rebellion was the national freedom struggle which led to the country's independence in 1963.

Kenyatta, Ngei and other members of the "Kapenguria Six" were a diverse group of political hopefuls who had little to do with the fighting in the Aberdare forests, as they were serving their prison terms; they had been rounded up by the colonial authorities as the usual suspects when the first signs of black unrest manifested themselves. All, however, were to be hailed as heroes of the revolution when independence was finally granted.

Ngei, in particular, was to prove a supreme political opportunist, often boasting in his later life that he had "at least nine lives". He needed them all in the vicious labyrinth of Kenya's post-colonial tribal politics. As a member of the small Kamba tribe, he made several powerful enemies among the ruling Kikuyu elite. But he always survived the many attempts to discredit him because of the close bonds he had forged with Kenyatta.

The youngest of the Kapenguria Six, Ngei was said to have kitted himself out with the same kind of leather jacket, fly whisk and walking stick as Kenyatta, whose life he claimed to have saved by preventing a fellow detainee from grabbing him by the neck and throwing him into a fire. He and Kenyatta had a falling out before independence, when Ngei threatened to lead Kamba out of the nationalist coalition. But after the failure of his party to make an impact, he joined the delegation to the independence talks in London.

A stocky, powerful figure with a rasping voice that was filled with menace yet rarely sounded angry, Ngei was never averse to using his fists on journalists and political opponents, or on rivals in his always complicated love life. He was fined by a Nairobi magistrate for pulling a gun on a Kenyan businessman and threatening to shoot him.

He was suspended from the government in 1966 amid allegations that he had been involved in smuggling maize, causing a shortage of the staple food in Kenya. Kenyatta instituted a commission of inquiry which, under pressure from his office, found no case to answer.

Ngei was an enthusiastic member of what Kenyans came to call the "WaBenzi" tribe, powerful and influential members of the new ruling class who were identified by the large Mercedes-Benz limousines they drove. Ngei acquired his Mercedes in 1971, telling the dealers to send the bill to the government. The Treasury refused to pay, insisting that the minister had acquired it for his personal use; and the dealers, aware of their customer's status, wrote off the deal to experience, leaving Ngei to use the car for another 20 years. It became known to Nairobi wags as "the longest test drive in history". He frequently used the same ploy in Nairobi's hotels and restaurants, telling the waiters to "send the bill to the government", knowing it would never be paid, but confident that no one would lay a complaint against him.

Ngei's capacity for political survival was never better illustrated than during the tense period after the death of Kenyatta in 1978. He actively and openly led a movement to prevent Daniel Arap Moi from succeeding as President. He failed, but swiftly set about mending fences with Kenya's new leader so smoothly that he was appointed to Moi's new cabinet.

Ngei was finally forced to resign his cabinet post and his parliamentary seat in 1991 after being declared bankrupt by the

Kenyan High Court. Numerous business ventures failed, and the trappings of power disappeared. His health began to fail and eventually he had to have both legs amputated following complications caused by chronic diabetes. He spent his last years wheelchair-bound and in penury.

Paul Joseph Ngei was born in 1923 at Kangundo in the Machakos district, a grandson of Paramount Chief Masaku. A bright, ambitious youngster, he attended the prestigious Alliance High School in Kikuyu and went on to Makere University in neighbouring Uganda. He initially opted for a military career, joining the King's African Rifles, but his rebellious nature was not compatible with Army discipline. Having studied drama at Makere, he tried his hand at acting, gaining a small part in the film, *Where No Vultures Fly* (1951), which starred Anthony Steel and Dinah Sheridan.

He moved to journalism, joining the *East African Standard* before starting his own Swahili-language newspaper. This was the era of political awakening in Africa, and Ngei was drawn into politics. He joined the executive of the Kenyan African National Union (KANU), which was to become the ruling party; his involvement led to his arrest at the outbreak of the Mau Mau insurgency.

On his release, Ngei briefly fell out with the KANU leadership and formed his own party, the African Peoples' Party (APP). This, too, was short-lived; it disbanded when he was persuaded to rejoin KANU as it came to power under Kenyatta. Ngei's first government job was as chairman of the Maize Marketing Board and, within a year, he was appointed to the cabinet as Minister of Co-operatives and Marketing.

Like many others in the governments of Kenyatta and, later, Moi, Ngei had taken full advantage of his position to enrich himself. He acquired a mansion on a five-acre plot in Nairobi, a 3,000-acre ranch at Oldonyo-Sabuk and a beach house at Malindi on the Indian Ocean coast. He owned more than 1,000 head of cattle and 2,500 goats, and regularly flew to London to add to a large collection of Savile Row suits.

But even when poverty-stricken and confined to his wheelchair in old age, he was still able to boast of having three lovers, telling his dwindling band of admirers:"You don't need legs to have a mistress."

Paul Ngei had four wives, three of whom were at his bedside when he died, and at least nine children.

# Joan Root

JOAN ROOT (who was murdered by intruders at her home in Kenya on January 12 2006, aged 70) made, with her former husband Alan Root, some of the most adventurous and highly acclaimed wildlife documentary films to emerge from the continent.

The Roots pioneered the wildlife film that weaves a story around its subjects, which varied from an animal and its habits to a tree and its inhabitants and the common termite. They produced 10 titles, mostly for Anglia Television's "Survival" series, sometimes taking two years to complete and involving many hair-raising encounters in the East African bush.

*Joan and her husband Alan facing danger behind the camera when making their documentary* Two in the Bush. *(Survival)*

The farm near Naivasha in the Rift Valley, north of Nairobi, that was their home became a destination not only for people involved in the film industry but also for sundry adventurers, hunters, conservationists and pilots. Alan Root was one of the first to operate hot-air ballooning "safaris" over Kenya's game reserves, he and Joan setting a record by flying a balloon over Mount Kilimanjaro, the highest peak in Africa.

She was born Joan Thorpe on January 8 1936, the daughter of a British settler who had come to Kenya as a coffee planter. From her earliest years, she developed a passion for the African wild and all of its inhabitants. It was while working as a safari guide that she met Alan Root, a Londoner who had come to the colony in search of adventure. He had been a trapper, a stunt motorcyclist and had learned to fly before picking up an 8 mm film camera and discovering a career as a cinematographer. Root found Joan "painfully shy", but when he heard she had successfully hand-raised an orphaned baby elephant he decided she was worth pursuing.

As he pithily put it later: "Before we were married she wore a monocle and so did I. Together we made quite a spectacle." In fact, Joan, quietly-spoken and self-effacing, made a perfect counterpoint to the ebullient and daredevil Root. Her modesty disguised a will of iron and raw courage, which was much needed in the frequently hazardous work they were undertaking.

She had a bitter taste of what her married life might hold on her honeymoon night. The couple were camped near the Tsavo River Bridge in eastern Kenya, listening to the roars of the lions which might have been descendants of the notorious man-eating cats that terrorised the area nearly a century before. They survived the lions but romance disappeared rapidly from their tent when Joan was stung by a scorpion.

The Roots' first successful film was *Baobab: Portrait of a Tree*, in which they caught the seasonal changes of growth and the myriad creatures that live in and off these trees. There followed *Mysterious Castles of Clay*, in which they spent months, day and night, filming termites building one of the towering mounds which dot the African savannah, only to have it destroyed in a matter of hours by an aardvark.

Joan Root knew that she could never curb her husband's risk-taking in the making of a film or in his flying or ballooning. "I just made sure I was there with, hopefully, the right medication or words of comfort until we could get him to hospital," she once said. Unlike Alan, Joan never readily put herself in the path of danger; but accidents did happen. When the couple were filming hippos underwater for *Mzima: Portrait of a Spring*, Joan had the face of her diving mask bitten off by an angry male hippo. Inches further and she would have lost her head to a pair of massive jaws; Alan was bitten in the leg by the same beast, and nearly lost it.

When Alan decided, between films, to set a ballooning record by flying over the 19,340-foot peak of Mount Kilimanjaro he belatedly had Joan join him, hauling her into the basket as the balloon lifted off.

They were in thick cloud for the first half hour as the balloon ascended. At one point the flame on the vessel's burner blew out, and Alan fumbled with the matches to relight it. As they broke into the sunlight, Joan became uncharacteristically snappy and clumsy. This puzzled Alan until he noticed that the tube from her oxygen supply had become snagged. A rapid repair job soon had Joan back to her normal, placid self, and the couple marvelled as they cruised at 24,000 feet over Kilimanjaro. They made a gentle descent to land in Tanzania, then in hostile relations with neighbouring Kenya. Their celebrations on landing were muted when they were arrested and held briefly as "astronaut spies".

The film which the Roots regarded as their favourite, *The Year of the Wildebeest*, about a mass migration through Tanzania, won international acclaim and many awards, although Alan, with his Cockney humour to the fore, referred to the project as "Brave Gnu World". During one shooting session in the Serengeti, he was bitten on the backside by a startled leopard. Joan, as always, was on hand to treat the wound until they could get her husband to a Nairobi hospital, where he was regarded as "a regular".

In making *Two in the Bush*, Joan and Alan were themselves filmed to show how they went about their adventurous life. At one point in the film, Alan insisted that Joan be the target of a captured spitting cobra, a compelling scene in which her spectacles were quickly coated with venom. The film was widely criticised as being too self-indulgent. The Roots agreed. "It was more of a home movie," said Alan.

Nairobi and the documentary film world were shocked when the Roots were divorced in the mid-1980s. "It was very saddening news. They had made such a name for themselves as a couple and it seemed an ideal partnership in every way", said one of their executive producers. The parting was amicable, and Joan stayed on at their Naivasha farm, throwing herself into conservation work. She campaigned vigorously to prevent the growing wave of human encroachment from spoiling the wildlife in, on and around Lake Naivasha. Her anti-poaching activities made her some enemies within the African communities around the lake, and may have played a part in her death.

In 2007 it was announced that the actress Julia Roberts was to star in a film about Joan Root's murder.

## Ralph Lownie

HIS HONOUR RALPH LOWNIE OF LARGO (who died on November 28 2007, aged 83) enjoyed 40 years on the bench, during which he sweltered in wing collar, wig and gown beneath the Kenyan sun and sampled the air-conditioned courts of Bermuda, before returning home to become a metropolitan magistrate and a circuit judge.

*Lownie enjoying a ride in Cairo while on holiday from the Kenya circuit.*

Lownie claimed to have heard a case under a palm tree only once. But in an article for *The Daily Telegraph*'s book *The British Empire* (1997), Lownie recalled decrepit court rooms where the tar dripped from the roof on to his notes; he remembered listening to witnesses suckling their babies as they gave evidence and an usher who was paid a small fee "for polishing the judge's chamber pot".

After starting as registrar of the Supreme Court in Nairobi, Lownie was promoted to senior magistrate, which enabled him to travel "up country", where he once spent an afternoon riding along a stretch of the Uganda railway by self-propelling trolley to check what an engine driver had seen from a level crossing.

He sometimes had to inspect men considered of unsound mind whom the police had trussed up in the back of their vehicles; and when staying in regulation bungalows he had to provide his own curtains. And, since the Mau Mau campaign was at its height, Lownie occasionally found himself being addressed by armed counsel and passing down sentences designed to eradicate the cancer of terrorism. But he was most impressed by the way imprisonment, in what was called "Hotelli King George", represented for many Africans a relief from everyday hardship; escapes were unknown.

With Kenyan independence approaching, Lownie was called to the Bar by Inner Temple and became an efficient and effective magistrate on Bermuda. But the island received a severe shock when the Governor, Sir Richard Shaples, was murdered by terrorists. Lownie was also a potential target, who was said to be No. 3 on a terrorists' list; but his only response was to take down the sign on his house and close the curtains.

After returning from Bermuda in 1972, his ability to hand down sure judgments (none of them successfully challenged on appeal) ensured a rise, over three decades, from Bow Street "beak" to circuit judge at Croydon. He sat under heavy police guard at Lambeth while remanding a group of nine people accused of firearms offences and an Irishman charged with the Harrods bombing. Whenever such hearings were coming up, his wife Claudine (with whom he had a son and a daughter) would cut his sandwiches with extra care because she knew that they would be examined by the security guards.

Ralph Hamilton Lownie was born in Edinburgh on September 27 1924 and educated at George Watson's College. He went up to the university, but in the week following his 18th birthday he joined up to serve with 584 Army Field Group, Royal Engineers, building bridges over the Maas and the Rhine in 1945.

After leaving the Army he returned to Edinburgh and his studies, then qualified as a solicitor. He also found time to act as a voluntary agent for the poor and to take a small part (alongside Stanley Baxter) in Tyrone Guthrie's production of Sir David Lindsay's *Pleasant Satyre of the Thrie Estaites* at the Festival. In the years that followed he became a Writer to the Signet before being called to the Scottish Bar.

A reticent man, who would put down his profession as "winkler" when asked to register at hotels, Lownie earned a doctorate on homicide and diminished responsibility from Kent University in his later years. He became a keen fan of the wrestler "Big Daddy" on television, and enjoyed "sneaking up" to London on Sundays to attend St Columba's, Pont Street.

At the age of 80 he published *Auld Reekie*, a highly evocative Edinburgh anthology, and had just completed a book on feudal baronies before his death.

# The Reverend Robert Philp

THE REVEREND ROBERT PHILP (who died on March 1 2008, aged 95) was a Church of Scotland missionary in Kenya, and the interpreter for Jomo Kenyatta at his trial in 1952.

*Philp delivering an address in Kikuyu in 1988 on the 90th anniversary of the first Scottish missionaries' arrival in Kenya.*

Kenyatta, later to become his nation's President, was charged with "managing and being a member" of Mau Mau, the insurgency against British rule. The trial was held in a remote area amid great security and an atmosphere of extreme political tension. Although he knew English well, Kenyatta determined to speak only in his native language, Kikuyu. The role of court translator was initially given to the archaeologist Louis Leakey, but his interpretations were continually challenged by defence counsel, and an exasperated Leakey finally walked out.

The job was then given to Philp, who had been born and raised amongst the Kikuyu of central Kenya, and was known for his mastery of their complex language as well as for the authenticity of his accent. In April 1953 Kenyatta was sentenced to seven years' hard labour; he remained in prison until 1959.

Robert Anderson Philp was born on February 25 1913, the only child of a Scottish missionary doctor, the Reverend Dr Horace Philp, founder of Tumutumu hospital near Nyeri, in the foothills of Mount Kenya. Robert was the first of the children born to the early Scottish missionaries in Kenya.

His mother Mary, a Latin scholar, taught Kikuyu to new missionaries. Her son's prowess in the language, however, derived from his upbringing as the only white child living amongst the Kikuyu people. Until the age of nine all his playmates were Kikuyu, and he grew up bilingual.

He was sent to George Watson's College in Edinburgh, and went on to read divinity at Edinburgh University. His curiosity and taste for adventure led him to explore Europe by motorcycle. He spent a year studying at the Budapest College of the Reformed Church of Hungary, then, in 1937, returned to Kenya as a missionary.

Philp's first posting was to his birthplace, Tumutumu, where he lived and worked as a bachelor missionary and Army chaplain throughout the war years. At Edinburgh University he had met a fellow student, Jeane Caddick, and after the war they renewed their friendship when he made a return trip to Britain. They married in 1946.

Philp had a deep affinity with the Kikuyu. During the insurgency of the 1950s those who refused to take the Mau Mau oath were in danger of being killed, and many suffered this fate. Others were detained by the British on suspicion of being rebels, and Philp successfully interceded on behalf of some of these with the authorities.

He would also visit Kikuyu Christians living deep in the bush in what was dangerous Mau Mau territory. On one occasion he was accompanied by Jeane, and they arrived at a village to find only one old, lame Kikuyu lady. "He has come, he has come. The *bwana* Philipo has come!" she exclaimed, as she abandoned her stick and danced with sheer joy at his arrival.

During the 1950s Philp worked alongside Anglicans and Methodists as the first Presbyterian tutor at St Paul's United Theological College at Limuru, preparing and equipping Africans to become ministers. Among his pupils were future leaders of the Presbyterian Church of East Africa (PCEA). Later he became the first Church of Scotland missionary resident at Nakuru in the Rift Valley, and then moved to Thogoto, near Nairobi, where he was tireless in his efforts to foster good relations between Africans and Europeans.

In 1960, after 23 years as a second-generation missionary, personal circumstances caused Philp reluctantly to resign from the Church of

Scotland Mission and leave Kenya. On the sea voyage to Britain his children so relished their time with him that he became known as "the man with the three adoring daughters".

Philp became a Church of Scotland minister at Stepps, near Glasgow. He brought a strong evangelical message, and many attributed their faith to his ministry; several in his congregation later themselves became ministers or missionaries. He began the now common practice of young people participating in services with musical instruments and in singing groups. He also took great pleasure in introducing the congregation to visiting African ministers.

When he retired at 69, Philp and his wife went to live in Leeds, where they became involved with a Congregational church, and later in Bath, where they became part of an Anglican church community.

In 1988 the PCEA celebrated the 90th anniversary of the first Scottish missionaries' arrival in Kenya, and asked Philp to attend as guest of honour. As part of the trip he returned to Tumutumu, discovering that he was still fluent in Kikuyu after 28 years in Britain. An old lady greeted him: "It's Roberti! It's our Roberti! He's come home", and recalled the day 75 years previously when, as a teenager, she had been invited into the Philpses' home by Robert's mother to see the new baby. The PCEA's service of celebration at Thogoto was attended by more than 5,000 people, including President Daniel Arap Moi. In his address, Philp spoke without notes in Kikuyu, and the crowd broke into spontaneous applause.

Jeane Philp died in 2005. As he entered old age, Philp reacted to increasing disability and frailty with typical resilience and dignity. He lived out his last days at a nursing home near Bath, but the pull of his heart was to Kenya, and it was his Kikuyu Bible that he chose to read, rather than an English one.

Robert Philp asked for his ashes to be buried in Kenya, amongst the Kikuyu people, because "after all, that is where I am from".

# CENTRAL AFRICA

~

## Doctor Hastings Banda

DOCTOR HASTINGS BANDA (who died on November 25 1997, aged 99) led the Protectorate of Nyasaland to independence as Malawi in 1964, and then became its absolute ruler for 30 years.

*Banda, Prime Minister of the newly-created state of Malawi, arriving at London Airport for a Commonwealth Prime Ministers' conference.* (PA)

For much of that time, he was revered as a messiah by his people, despite the despotic nature of his administration. Appointed President for Life in 1971, he liked to take the salute of his public from the back of an open-topped, scarlet Rolls-Royce. This taste for luxury was at odds with a puritanical nature, one of the many contradictions that marked both Banda and his regime.

Malawi was run not just as a one-party state, but as a one-man state; he was not only President and head of the Malawi Congress Party but also Minister of External Affairs, Justice, Public Works, Agriculture, Community Development and Social Welfare. This grip on power was compared to that of a Roman emperor, but Banda's excesses did not match those of such tyrants as Idi Amin of Uganda or Bokassa, the self-appointed Emperor of the Central African Empire.

Habitually clad in a Homburg hat and a dark three-piece suit, the only concession to his African heritage an ivory-handled fly whisk, Banda imposed strict censorship on newspapers and morals. Women were banned from wearing skirts above the knee, men from wearing flared trousers. Men with long hair were denied entry to the country unless they were shorn by airport barbers. He prohibited the playing of the Simon and Garfunkel song "Cecilia", because its lyrics were adapted by opponents to poke fun at his relationship with his Junoesque companion, Cecilia Kadzamira, whose uncle, John Tembo, was his right-hand man. More sinister was the frequent disappearance of those who disputed Banda's rule; he joked that they were "food for the crocs".

Although physically small, Banda possessed great presence and was capable of impressive rages. When Ugandan players stormed off the pitch in a football match he was watching, because they disagreed with the referee's decision, Banda went to their dressing room and ordered them back on to the field. In 1973, a delegation of representatives from Western oil companies was treated by him to an impromptu and well-informed briefing on oil supplies. He then dismissed his watching cabinet, saying: "You must excuse them, they are just children," and handled the negotiations in person.

The repression of any opposition brought political stability. His domestic policy of paternalistic capitalism was reinforced by a conduct of foreign affairs based on opportunism rather than ideology. He saw the necessity of doing business with neighbouring countries, including South Africa under apartheid, which provided 40 per cent of Malawi's imports. Banda became the only black leader to establish diplomatic relations with Pretoria, and was also friendly with the Israeli government. He successfully steered the country through the crises that engulfed the region, notably Rhodesia's unilateral declaration of independence.

While he was genuinely popular in the early years of his rule, he later relied on the cult of his own image. Whenever he appeared in public he was surrounded by hundreds of dancing women, the *mbumba*, who sang his praises and dressed in cloth stamped with his likeness.

One improbable source of inspiration for his style of government was the Classics. His favoured reading was Caesar's *Gallic Wars*; he particularly admired the Roman dictator's political ruthlessness. Banda used to harangue his audiences on the need to read Plato, holding that no man was educated until he knew Latin and Greek. He even founded Kamuzu Academy, which he called the "Eton in the Bush", where Malawi's future rulers were given a traditional European education; no native teachers were allowed. The school library was built as a miniature replica of the Library of Congress in Washington. The Academy became the source of much ridicule.

From the late 1970s Banda began to withdraw a little from power, like Tiberius at Capri, ruling through minions. As his grip weakened, so Malawi became less stable. The detention of a dissenting trade union leader in May 1992 provoked riots in Blantyre, the country's biggest city, and Lilongwe, its capital. Roman Catholic bishops published a document deploring official repression, and all aid from the West was withdrawn. At the same time the Church of Scotland made it clear that people should no longer regard Banda as an elder.

Banda's opponents staged demonstrations and made noisy criticisms of the regime for the first time in three decades. He duly made some concessions on censorship, which resulted in 24 newspapers being set up overnight. Eventually he was forced to agree to a referendum on whether to retain his one-party state, and 63 per cent of the population voted against the man they knew as *Ngwazi*, the conqueror and chief of chiefs. But he refused to step down, even after losing the subsequent elections and the presidency in December 1993.

The son of poor Chewa peasants, Kamuzu Banda is thought to have been born near the town of Kasungu, Nyasaland, in February 1898, during the Angoni uprising at Fort Jameson (now Chipata). In later life, he would claim to have been born in 1906, celebrating his official birthday on May 14. The infant Banda was named Kamuzu, "the little root", because root herbs were believed to have cured his mother's barrenness. He later took the name of Hastings from a missionary, having been taught English at the mission of the Church of Scotland at Livingstone.

At school Kamuzu was accused of cheating in an examination by looking over the shoulder of another pupil; he was summarily expelled. Of small stature, he had in fact been standing up so that he could see the blackboard. He had nurtured a hope that he might one day become a professor of Classics; shattered to discover all further avenues of learning cut off, he set out on foot for South Africa, a journey of 1,000 miles. He did not tell his family, who thought he had been eaten by lions. It was two years before they heard of him again.

He interrupted his journey to work as an orderly in a native hospital in Southern Rhodesia, where he suffered racial discrimination that made him determined to become more astute and better educated than his persecutors. For the next eight years he worked in the Rand goldfields as a clerk and interpreter, and attended night classes at a Methodist school. In 1924 he won a scholarship to study at their college in Ohio.

Banda spent the next 12 years studying in America, supporting himself by odd jobs and teaching in Sunday schools. He went on to medical college in Chicago, where he was the only black student, and at Nashville, graduating in 1937 with marks of 99.45 per cent in surgery. In the Deep South Banda witnessed a lynching by the Ku Klux Klan, but the greatest influence on him was Dr J. E. K. Aggrey, an American-educated Ghanaian, who preached that to achieve racial harmony "you had to play on the white keys as well as the black".

Banda's ambition was to return to Nyasaland as its first native doctor, but since the only offer he had required him not to socialise with his European colleagues, he decided instead to enrol as a medical student at Glasgow and Edinburgh universities. He also became an elder of the Church of Scotland. After qualifying at the Royal College of Surgeons in 1941 he went on to study tropical medicine in Liverpool. As a pacifist during the Second World War, he was drafted to work as a general practitioner on Merseyside and Tyneside. In 1945 he moved to Harlesden, north London, where he served 4,000 patients, mostly white, and was highly respected. He used money from richer patients to subsidise those who could not afford treatment and to fund the schooling of Nyasaland children.

After the war he became deeply interested in African affairs, and his house in Brondesbury Park, north London, was used as a meeting place for Fabians, African students and such nationalist leaders as Jomo Kenyatta of Kenya and Kwame Nkrumah of the Gold Coast (which became Ghana on independence in 1957). Banda and Nkrumah agreed that since the Gold Coast's mosquitoes were the worst in Africa, it was a colony the British would not be reluctant to quit. Banda, though, remained fond of Britain, and when he had come to power would stay at Claridge's for a month every year.

In the late 1940s he began conducting his own political campaign in London, writing letters and pamphlets for the native leaders in Nyasaland. This led to the creation of the nationalist Nyasaland African Congress in 1950, whose leader he was generally accepted to be. He first clashed with the British authorities when he vehemently opposed plans for a federation of Northern and Southern Rhodesia and Nyasaland, based on white supremacy. When this was set up in 1953, Banda accused the British of betraying his country. In the same year he went to the Gold Coast to practise medicine and to continue his correspondence with the nationalist leaders in Nyasaland.

Shortly before leaving Britain, Banda had been cited as co-respondent in a divorce case. The woman had been his secretary in London and followed him to the Gold Coast, where she bore his son; later she returned home. He was still regarded in Nyasaland as a potent political force, and when, in the summer of 1958, widespread unrest broke out, the young Nyasa leaders invited him to return home. The small figure in the Homburg hat spoke in English, as he would continue to do in all public pronouncements. But a crowd of 4,000 at Blantyre greeted him as a liberator.

Banda's dynamism and willpower were soon evident: he called for friendly negotiations between Europeans and Africans, while demanding elections and freedom from the federation. Within nine months he had been elected president-general of the Nyasaland African Congress and had purged the leadership of all but his most loyal lieutenants; he bluntly admitted he was an extremist, styling himself on Cromwell. At other times he took Churchill as his professed model.

In early 1959 a state of emergency was declared by the Governor. The Congress was banned and Banda was jailed without trial. He was later accused of being involved in a plot to massacre the white population. A clamour for his release was mounted in Britain and Africa against the federal Prime Minister, Sir Roy Welensky, who claimed that freedom for Banda would mean renewed unrest and violence. On

April 1 1960 Iain Macleod, the new Colonial Secretary, ordered Banda's release.

Banda held no grudge against his jailers, and became friendly with one of them, a Rhodesian named Tony Barnard, whom he invited to Malawi's fifth anniversary of independence celebrations in 1969. "I was Mr Barnard's guest, and he looked after me very well," Banda told the cheering crowd. "Now he is my guest in Malawi." This was typical of Banda's humour at its most generous, and it was widely appreciated.

In June 1960, two months after his release, the state of emergency was lifted, and he attended a string of conferences in London on the future of Nyasaland. The result was a constitution which gave the vote to 100,000 Africans with property, income and literacy qualifications, enough to give them a solid majority on the legislative council. The first elections served as a referendum on whether Nyasaland should stay in the federation, and there was an overwhelming victory for the nationalists. Banda was appointed Minister of Natural Resources and Local Government and developed a close relationship with the Governor, Sir Glyn Jones. He became Prime Minister in February 1963, and led his country to independence, as Malawi, in June the following year.

Within two months of independence Banda introduced a preventive detention law enabling him to arrest dissenters on the spot. He also sacked cabinet members opposed to his belief that, for its economic survival, Malawi needed to maintain relations with Portuguese Mozambique and South Africa. The dispute caused a brief civil war, but the rebels were routed.

His principal aim was political stability, and he detained anyone whom he deemed a threat to the country's efficient administration. Journalists, lawyers, lecturers and even relatives of exiled ministers were imprisoned or disappeared, murdered by the police or by Banda's private thugs, the Young Pioneers. In 1976 hundreds of Asians were expelled, after a group of Goans in a club bar demanded that a radio broadcast he was making should be turned off. The barman obeyed, but reported the incident to the police, who rounded up 66 members. They were the first victims of wholesale expulsions. The persecution of Jehovah's Witnesses, which had begun shortly after independence, reached new heights in 1975 and 1976; 12,000 fled while some 5,000 were sent to detention centres.

Compared with many African countries, however, Malawi prospered. "I want my people to have three things: enough food to eat, decent clothes to wear and a house that doesn't leak when it rains. That is what independence means to me," Banda said repeatedly. Agricultural production increased, and in most years there was a surplus for export. Banda prevented the flow of rural workers to the cities with incentives to grow more crops at guaranteed prices, efficient marketing and distribution, and controls that allowed rural incomes to rise faster than those in urban areas, which were deliberately kept at a low level.

Rural development schemes, the envy of the Third World, sprouted with such success that the World Bank, the Commonwealth Development Corporation and European banks queued up to offer funds. Aid from Britain had pumped more than £40 million into Malawi's economy by 1978, helping the country to become that African rarity, a self-sufficient economy that produced surplus food for export.

By moving Malawi's capital from Zomba to Lilongwe, about 200 miles north of Blantyre, Banda also provided thousands of jobs. The project was principally financed by South Africa. Construction began in 1968, and two years later Banda became the first black African President to visit South Africa. By Inauguration Day, January 1 1975, the population of the new capital had jumped from 20,000 to 130,000, and a decade later the capital's £70 million airport was opened.

After Banda had been replaced by the United Democratic Front of Bakili Muzuli in 1994, he and John Tembo were placed on trial for the murder the previous year of three cabinet ministers and an MP; their executions were said to have been disguised as a car accident. However, when Banda came to give evidence, he claimed that he could no longer remember what had happened. This loss of memory (he had undergone brain surgery in 1993) and the lack of any direct connection to the crime, led to both his and Tembo's acquittal in 1995.

During his last year, when he was clearly near the end of his life, Banda apologised to his countrymen for any atrocities committed during his time in office.

~

# Joshua Nkomo

JOSHUA NKOMO (who died on July 1 1999, aged 82) was known as "the Father of Zimbabwe", but never achieved his ambition of becoming his country's first black leader. After enduring imprisonment and exile in the struggle for Rhodesian independence, he was defeated by Robert Mugabe in the new nation's first democratic elections in 1980.

*Nkomo in talks with the Foreign Secretary, James Callaghan, in London.* (PA)

Mugabe's Zimbabwe African National Union (ZANU) won 57 of the 80 seats, while Nkomo's Zimbabwe African People's Union (ZAPU) gained only 20, all but one of them in his native Matabeleland. The electorate had divided on tribal lines. Mugabe's Shona tribe constituted nearly three-quarters of the population. Against this reality, Nkomo's reputation as a freedom fighter and a jolly extrovert was powerless.

He became Minister for Home Affairs in the first Mugabe administration. But, after two years, he was sacked when caches of arms were found on the farms of his party members. When he was seized at Bulawayo airport in 1983 the police could find no evidence to justify a charge of plotting against the government, but this did not prevent them from menacing his home and family. He fled on foot in disguise to Botswana, and later travelled on to Britain, where he remained for five months rallying opposition to the dictatorial Mugabe.

In *The Story of My Life* (1984), Nkomo wrote that the hardest lesson had come to him late. "It is that a nation can win freedom without the people becoming free." Members of his party began an armed rebellion, in which 10,000 people were tortured or killed, and eventually Nkomo and Mugabe struck a Faustian bargain. In 1988

Mugabe declared himself President (replacing Canaan Banana) and took his old rival into the government as "senior minister in the President's office". The price was that ZAPU should be totally integrated into his own ZANU to make Zimbabwe a one-party state, and that Nkomo, the former apostle of liberation, accede to the destruction of democracy.

Joshua Mqabuko Nyongolo Nkomo was born in Matebeleland on June 19 1917, the third of eight children of workers for the London Missionary Society. He grew up on his parents' farm, which supported 1,000 cattle in the Matopo district, and attended the mission school. Becoming an active Methodist, he worked as a carpenter and a lorry driver to earn money for his secondary education at the Tjolotjo Government School of Adams College in Natal. He then attended the Jan Hofmeyer School of Social Work in Johannesburg, where he met leaders who were to help shape his political aspirations.

On returning home in 1947, Nkomo became the first African to be employed by Rhodesia Railways in staff welfare. He took a correspondence course with the University of South Africa to obtain his bachelor's degree in social science. Everywhere he went he wore his cap and gown with flamboyant pride.

In 1951, Nkomo was appointed general secretary of the Rhodesian Railways African Employees' Association, one of the strongest black organisations in the country. In his lion-skin hat and carrying a carved ceremonial baton, he cut a paternal figure. Even to Southern Rhodesia's white leaders, he appeared a man of reason and moderation, someone with whom they might do business.

The next year he was invited to talks in London on the proposed federation of Northern and Southern Rhodesia with Nyasaland. He rejected the plan, which would have left all government power in the hands of the whites, and returned to Salisbury in high dudgeon. But his protest could not stop the creation of the Central African Federation the following year. By now Nkomo was President of the African National Congress (ANC) in Southern Rhodesia. But when he stood as a candidate for the first Federal Parliament he was swept aside by the white electorate. Disillusioned, he left his job with the railways and turned to insurance and auctioneering in Bulawayo.

As tensions between blacks and whites increased, the ANC began to gain authority. He launched a campaign against the Native Land Husbandry Act, which aimed to force blacks from the farms in order to create cheap labour in the cities. In February 1959, while he was abroad, the government declared a state of emergency, arrested ANC leaders and banned the organisation. For the next two years Nkomo remained in exile. Then, when the ANC in Southern Rhodesia was replaced by the National Democratic Party, which elected him President, he defied a warrant for his arrest and returned home to receive a hero's welcome.

At the Southern Rhodesian constitutional conference in London and Salisbury in 1961–2, Nkomo accepted a draft constitution that provided for two electoral rolls. One was for whites, which would elect 50 deputies, and another for blacks, which would elect 15. But when his party protested, he immediately altered his position and led the black campaign against the measure.

Undaunted by the banning of his National Democratic Party at the end of 1961, he announced the formation of ZAPU. He went to the United Nations, and won support for a demand that Britain and Southern Rhodesia should produce a fairer constitution. This diplomatic triumph, however, sparked more racial unrest. ZAPU was banned, and Nkomo arrested. For three months he was restricted to a three-mile radius of his home.

The first elections under the new constitution, in December 1962, resulted in a victory for the white Rhodesian Front, led by Winston Field, who pressed for independence. Black Rhodesians insisted that there could be no independence without majority rule. Nkomo was arrested and tried four times, but through appeals and bail avoided imprisonment. ZAPU, however, was beginning to fall apart, with its militant wing splitting off to form ZANU. Nkomo responded by creating the People's Caretaker Council and, when there were clashes between the rival groups, both movements were banned. In April 1964 Field was ousted by Ian Smith, whose first official act was to put Nkomo and three of his aides into a detention camp for a year. When, after six months, a court ruled that Nkomo's detention was illegal, Smith had him moved to Gonakudzingwa restriction camp, where he was held for 10 years.

On November 11 1965, Smith, despairing of reaching a constitutional accommodation with Britain, unilaterally declared Rhodesia independent, initiating years of strife, guerrilla warfare and economic sanctions. In camp Nkomo supervised a school, ran the newspaper and held meetings of ZAPU, which had reverted to its original name. It joined ZANU, now led by Mugabe, in guerrilla operations.

John Vorster, Prime Minister of South Africa, pressed Smith to make concessions, which included the release of Nkomo who, despite his long detention, adopted a moderate stance in failed negotiations on a timetable for black majority rule. Late in 1975 he opened secret talks with Smith, while other black groups wrangled over ways of continuing the guerrilla war. These negotiations collapsed after black rebels shot down an Air Rhodesia plane and massacred the civilian survivors.

Finally the combined pressure of ZANU and ZAPU forced Smith to seek a settlement, and Nkomo was one of the leaders present at the Lancaster House conference in London late in 1979. But Mugabe proved too strong for him, though he never entirely eliminated the threat that Nkomo posed to him. The two thus became locked in their unholy embrace, and in 1990 Nkomo was appointed second Vice-President. It was noted that, when the government began to confiscate farms, Nkomo's vast holding of 800,000 acres was not merely exempted but accorded tax-free status.

When one of his sons died from AIDS in 1996, Nkomo, 21 stone and increasingly fond of drink, accused the white population of having introduced the virus into Zimbabwe with the aim of wiping out the black population. Later that year he underwent an operation for prostate cancer in Cairo.

Joshua Nkomo married Johanna Fuyana in 1949; they had two sons and five daughters.

~

## Lady Gore Browne

LADY GORE BROWNE (who died in December 12 2001, aged 93) was the spirited chatelaine of Shiwa Ngandu, a manor house deep in the Northern Rhodesian bush.

The remarkable story of Shiwa Ngandu, which is vividly told in Christina Lamb's book *The Africa House* (1999), began in 1914, when Lorna Gore Browne's future husband, Stewart, stumbled upon his "personal paradise". A colonial boundary commissioner, he heard that land was being sold cheaply to white settlers and set off from Ndola by foot and canoe to retrace Livingstone's last footsteps and search for a place to settle. He found it at Shiwa Ngandu ("Lake of the Crocodiles"), a cobalt lake five miles long and surrounded by hills teeming with game. It was 350 miles from the nearest railway station.

He had dreamed of building his own house as a boy at Harrow where, aged 16, he had sketched in his diary "House to be built at some future date for S. Gore Browne Esq". With his private income of £500 a year, Gore Browne had long reckoned he could make little impact in England yet "live like an emperor" in Africa.

Six years, during which he won a DSO in the First World War, elapsed before he returned to Shiwa. In 1920, after buying 23,000 acres, he made his way back with two Army colleagues, intending to farm with them in partnership. It took them and their bearers three weeks to get there, marching across crocodile-infested swamps and canoeing along rivers. In due course, they began work on the house, employing Bemba tribesmen who lived around the lake and using clay from anthills to bake hundreds of red bricks each day. Gore Browne acted as architect, relying for engineering tips on an Army building manual.

By 1926, he was able to report to his aunt: "The walls are good and solid, and with plenty of antiques and paintings around it, as well as some Persian rugs, it all looks opulent and ancient and established, not at all parvenu." His farming partners had long since left, and his family was now pressing him to find a wife.

As a young man, Gore Browne had been in love with Lorna Bosworth Smith, a Dorset girl whose smiling face and serious eyes recalled for him "a Madonna in an Italian painting". Their three-year courtship ended when she married, in 1906, Edwin Goldmann, a Polish Jewish surgeon. Thereafter, Gore Browne's chief emotional outlet was his beloved aunt, Ethel Locke King, 20 years his senior and married to the man who built Brooklands race track. Addressing her as "My Darling", he wrote letters to her almost daily, beseeching her to come and share his life in Africa.

In 1927, on a return visit to England, Gore Browne attended the funeral of Lorna Bosworth Smith's grandmother in Dorset. In the church he had to keep himself from staring at a strangely familiar girl in a nearby pew. After the burial, seeing a woman he vaguely recognised, he ventured to ask the girl's identity. It was Lorna Goldmann, the orphaned daughter of Lorna Bosworth Smith.

Lorna Grace Goldmann had been born on March 2 1908 at Freiburg, Baden, and had later moved with her parents to South Africa. Her father died when she was five, her mother when she was 11. She and her brother Bos were adopted by their uncle, Major Charles

Goldmann, who took them to live in London. According to Gore Browne's informant in the churchyard, Lorna's uncle and aunt treated her "like a housemaid"; Lorna particularly resented being accused of stealing her cousin's stamp collection. She was furthermore "a bit of a trouble maker", who had been expelled from various boarding schools and was now at Sherborne.

Though far from spontaneous by nature, Gore Browne felt impelled to act. Introducing himself to Lorna as a friend of her mother, he asked if he might call on her in London, adding that he was only in town for a short time as his real home was in Africa. With his leathery, suntanned skin and monocle in his right eye, he looked to Lorna, she later told friends, like a character out of the adventure books her mother used to read to her in Johannesburg. He then pulled out a photograph of Shiwa Ngandu and said: "Maybe I could show it to you one day."

Whatever misgivings Lorna may have had about this rather stiff man 25 years her senior, they were eventually overcome by her longing to return to Africa. Her happiest memories were of the times she had spent in the Kalahari Desert, where her mother sought a cure for her consumption. One evening, Gore Browne turned up at Sherborne and asked the headmistress if he could take his "fiancée" out to dinner. "We don't have fiancées at Sherborne," said the headmistress. "You do now," he replied.

Three months later, in July 1927, they were married, and, after honeymooning in Venice and Egypt, they arrived in October at Shiwa. Hundreds of staff had lined up in their white cotton shirts, scarlet Bermuda shorts, waistcoats and cummerbunds, to greet them.

Their first night together at Shiwa was not altogether auspicious, Gore Browne leaving his young bride at bedtime to shoot a leopard, and on his return at four in the morning, sitting down in the library to write a letter to Aunt Ethel. "I'm feeling pretty bucked tonight," it began. "Once again, I only wish you had been here." Lorna, meanwhile, spent a restless night thinking about Livingstone's dog Chitane, who, so her husband had told her over dinner, had been eaten by Shiwa's crocodiles in 1867.

If they were still a little awkward in one another's company, there were signs of growing affection, she calling him "My Man", he describing her as "One in Ten Thousand". She did not really like her husband's "Lord-of-the-Manor stuff", the sounding of a gong for dinner, the dressing in black tie, and the hoisting of the Union Flag each morning, but she enjoyed their moonlit canoe trips on the lake, and romantic nights beside the hot springs.

She took a vigorous part in the running of the estate, and soon spoke Bemba more fluently than her husband. She threw herself into the farming (growing eucalyptus and bigarade oranges to produce essential oils), oversaw the kitchen and vegetable garden, and helped to supervise building work on the house. With the addition of a wine cellar, cloistered courtyard, additional guest rooms, tower and swimming pool, plus the employment of some 300 staff, Shiwa was costing £4,000 a year to run, and was heavily reliant on a constant flow of cheques from Aunt Ethel at Brooklands.

The Gore Brownes' first child, Lorna Katharine, was born in 1929, and the next year Gore Browne wrote to his aunt: "I don't know why Lorna married me, but I thank the Lord daily and hourly that she did." Yet by 1932, the year that Lorna gave birth to a stillborn son, Gore Browne was beginning to suspect that his wife was no longer happy at Shiwa.

On returning from England after the birth of their second daughter, Angela, in 1931, she had stayed in bed for days on end. When he showed her the initials he had had carved over the front door "L 1932 S", she had reacted by asking: "Does that mean we have to live here forever?" Gore Browne was also exercised by a young anthropologist from Cambridge, Audrey Richards, who had come to Shiwa to study the Bemba in 1931 and who, he thought, "gives Lorna all sorts of ideas".

In 1934, Lorna Gore Browne was easily persuaded to follow her new friend back to Cambridge, leaving the children in the care of a governess. She intended to rid herself of her post-natal depression, to sample some independence and to study agriculture, music, German and medicine. Her husband later complained that she seemed to be doing "nothing but wining and dining". When she did return to Shiwa after 18 months away, she immediately felt "as if I was entering a prison".

Over the next few years Lorna Gore Browne witnessed the opening of a school and a hospital at Shiwa, both her initiatives. Her husband, meanwhile, was often absent on political business, having been elected a member of the Legislative Council in 1935. When they were together, Lorna Gore Browne tended to be wilful and unpredictable. One moment she was in sparkling form, charming their guests, the next she would make inappropriate jokes in front of the Governor. One (male) friend from those days said: "She was beautiful, eccentric and trouble. There was a wicked streak in her. I wouldn't have been at all surprised if she had asked me to run off with her."

In the early years of the Second World War, with her husband again away much of the time, Lorna Gore Browne was left to run Shiwa. But in 1942 she took off on a solo canoeing trip to Lake Bangweulu, 100 miles away, where she resided for months in a simple house she had built on an island; she wrote of setting up home there with just her violin and radio for company. On returning to Shiwa, she left immediately for Johannesburg (where her daughters were at boarding school) and enrolled on a university biology course.

When she returned to Northern Rhodesia in 1945, she went not to Shiwa but to Lusaka, where she took a job as a technician in the government pathology laboratory. The city was full of bachelors, and Gore Browne would occasionally glimpse Lorna on the arm of a handsome young officer. Aged 63, the arthritic (and recently knighted) Gore Browne felt powerless to win her back. When they did meet, she pointed out that Shiwa had always been his dream, not hers, and that he had "married the wrong Lorna".

In due course, Lorna Gore Browne made her way back to London, where she rented a flat in Notting Hill. In 1948, she wrote a sympathetic letter to her husband after he had come in for criticism over his plans for home rule in Northern Rhodesia by minority white settlers. "I so much fear that you'll go because you are hurt, and please, please stay Dear because you are much too valuable to them even if they are Beastly sometimes."

After the Gore Brownes divorced two years later, Sir Stewart stayed on at Shiwa, acting as mentor to Roy Welensky, who was to become Prime Minister of the new Central African Federation, and to Kenneth Kaunda, the first President of Zambia when Northern Rhodesia became independent in 1964.

When he died in 1967, aged 84, he was given a state funeral and a chief's burial (the only white man in Central Africa to have been accorded that honour). The *Times of Zambia* described how he had lived in "semi-feudal splendour" with servants who "wouldn't have disgraced London's Dorchester Hotel". Yet he was a man "who judged his fellow men on their merits alone and not on the colour of their skin".

Lady Gore Browne, or "Mrs Browne" as she preferred to be called, lived for the remainder of her life in a flat in north London, and continued to travel with great gusto. She learned Serbo-Croat and Greek, played and composed on elaborate musical instruments, and did apple-picking to help make ends meet. To visitors, her flat recalled a student's digs, with posters on the wall and cushions on the floor.

Intelligent and articulate, she would listen and then add a succinct comment on any subject. Although as a mother she had been a shadowy and often absent figure, she had a direct way with other people's children, never patronising them, and was a wise adviser to many a troubled teenager. Men continued to be attracted to her. Some loved her and she them, but a lasting relationship eluded her. Occasionally, after several vodkas, she could be persuaded to talk about her time in Africa, but mostly she preferred to look to the future.

Lady Gore Browne was survived by her second daughter, Angela. Her elder, Lorna, who had taken over Shiwa, was murdered in 1992, along with her husband, John Harvey, during a robbery. Lady Gore Browne's eldest grandson now lives at Shiwa, where he has set about completely renovating the house.

—

## Sir Garfield Todd

SIR GARFIELD TODD (who died on October 13 2002, aged 94) was the missionary and former Prime Minister of Southern Rhodesia, whose commitment to African advancement exasperated his political successors.

He was locked up twice by Ian Smith's government for supporting black majority rule. Yet later, after being created a senator by President Robert Mugabe in 1980, Todd became increasingly appalled by the suffering, torture and humiliation being inflicted on Zimbabweans. During the general election of 2002, he was stripped of his Zimbabwean citizenship.

A curt note informed him of the decision only days after three schools, near his home at Bulawayo, had been named after him and his wife Grace. In an interview with *The Sunday Telegraph* Todd said that he was grateful that his wife, who had died two months earlier, had not lived to witness this insult, since she had high hopes of Mugabe when he was a young teacher. "What is that expression about power corrupting, and absolute power corrupting absolutely?" he asked. On arriving at his polling station to vote he was turned away by an election officer whom he had once taught.

It is doubtful whether the policies aimed at achieving a genuine multi-racial society, which Todd introduced as Prime Minister of Southern Rhodesia from 1953 to 1958, could have succeeded for long; the pan-African desire for independence had been fanned by Harold Macmillan's "Wind of Change" speech. But Todd's fall from power certainly ended any chance that the blacks would perceive the white-led Central African Federation as the appropriate channel for their aspirations.

*Todd being greeted by his daughters, Judith (left) 24, and Cynthia, 19, on arriving from New York at Heathrow Airport in 1967.*

His rise to the colony's premiership was proof of his remarkable abilities and charismatic personality, since the white electors had a strong antipathy towards missionaries such as himself. Even after they had rejected the pace of African progress which Todd demanded, a policy dictated by his own autocratic character as much as by his principles, some believed the white majority found it impossible to ignore him.

Long before Ian Smith declared independence, Todd found himself increasingly harassed: he was subjected to house arrest, imprisoned and charged with treason for aiding terrorists. Each threat only strengthened his resolve and drew the world's press to his comfortable farm in the bush.

Reginald Stephen Garfield Todd was born at Invercargill, New Zealand, on July 13 1908, the grandson of a Scottish brickmaker who had been employed on the Marquess of Bute's estate before emigrating. Young Garfield began work in his father's brickworks, swinging a pick for 22s 6d a week, before going to Otago University and Glen Leith Theological College. After two years as a Church of Christ minister at Oamaru, where he married Jean Wilson, with whom he was to have three daughters, he set out for Southern Rhodesia in 1934.

As superintendent of the mission at Dadaya, 300 miles south of Salisbury, Todd put his practical skills as a bricklayer, stonemason and carpenter to good use in expanding the local school. He also found himself regularly acting as a doctor, binding up wounds and assisting at births. Such tasks became so frequent that he felt obliged to take a year off to go on a medical course at Witwatersrand University in South Africa.

But, if Todd joined in every aspect of the Africans' lives for the 14 years his family had no white neighbours, he also had a strong Christian belief in the duty to chastise wrongdoers. This led to trouble when he personally caned on the buttocks a group of rebellious girl students, much to the consternation of their parents who regarded them as of marriageable age. A brief strike in protest was led by one of the teachers, Ndabaningi Sithole, the future founder of the Zimbabwe African National Union.

Unlike other missionaries, who rejoiced in embracing as closely as practicable the Africans' poverty, Todd not only shared the settlers' belief in their value to the country but was willing to take up land for a private farm. For a time he owned 90,000 acres, though later he gave many of them Africans.

His first foray into politics came at a meeting in October 1942, when he heckled the Prime Minister, Sir Godfrey Huggins, so forcibly that four years later Huggins wrote inviting him to make amends by standing as a candidate for the governing United Party.

Not long after his election, Todd proposed giving an address on "The Native as a Human Being", but withdrew gracefully after Huggins made it known that the subject might prove embarrassing. Over the following years Huggins talked freely to Todd about his colleagues, making it clear that he had no intention of offering him a post. But when Huggins resigned in 1953 to become Prime Minister of the new Central African Federation (made up of Nyasaland, Northern and Southern Rhodesia), Todd was chosen to be his successor as leader of Southern Rhodesia.

On forming a United Rhodesia Party government and decisively winning a general election, Todd settled into office without any sign of self-doubt. He showed little reluctance to call in territorial troops to suppress a strike by black miners and white railwaymen, which he said followed a "Communistic pattern". A trouble-making union leader was sent back to Britain. Todd also threatened to suppress the local African National Congress. But, while recognising the colony's need for skilled white labour, he soon began to express disappointment that Commonwealth countries failed to provide £5 million for African housing projects.

He attacked Huggins for faltering over the location of the Kariba dam in Southern Rhodesia, and made a speech calling for his retirement, which made Huggins stay on an extra year. "Why did you do that?" Todd was asked by Roy Welensky, Huggins's acknowledged successor. "You knew he was going." "God told me to make that speech," Todd replied.

Unlike white South Africa to the south and the newly emerging black autocracies to the north, the Central African Federation was committed to partnership between the races, intended to lead at some unspecified date to equality. Todd encountered no difficulties when he introduced the appellation "Mr" for Africans instead of "AM" (African Male), or when he permitted blacks to drink European beer and wine, though not spirits. But, as the white electorate became aware of the high hopes he was creating in the black population, trouble surfaced in cabinet over a Private Member's Bill to make sexual relations between white men and black women legal. It took a more serious turn when Todd managed to push through a measure increasing the number of African voters by threatening to resign if it failed. There was more dissent during talks about amalgamating his party with the Federal United Party; it emerged that he had been talking privately to the African leaders Ndabaningi Sithole and Joshua Nkomo, as well as to the white liberal Guy Clutton-Brock.

Eventually Todd demanded the resignation of his four cabinet ministers and governed alone for a week, a unique achievement in the parliamentary history of the Empire. He then appointed new, more liberal colleagues. Instead of meeting the Assembly, he chose to face a party congress. Here Todd was at his best. A tall, commanding figure with a noticeable New Zealand twang emphasising his difference from those present, he drew applause for his eloquent and witty speech. But he decisively lost a vote of confidence, and resigned his office.

It became an article of faith for white Rhodesians that Todd's successor, Sir Edgar Whitehead, advocated equally liberal policies. But the fall of Todd, already considered "the Moses of our times" by some Africans, was marked by a popular African record which had the refrain: "Todd has left us / Go well old man."

Freed from the necessity of carrying the support of white electors, Todd made some show of supporting Welensky's efforts to hold the federation together. But within two years he was describing it as a police state. His attempt to form a genuine multi-racial Central African Party failed. Todd's strident warnings put off white recruits, while black members soon decided to switch to their territorial African National Congresses.

By 1962, he was appealing at the United Nations in New York for Britain to retain its powers in Southern Rhodesia, even if it granted independence to Northern Rhodesia and Nyasaland, the future Zambia and Malawi. The narrow-minded Ian Smith found such behaviour quit unacceptable after the colony made its unilateral declaration of independence in 1965 under the name of Rhodesia, and had Todd served with an order restricting him to his farm. He was about to fly to Britain to address a teach-in at Edinburgh University with Sir Alec Douglas-Home.

Ian Smith, the Prime Minister, feared that if Todd was abroad when UDI was declared, Harold Wilson might try to set him up as an exiled leader. But the order attracted far more attention and sympathy for Todd than he would have received if he had been able to go. Fourteen television crews appeared on his lawn to record his comments and admire the persecuted man's Mercedes and gardens, beautifully tended by African servants.

His 22-year-old daughter Judy flew to Edinburgh to capitalise on the righteous indignation being expressed in Britain, though Douglas-Home pointed out that Todd's views had been far less radical when he was Prime Minister only eight years earlier. On her return home, in a black leather coat and Dior dress, she told reporters at Salisbury airport that white Commonwealth troops should be sent in to end UDI. By now Todd was a hated figure among the whites in Rhodesia, despite the contempt he shared with his former colleagues for the pusillanimity of all British governments. He had 30 pieces of silver hurled at him at Salisbury airport; a baboon was loosed in the centre of Bulawayo with "Garfield Todd" written on its back.

In 1971, Todd warned Lord Pearce's committee that any new settlement arrived at with London should not be rammed down

African throats. Smith then locked him up for two months, and placed him under house arrest for another four years. Every afternoon Todd sat on his verandah counting the number of railway tankers carrying sanctions-busting petrol to Salisbury, then passed the information on to MI6 contacts. He finally emerged to join Joshua Nkomo's team visiting London in search of a settlement, and found Smith's hatred as strong as ever. Just as the transition to direct British rule was finally being effected, Todd was arrested for supplying food and a motor car to terrorists near his farm. The charges were dropped only at the insistence of the Governor, Lord Soames.

After an independent Zimbabwe was achieved, Todd told *The Guardian* that a one-party state might indeed be best for the country. But, as the standard of living for the ordinary African declined, he was so appalled by the spread of corruption that he declared that Mugabe should go. He was not reappointed to the Senate.

In his later years Todd surprised many by his ability to greet former enemies as though there had been no rift between them. Britain might not have appreciated his efforts, but his fellow New Zealanders showed they had not forgotten him when he was recommended for a knighthood in the dominion's 1986 honours list.

If at times his actions seemed inspired as much by his own personality as his principles, he was steadfast in his Christian belief in the goodness within every man; and he retained, in private at least, an awareness of what a sacrifice had been demanded in expecting the whites to give up all they had built up in Africa. "Living as we do," he told the historian Lord Blake, "all of us are guilty", that phrase which summed up the comfortable funk of postwar consensus.

# SOUTHERN AFRICA

~

## Lady Khama

LADY KHAMA (who died on May 22 2002, aged 78) was the London secretary whose marriage to Seretse Khama, heir to the chieftainship of the Bamangwato tribe in the British protectorate of Bechuanaland, caused a political storm in 1948.

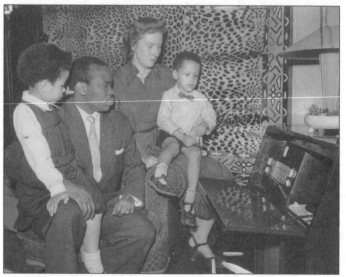

*Ruth Khama and her family in Croydon listening to a news bulletin announcing that her husband had renounced the chieftainship of the Bamangwato tribe in Bechuanaland.* (PA)

As a result, Britain's Labour Government refused to recognise Seretse Khama, a former undergraduate at Balliol College, Oxford, and sent him into exile. The Colonial Secretary, Patrick Gordon Walker, assured the Commons that there was no outside pressure but, in reality, the government was keen to avoid upsetting the new National Government in South Africa, to the south of Botswana. Bent on introducing apartheid, South Africa's leaders were horrified by the prospect of a mixed marriage. What was more, they had the power to withhold supplies of uranium that were vital for Britain's nuclear industry.

Dr Daniel Malan, the new South African Prime Minister, pronounced the marriage "nauseating". Even the Reverend Trevor Huddleston, later Archbishop of the Indian Ocean and a sainted opponent of apartheid, advised Sir Evelyn Baring, the High Commissioner to South Africa as well as Bechuanaland, against recognising Khama as chief, though he later regretted it. The exasperated Prime Minister, Clement Attlee, complained privately: "We are invited to go contrary to the desires of the great majority of the Bamangwato tribe, solely because of the attitude of the Union of South Africa and Southern Rhodesia. It's as if we had been obliged to agree to Edward VIII's abdication so as not to annoy the Irish Free State and the USA."

Lady Khama was born Ruth Williams at Blackheath, south-east London, on December 9 1923, the daughter of a former captain in the Indian Army who worked in the tea trade. She was in the family home when it was bombed during the Blitz, and left Eltham High School to join the Women's Auxiliary Air Force. She drove ambulances at the airfields of No. 11 Fighter Group and served at the emergency landing station near Beachy Head.

After the return of peace, Ruth Williams became a confidential clerk in the claims department at Cuthbert Heath, the Lloyds underwriters. She rode, ice-skated and went ballroom dancing in her spare time, meeting her future husband, a law student living in a hostel near Marble Arch, through their mutual interest in jazz. Although their initial meeting, when they were introduced by her sister, was not a success, the friendship matured through their enthusiasm for the Inkspots, the singing group.

The sight of a black man with a white woman was then a rarity in London, and there were some unpleasant incidents in which she was branded a cheap slut by strangers. After Seretse proposed and she accepted, the couple assumed they would return to Bechuanaland. But problems quickly developed. Her father said she could stay in the family home, then ordered her out; her boss offered a transfer to New York or the sack; she left at the end of the week.

When Seretse wrote to his uncle Tshekedi, the Regent in Bechuanaland, the London Mission Society was pressed to try to prevent the wedding. Baring sent warning telegrams from Cape Town to the Commonwealth Office. Three members of the Mission Society turned up at St George's, Campden Hill, and threatened to object during the ceremony. When Seretse and Ruth complained, the vacillating vicar referred them to the Bishop of London, Dr William Wand, who was conducting an ordination ceremony nearby at St Mary Abbot's in Kensington. The young couple sat through this ceremony, to be told by him that a marriage could not take place until the British government agreed. In the end they were married, after some difficulty, in a register office.

The couple headed for Bechuanaland, where Seretse told a tribal rally: "Stand up those who will not accept my wife"; he counted them and shouted, "40". He then asked: "Stand up those who want me and my wife"; 6,000 stood up and applauded for 10 minutes. But as the couple awaited the birth of their first child, Gordon Walker told Khama that he was being exiled from Bechuanaland for five years, which Winston Churchill, Leader of the Opposition, described as "a very disreputable transaction". But when the Tories returned to power, "not less than five years" of exile was changed to "indefinitely".

The Khamas returned to Britain in 1950, where Seretse continued his legal studies and Ruth kept house at Addiscombe, Croydon. Although she didn't really believe it, she used to tell him she had a telepathic feeling they would be allowed to return. Anthony Wedgwood Benn steered a motion through a Labour Party conference calling for their return. Not to be outdone, the Conservative government offered Khama a diplomatic post in Jamaica. In reply he asked why, if he was not considered good enough to rule his own people, he should be allowed to play an administrative role in the West Indies.

One happy result of the exile was that Seretse and Ruth's father became reconciled. Then, in 1956, Seretse heard that he was being allowed back after his people had cabled Her Majesty the Queen: "The Bamangwato are sad. Over our land there is a great shadow blotting out the sun. Please put an end to our troubles. Send us our real Chief the man born our Chief Seretse."

Before the government could change its mind, Seretse hurried to London Airport, leaving Ruth to sell their house and car and to follow three weeks later. They settled down in Serowe, where Seretse consolidated his cattle farm and formed the Botswana Democratic Party; although he disclaimed a desire for the chieftainship, he gradually took over from the Regent. As such he was knighted, became first Prime Minister of Bechuanaland, and then President of the Republic of Botswana, which remained in the Commonwealth.

Lady Khama never spoke any local languages, and remained a keen reader of *Reader's Digest* and *National Geographic*. But she was kept busy bringing up their four children and playing a leading role in charity work. One of her particular delights lay in attending Commonwealth conferences.

After her husband's death in 1980, there was some speculation that she might settle in London, but she had no intention of leaving. She had played a key role in the Queen's visit the year before and was President of the Red Cross of Botswana and the Botswana Council of Women, while running the Lady Khama Christmas Charity Fund. Lady Khama was known as Mohumagadi Mma Kgosi ("Mother of the Chief") since her eldest son is chief, but also, colloquially, as "the Queen Mother".

Ironically, there was a ripple of surprise in 1990 when her son Tony, named in honour of Tony Benn, announced that he wanted to marry a South African white girl from the rural Afrikaner stronghold of Rustenburg across the border. Lady Khama warned that there might be some trouble with conservative tribal elders, though once again fear of South African hostility played a part in it.

Lady Khama was survived by her daughter and three sons, of whom the eldest, Lieutenant-General Ian Khama, became President of Botswana.

# SOUTH AFRICA

—

## Robert Snowden

ROBERT SNOWDEN (who died on May 11 1998, aged 82) became a colonial officer in Uganda after the Second World War and, 41 years later, was elected a local councillor in Durban, by a substantial number of Zulu voters. With a reputation for drawing on his own experience rather than adhering to party policy, he topped the voting for the Inkatha Freedom Party at Greater Durban (Outer West) in the 1997 council elections.

Robert Eccles Snowden was born in Hobart, Tasmania, on May 18 1915, the only son of Colonel Sir Eccles Snowden, a Mayor of Hobart and Tasmanian Agent-General in London, who died while making a speech at Guildhall. Young Bobby was educated at Harrow and, after an agriculture course at Reading University, went to Paarl, South Africa, to make a career in fruit farming.

In 1939, Snowden was commissioned into the 4th South African Armoured Car Regiment and posted as a tank instructor to Nairobi, where he was billeted in the Muthaiga Club, which was humming with the trial of Sir Evelyn Delves Broughton for the murder of the Earl of Errol. Snowden visited the court, and formed a dim view of the Happy Valley set.

On joining his regiment in North Africa just before the Battle of El Alamein, Snowden was advised by the diamond magnate and his fellow officer, Harry Oppenheimer, to buy some gold shares. As a result Snowden spent the battle worrying whether a cable to his broker had arrived. Twelve days later he found he had made enough to pay his children's school fees. Later, when the regiment was placed in reserve because of losses, Snowden took a drop in rank to join the 17th/21st Lancers in fighting at Monte Cassino and up the Po Valley.

On demobilisation in 1946, he joined the Colonial Service as a district officer in the West Nile province of Uganda. He then transferred to the Basutoland Protectorate, where he served until the country became independent as the Kingdom of Lesotho in 1966. Under an agreement with Queen Victoria, the Basuto were given protection from the Boers, with no white settlement allowed and native law and custom respected. Inevitably there were tensions. On one occasion Snowden attended a meeting where the South Africans refused to speak English. As he refused to speak Afrikaans, they compromised by using Sesuto, the Basutoland language.

Snowden found that administration was best managed by persuasion rather than instruction. He greatly enjoyed the business of the "district trek", which involved travelling on horseback accom-

*Snowden ran a small farmer credit scheme in Sierra Leone that was so successful it was investigated for fraud.*

panied by a couple of Basuto mounted police, armed only with ceremonial lances. On arrival in mountain villages there would be lengthy parleys with village elders.

After a spell back in England, where he became Secretary of the Dorneywood Trust, Snowden joined a small farmer credit scheme in Sierra Leone. This was funded by the World Bank, and Snowden was placed in charge of finance. Loans, in the form of seed and tools, were granted for a five-year period, together with technical and marketing assistance. When Snowden reported to Washington that 90 per cent of the loans had been repaid in three years, the response was to send out a team of auditors to find out how he was cooking the books.

In 1976, Snowden became a contract officer with the Ministry of Overseas Development and was posted to the Solomon Islands, where he organised the independence ceremony before becoming private secretary to the first Prime Minister and later to the first Governor-General. His last task before retirement was to arrange Her Majesty the Queen's visit to the islands. When it was found that there was no court sword on the royal yacht *Britannia*, she had to use Snowden's to knight the Governor-General.

Appointed OBE in 1965, Snowden finally retired to South Africa where he became an election agent for the Progressive Reform Party, then joined the Inkatha Freedom Party when multi-racial parties were legalised. While an admirer of Nelson Mandela, he feared that the ANC would promote an over-centralised form of government.

In 1943 Robert Snowden married Marygold Newman, who died in 1974. He was survived by two sons and a daughter. His eldest son predeceased him.

## Walter Sisulu

WALTER SISULU (who died on May 5 2003, aged 90) played a key part in undermining apartheid, as Secretary-General of the African National Congress and as mentor to Nelson Mandela.

*Sisulu* (centre) *appearing with the Libyan leader Colonel Gaddafi.*

Sisulu's special contribution was his persistence in converting the ANC from a narrow political agenda designed to serve the African population alone to one which envisaged full democratic rights for all races in South Africa. This was a lesson of which Mandela, who in his thirties was still capable of driving an Indian off an ANC platform, stood in particular need. The two men had first met in 1941 when Mandela, recently thrown out of his job at Crown Mines in Johannesburg, turned up in desperation at Sisulu's office.

Sisulu, who was working as an estate agent, immediately recognised Mandela's potential – "I saw a bright young man with high ideals" – and recommended him to a lawyer called Lazar Sidelsky. A job in Sidelsky's office and loans from Sisulu enabled Mandela to complete his degree at Witwatersrand University by correspondence course. A fast friendship developed; and it was at Sisulu's house in Orlando that Mandela met his first wife.

Nevertheless, Mandela was still a political novice when, in 1944, Sisulu and others founded the Youth League, which aimed to "light a fire under the leadership" and to convert the ANC to more aggressive policies. Mandela was co-opted on to the executive committee. "While I was not prepared to hurl the white man into the sea," Mandela has written of his political attitudes at this time, "I would have been perfectly happy if he had climbed aboard his steamships and left the continent of his own volition."

Sisulu, by contrast, understood early the necessity of making common cause with all potential allies. A small, stocky and bespectacled man with a calm and measured demeanour, he possessed the doggedness to stick to this point of view through fierce arguments with Mandela, without ever losing faith in the younger man's star.

In 1948, the National Party won power in South Africa and began to erect the statutory apparatus of apartheid. Anxious for a more vigorous opposition, in 1949 the Youth League achieved a coup at the ANC conference, and installed Sisulu as Secretary-General, and he lost no time in co-opting Mandela on to the executive. "Essentially he [Mandela] is a moderate in his approach," Sisulu wrote of his young disciple at this at this period. "But then there is this contradiction of his stubbornness. When it comes to the final point, he can become very stubborn, very arrogant. His anger becomes extreme. It is not in argument that he becomes angry. It is when he suspects people's motives, as he did with the Communists."

Sisulu always denied being a Communist, and professed himself revolted by the cult of Stalin. In the early 1940s he had insisted that Communists should resign from the party if they were to join the

ANC. On the other hand, he advocated widespread public ownership, and was given to careful intellectual formulations of socialist dogma.

In 1952, he produced a plan to combat the National government with a campaign of defiance against its apartheid legislation. His idea was that protesters should deliberately court arrest by breaking the racist laws, so that the jails would overflow and the system break down. In five months some 8,000 people went to prison, and membership of the ANC soared from 7,000 to 100,000. But after Sisulu and other leaders were arrested in July 1952, the campaign fell to pieces for want of proper direction.

Though Sisulu received only a suspended sentence, in 1953 he was removed from his post at the ANC under the Suppression of Communism Act. Later that year he went to Prague, Bucharest, Warsaw, Moscow and Peking in search of support and weapons, though his Communist hosts counselled against armed revolt. On returning home he was derided as "Mao Tse-tung" by the Africanists anxious to preserve the purity of their own cause. Mandela, however, followed Sisulu in drawing closer to the Communists as well as any other group prepared to resist the National government. His first reaction to any political dilemma was invariably to ask: "What does Walter think?"

In 1955, Sisulu toured the Transkei and the Ciskei to drum up support for a Congress of the People, drawn from a wide variety of organisations. Though banned from public meetings, he managed to attend the Congress, which issued a charter affirming the right of all citizens to equality and calling for a wide degree of public ownership.

As the revolt against the National government spread the ANC's senior leaders, including Sisulu and Mandela, were charged with high treason. The ensuing court action, which became known internationally as the Treason Trial, lasted for more than four years and ended with the acquittal of all concerned.

As late as 1957, Sisulu had been convinced that the National Party was on the brink of collapse. "The Europeans of the country", he wrote, "are gradually beginning to see that South Africa has no choice but to follow the road to a multi-racial society." But the Sharpeville Massacre of 1960, in which police fired into a crowd of demonstrators, killing 67 and wounding 146, annihilated such optimism. Thenceforward the leadership of the ANC (which was banned shortly after Sharpeville) became firmly convinced that change in South Africa could no longer be achieved by peaceful means. It resolved to set up a secret military wing, Umkhonto We Sizwe ("Spear of the Nation"), and Sisulu became its political adviser.

Under constant supervision by the security police, he was arrested six times in 1962. "Just routine," the police officer explained, when asked why Sisulu's house was being raided. For a while Sisulu went underground, but in July 1963 he was arrested at a meeting of conspirators at Lilliesleaf Farm, Rivonia, near Johannesburg, where incriminating documents were found. Subsequently Mandela and Sisulu were the leading figures among 156 accused of conspiring to conduct warfare and sabotage against the government of South Africa. It was a charge that carried the death penalty, and many were surprised when Mandela and Sisulu were sentenced instead to life imprisonment.

Although Mandela had been the acknowledged leader of Umkhonto We Sizwe, it was observed that, when preparing his defence at the trial, he never made any decision without first seeking Sisulu's opinion. And, according to one lawyer acting for the defence, Sisulu was worthy of this trust: "At no time did I ever hear Walter make a hasty judgment, or venture an appraisal of anybody or anything without first weighing it carefully, deliberately, generally against his own immediate, instinctive reactions."

In court Sisulu proudly admitted that he had planned to overthrow the government: "We could not continue to preach non-violence", he declared, "when the situation was becoming desperate." His dignity under cross-examination was a triumph of willpower, for as a young man he had been intemperate in the violence of his views. Whereas Mandela's origins had been aristocratic, even regal, Sisulu came from a modest background which might have given him every excuse for stultifying bitterness.

Walter Max Ulyate Sisulu was born at Engcobo, Transkei, on May 18 1912, the year in which the ANC was founded. His mother was a Xhosa; his father was believed to be a white road-building foreman who had abandoned the family. The boy was therefore brought up by his mother's family, who were devout Anglicans and inclined to treat visiting white churchmen with exaggerated deference. Walter, sensitive about his mixed-race origins, went out of his way to be especially rude to them.

Educated at a mission school in Transkei, he left at 16, and for a while worked underground as a goldminer, a job he abhorred. He went on to a series of factory jobs, in which he continually clashed with his white employers. After attacking a ticket collector who was trying to confiscate a black child's ticket, he served a spell in prison. Meanwhile Sisulu had become fascinated by Xhosa history, on which he wrote articles for *Bantu World*. But it was only when he joined the ANC in 1940 that he found his true métier.

For all Sisulu's importance in the subsequent development of ANC policy, it was during his imprisonment on Robben Island from 1964 to 1982 that he showed his finest qualities. Conditions were harsh, especially at first, with the prisoners being required to work for hours smashing up stones into fine gravel with five-pound hammers, or labouring in a lime quarry. A light was kept on in the cells all night. Sisulu was allowed only one visitor every six months, and to receive and write only one letter every six months.

Yet he proved a constant source of strength to the other prisoners, always ready to forget his own problems to help combat the despair of others. He was particularly adept at keeping up Mandela's spirits, being the only man with whom Mandela was prepared to drop the mask of leadership. Yet even then, Sisulu confessed, he could be harsh.

The two men spent 18 years on Robben Island, before being moved in 1982 to Pollsmoor prison in Cape Town. In 1987, when the question arose of Mandela starting talks with the government, Sisulu urged that this should occur at the government's, not the ANC's, instigation. Mandela was no longer bound by Sisulu's opinion; nevertheless, their discussion prompted a heartfelt tribute in Mandela's autobiography: "I have been through thick and thin with Walter. He was a man of reason and wisdom, and no man knew me better than he did. There was no one whose opinion I trusted or valued more."

Sisulu was released in October 1989. Typically, he used the attendant publicity to call for economic sanctions to be intensified. Since Mandela remained in prison a few months longer, he briefly became the ANC's *de facto* leader.

As negotiations with F. W. de Klerk's government got under way, Sisulu was responsible for holding the ANC membership together. This was a delicate task, balancing the extreme demands of the angry township youth and the compromises imposed by political necessity.

Appointed vice-president of the ANC in 1991, Sisulu remained Mandela's most trusted and constant adviser. In 1992, on Sisulu's 80th birthday, Mandela paid another tribute. "You personify", he declared, "the dignity and respect we want for all South Africans." Sisulu retired from the ANC's vice-presidency in 1994, after the first general election held under universal franchise.

He married, in 1944, Albertina Nontsikelelo, herself a formidable anti-apartheid campaigner who was appointed President of the World Peace Council in 1993; they had a son and a daughter. "The only time we were together as a family," she told Margaret Thatcher in 1989, "was when he was under house arrest."

~

## Hamilton Naki

HAMILTON NAKI (who died on May 29 2005, aged 78) was a poorly-educated gardener who became one of South Africa's most skilled surgeons; he contributed to pioneering research at Cape Town's Groote Schuur hospital, where he helped Professor Christiaan Barnard to carry out the world's first successful heart transplant.

The tragedy of Naki's career was that his surgical brilliance was only appreciated within the confines of Cape Town's medical community. It could never be publicly acknowledged because of the apartheid doctrine denying black people any formal training for careers deemed suitable only for whites.

As a result, Naki was an unsung hero who retired to a tiny shack-like home in the teeming Cape Flats township, near Cape Town, on a £70 a month gardener's pension. It was well after South Africa's transition to democracy that his achievements were made more widely known, and that he was recognised with an honorary degree in medicine from Cape Town University, a Presidential Life Achievement award, and a television documentary about his life.

Barnard himself was instrumental in seeing that Naki finally gained the recognition he deserved. "Hamilton Naki had better technical skills than I did," he said. "He was a better craftsman than me, especially when it came to stitching, and had very good hands in the theatre."

Hamilton Naki was born to devoted but impoverished parents on June 13 1926 at the village of Ngcangane, in the Transkei region of the Eastern Cape. Barefoot, he helped to herd cattle before and after lessons at the village school. There was no money available for him to move on to secondary education so, at 14, he made his way to Cape Town to find work.

He was eventually successful in becoming an assistant gardener in the grounds of that city's distinguished university, tending lawns, tennis courts and flowerbeds. When Dr Robert Goetz asked the head groundsman if he could spare a strong young man to help with the laboratory animals at the university's medical faculty, Naki, who had proved himself a diligent and intelligent worker, embarked on his unofficial medical career. He started by cleaning cages and helping with the weighing, shaving and injection of the dogs, rabbits and pigs which Goetz used in demonstrations to medical students.

Naki's innate skills in handling animals and his steady, dexterous hands impressed the surgeons, and he was soon slicing, stitching and using drips on the animals. He once helped to operate on a giraffe, dissecting the jugular venous valves to discover why creatures with such elongated necks did not faint when they stooped to drink. On another occasion he insisted on rocking the pram of a medical student's baby daughter with one hand while he performed a liver transplant on a pig with the other.

Naki's skills became famous among Cape Town's young medical students, who were astonished at his grasp of anatomical terms and his instinctive, analytical mind. When questioned about his lack of formal education, Naki would smile and point to his head: "My eyes and ears are my university," he would say with a chuckle. Despite his slum-like living conditions in the often riot-torn Langa township, he always turned up for work punctually, and immaculately dressed in neatly-pressed trousers, shining shoes and a Homburg hat.

When Christiaan Barnard, then an ambitious young cardiac surgeon, returned from America intent on pioneering open heart surgery in Cape Town, he made a point of asking for Hamilton Naki as a member of his team. As Barnard performed his ground-breaking heart transplant on Louis Washkansky at Groote Schuur hospital in 1967, Naki was a key member of the team that worked around the clock on the heart of the donor, a young woman who had died in a motor accident. Barnard, with his toothsome smile and dashing air, became an international celebrity overnight; Naki, the black man who was by his side during the pioneering surgery, remained officially a gardener at the university, although he had been quietly appointed a laboratory assistant in the medical faculty.

Despite this, Naki harboured no resentment: "The government then would not allow me to go any further with my education, and would probably have been very angry that I had been given such responsibility as I had in the university. As far as the authorities were concerned I was employed as a gardener." It was years later that Barnard told Dirk de Villiers, a film producer, the remarkable story of his assistant. "I could see he was a very capable man," the surgeon said. "I gave him more and more to do, and eventually he could do a heart transplant sometimes better than the junior doctors who came here."

Even so, it was as a gardener that Hamilton Naki retired, drawing the meagre pension with which he maintained his family at the home in Langa, where he died from complications brought about by a heart problem. He received his honorary master's degree in medicine from Cape Town University in 2003. At the same time, President Thabo Mbeki presented him with the Order of Mapungubwe, one of South Africa's most prestigious awards. In retirement, Naki helped to establish a mobile clinic to treat children in his home area in the Eastern Cape, and used his new prestige to help young blacks to become medical students.

Hamilton Naki was survived by his wife Joyce and by their four children.

~

## Queen Modjadji VI

QUEEN MODJADJI VI (who died on June 12 2005, aged 27) was the youngest of South Africa's rain queens, one in a line of matriarchal monarchs stretching back at least 200 years and probably beyond in the mists and myths of African legends.

The rain queens, believed to have been bestowed with the powers to control the rains and rivers, were immortalised by the 19th-century adventure writer Rider Haggard in *She*, the novel about a beautiful, immortal queen ruling a hidden kingdom with supernatural powers. The story gave rise to the phrase still used today: "She who must be obeyed".

Queen Mokobo Modjadji was the first of that line to receive a formal education, although she admitted, in a rare interview, that she had never read Rider Haggard. She was enthroned in 2003 after the death of her grandmother Modjadji V, in an elaborate formal ceremony conducted in the royal village deep in the forested mountains and valleys of the north-eastern province, now named Limpopo.

The traditional drums beat far and wide for the ceremony, which was attended by royal families and dignitaries from all corners of southern Africa though, for the Balobedu people of the 140 villages that make up

*Queen Modjadji enjoyed discos and wearing jeans, but her Royal Council disapproved of her boyfriend because he was a commoner.* (AP)

the tiny kingdom, the celebrations were clouded not by rain but by controversy and scandal. The new queen, a modern miss who enjoyed visiting discos in nearby towns wearing tee-shirts and jeans, had a son by her long-standing boyfriend, a respectable young man with a good job in local government. But he was a commoner, of whom the Royal Council disapproved.

By strict custom, the rain queen must remain unmarried, living a mostly reclusive life in the royal village attended by a number of "wives", ladies-in-waiting who fulfil the household chores and functions on her behalf. Should she wish for male companionship, a suitor of royal blood must be chosen and thoroughly vetted and approved by the Royal Council. The tribe then prays for a girl-child as the hereditary succession is matriarchal.

The origins of the Modjadji royal line stretch back to the 16th-century Karanga kingdom of Monomatapa, in what is now south-eastern Zimbabwe. Centred on what are now the renowned Zimbabwe Ruins, the Monomatapa empire is known to have traded gold and ivory with India and China and to have reached an astonishing level of civil order and development in the heart of Africa.

Oral tradition holds that the son of a Monomatapa ruler had a relationship with his sister, Dzugundini, and produced an heir. His half-brothers plotted to kill the heir to prevent him succeeding to the throne. The old king, anxious to avoid a civil war, gave Dzugundini a magic horn for making rain and defending herself against enemies, advising her to take her child and followers southwards to establish their own kingdom.

The resulting tribe, known as the Balobedu, settled in the fertile Molotsi Valley in the north-eastern corner of what became South Africa, where the northernmost slopes of the Drakensberg mountains drop down towards the low veld. In the early 19th century, the tribe was ruled by Mugudo, a descendant of Dzugundini. Warned by his ancestors of family rivalries, he killed his sons and married his daughter, founding a dynasty of women. If the queen gave birth to a son, that child was strangled. Her first daughter, Modjadji, started the matrilineal tradition.

She remained in complete seclusion deep in the misty forests of an area that normally has an above-average rainfall; but in periods of drought, ambassadors and supplicants came from afar to consult and to beg her to use her powers to summon the rains. So respected were the rain queen's powers that warring tribes never troubled the Lobedu tribe, not even Shaka, the Zulu warrior king, but sent emissaries to seek her blessings.

Christian missionaries sought to debunk the myths and reduce the powers of the rain queen, but South Africa's ruling National Party promoted the role of traditional leaders, seeing their powers as a way of promoting apartheid. The rain queen was visited by several Afrikaner leaders, and was given a government salary. Her son was made a member of the Lebowa homeland parliament, specifically to represent her interests.

Queen Modjadji V, Mokobo's grandmother, was deeply suspicious of the African National Congress as it moved towards power. She viewed it as a force that would mobilise the youth against traditional leaders and undermine their authority. She even rebuffed the persuasive powers of Nelson Mandela (who, being of Xhosa royal blood himself, was sympathetic to her views). She turned her back on him when he visited the royal village, to seek her endorsement for the 1994 elections which saw him become South Africa's first black president.

When the ANC-controlled provincial government came to power, it was sympathetic and supportive of the Modjadji royal household, not least because it was keen to promote tourism to the scenically spectacular region, based around the myths and legends of the Rain Queen. The Balobedu area is rich in cycads, an ancient cross between tree and fern. To preserve the giant of the species, *encephalartos transvenosus*, the Modjadji Nature Reserve was established with her blessing.

Mokobo Constance Modjadji was born in the royal village in 1978, the daughter of Princess Makheala, who was the heir to the throne until she died two days before the old Queen in 2001. Mokobo, who had achieved matriculation level at the local high school and enjoyed the life of a modern teenager, found herself the new reluctant heir to the Rain Queen's throne, even though she secretly shared the scorn and scepticism of her contemporaries about the supernatural powers that supposedly came with the throne.

On ascending the throne, Queen Modjadji had to obey the demands of the Royal Council to continue the line, and she attempted to do her best, attending the many meetings of local tribal council, and traditional leaders and contributing what she could to promote their interests and those of the Balobedu people. Her duties precluded her from taking up Nelson Mandela's offer to fund her further education; and she was soon dogged with ill health.

Queen Modjadji VI died in the Polokwane Medi-Clinic. Medical staff declined to discuss her illness, but local rumours abound that her symptoms were those of the complications caused by HIV/AIDS, which is ravaging much of South Africa.

She was survived by a son and a duaghter; since they were believed to be the offspring of her commoner lover, they have not been recognised by the deeply traditional Modjadji Royal Council.

~

# David Rattray

DAVID RATTRAY (who was murdered on January 26 2007, aged 48) was the internationally renowned expert on the 1879 Anglo-Zulu War, responsible for putting the remote battlefields of the eastern province of KwaZulu Natal on the tourist map.

The Battle of Isandlwana, on January 22 1879, was the most humiliating defeat in British colonial history though, hours later, 139 British soldiers successfully defended their garrison at Rorke's Drift against an intense assault by 3,000 Zulu warriors. Rattray interpreted Isandlwana as a Zulu triumph rather than as a British disaster, tempering textbook accounts with authentic testimony he had personally collected from the Zulu side.

A fluent Zulu-speaker, he deconstructed the gung-ho version of events that had informed the empire's children for more than a century, infusing it with fizzing anecdotes told to him by the grandchildren of Zulu survivors, who now work the land as farmhands and goatherds. Rattray used these oral histories as the basis for talks and lectures,

*Rattray on the Isandlwana battlefield vividly recounting the great Zulu victory of 1879.* (Graham Boynton)

which he gave, both at his tourist lodge near the battlefield site and to specialist and academic audiences around the world. The result was as moving as it was electrifying, for Rattray was a gifted storyteller, and his narrative skills were known to have reduced even visiting British officers to tears. "To listen to David Rattray narrate the story of Isandlwana was akin to watching the best-scripted, best-directed and best-produced movie Hollywood's finest studios could put out," one South African commentator recalled. "It was goose-bump stuff."

Rattray's remarkable ability to transport his listeners back to the day of the battle, and to recreate its sights and sounds, earned him the accolade of "the Laurence Olivier of the battlefield". He addressed capacity audiences at the Royal Geographical Society in London on more than 20 occasions, and was elected a Fellow in 1998.

When he was 30, Rattray moved to his family's farm near Rorke's Drift with his wife Nicky, to start Fugitives' Drift Lodge, from where they guided tourists around the battlefield sites. In its original state, the guest house had been the home of Johan Potgieter and his family. Rattray's mother Gillian, a writer and artist, had immortalised "Mr Pot" in her award-winning book *The Springing of the Year* (1980).

In the early days Fugitives' Drift was slow to attract custom; then, in 1995, a travel article in *The Sunday Telegraph* brought it wider attention. As the lodge's facilities expanded and grew, so did Rattray's reputation as one of the country's great storytellers. His account of the Isandlwana massacre – with the Zulu impis humming like bees as they charged across the plain and the bravery of two officers, who were awarded posthumous VCs for trying to save their regiment's colours – struck one visiting journalist as "a timeless indictment of man's stupidity, and yet at the same time a tribute to his nobility of spirit". "He created a picture in the mind's eye," explained another, "in the way that only a great storyteller can do."

David Grey Rattray was born in Johannesburg on September 6 1958. His interest in Isandlwana was kindled when his father, Peter, a Johannesburg lawyer, bought 10,000 acres on the banks of the Buffalo River, including the ford (or drift) across which most of the survivors from the battle escaped to safety. The boy learned Zulu and listened to the stories of a local tribal chief whose father had fought in the battle. Rattray was educated at St Alban's College, Pretoria, then read entomology at the University of Natal, Pietermaritzburg. It was while looking for beetles and other insects at Umzinyathi House, an old farm near the Zulu battlefields, that his interest was nurtured by a lifelong friend, Mzunjani "Satchmo" Mpanza, who accompanied him on expeditions. Such was Rattray's obsession with what he considered to be the untold story of Isandlwana and Rorke's Drift that he determined to make it his life's study. This decision was accelerated by the accidental destruction of his beetle collection: when his mother left the door of the cabinet open, other parasites got in and reduced the contents to dust.

He worked as chief executive of the Mala Mala game park before marrying and starting a tourist lodge business in Namibia. This did not prosper, and after the couple's first son was killed in an accident in infancy, they returned to South Africa, settling at the family property in 1989.

Rattray spent several years writing *A Soldier Artist in Zululand*, based on paintings by a British officer who had served in the Anglo-Zulu War. The pictures had been found in Britain by some guests who had visited the lodge; although they offered them to Rattray as a gift, he insisted that they share in the royalties of the book, which was published just after his death.

More than anyone else, Rattray established battlefield tours as a mainstay of the South African tourist industry. He had Martini-Henry rifles and assegais on the lodge's walls and kept snakes on the terrace at Fugitives' Drift for the benefit of guests; he also created a game reserve as part of his lodge complex, and welcomed many dignitaries, including Prince Philip, the Oppenheimers, the millionaire business-man Cyril Ramaphosa and Chief Mangosuthu Buthelezi. In addition he arranged several meetings between the men of the Royal Regiment of Wales and the descendants of the Zulu warriors.

In 1997 the Prince of Wales and his two sons took a short holiday at Fugitives' Drift, following the death of Diana Princess of Wales; Rattray subsequently stayed at Balmoral and was invited to attend the private funeral of Queen Elizabeth the Queen Mother in 2002.

The Prince also supported Rattray in his fund-raising efforts to modernise a local school overlooking the battlefields, and attended an auction at Sotheby's in London in 2000 alongside two Zulu princes and the Education Minister for KwaZulu Natal. The following year, at the Prince's invitation, Rattray delivered the inaugural lecture in the Laurens van der Post memorial lecture series at St James's Palace.

Rattray received the Royal Geographical Society's Ness award in recognition of his work in widening popular understanding of Zulu culture in southern Africa. In 2002 he returned to London to receive a *Tatler* travel award for "Vision in Tourism".

David Rattray – whose body was found not far from where the two officers died trying to save their colours – was survived by his wife Nicky and three sons.

—

# Helen Suzman

HELEN SUZMAN (who died on January 1 2009, aged 91) came to symbolise the white opposition to apartheid, during a long parliamentary career in which she was South Africa's lone Progressive MP.

Regularly dismissed as a woman, a Jew and a "Mother Superior" who stirred up violence, Helen Suzman resembled a cheeky terrier on the floor of the House of Assembly, as she challenged the dour Afrikaners on the government front bench. She displayed a firm grasp of parliamentary procedure and a razor-edged tongue that earned their respect. As violence steadily grew in protest against the policy of segregation, she savaged the Nationalist government for its

*Helen Suzman with Nelson Mandela, whom she ticked off for making sexist remarks.* (AP)

introduction of repressive legislation such as the Sabotage and the Ninety-Day Detention Acts, and also condemned Rhodesia's unilateral declaration of independence.

Helen Suzman had a capacity for oratory that some experienced parliamentarians compared with that of Lloyd George at Westminster. She dismissed the government as "narrow-minded, prejudiced bullies"; described the head of the Bureau of State Security as "South Africa's very own Heinrich Himmler"; and told John Vorster, the Justice Minister, that he should visit his constituency "heavily disguised as a human being". "If my wife chattered like that honourable member I would know what to do," commented the exasperated future President, P. W. Botha. "She is like water dripping on a tin roof."

While Helen Suzman had little chance of achieving any immediate changes to legislation, she gradually attracted attention abroad as the representative not only of her constituents and her party but also of the millions of unenfranchised blacks. In addition, her cause was helped by the Nationalist government's reluctant introduction of television ("the devil's box" for many hardline Afrikaners) and also by the success in London of her niece, the actress Janet Suzman.

The daughter of a Lithuanian immigrant who made a fortune as an estate agent, she was born Helen Gavronsky at Germiston, Transvaal, on November 7 1917 – the day the Russian Revolution began, she liked to remark. She was sent to Parktown Convent, Johannesburg. Later, when asked where her campaigning fire came from, she had no doubt who to credit. "When I shirk something I know I ought to do, the ghost of Sister Columba, the head nun, whispers in my ear 'Do it child', and I do."

Afterwards, she went to Witwatersrand University, from which she dropped out, aged 19, to marry Mozie Suzman, a successful neurologist. After having two daughters, Helen Suzman returned to her course and completed her economics degree. It was while studying the laws being established to rule over black people that she was first "roused to the discrimination" against which she would protest for the rest of her life. Her feelings were reinforced in 1945, when, as a part-time lecturer at Witwatersrand, she gathered information for a report on black labour for the South African Institute of Race Relations.

She began to translate that indignation into political action following the 1948 election, which brought to power the National Party, and with it the ideology of segregation. She campaigned among fellow staff at Witwatersrand; and when a candidate could not be found for the ruling, liberal-minded United Party in the "silk stocking" Johannesburg constituency of Houghton, with its large Jewish population, she agreed to stand herself.

Duly elected, she entered the House of Assembly in 1953. Supported by her husband and some excellent domestic help, she made a point of cementing her local links by holding report-back meetings in a local school at the end of each parliamentary session. Her maiden speech was on a bill amending women's matrimonial rights.

When it became clear that the United Party, under the leadership of Sir De Villiers Graaf, Bt, was not going to regain power, despite its cautious refusal to condemn outright the creation of the racially segregated state, a group of 12 backbenchers, encouraged by the millionaire Harry Oppenheimer, broke away to form the Progressive Party. This rejected racial segregation and proposed a franchise based on educational standards or economic achievement. But the white electorate, mindful of the chaos descending on the newly independent colonies to the north of South Africa, was not impressed. In the 1961 election all of the Progressives, bar Helen Suzman, were defeated.

As the government introduced increasingly repressive legislation to cope with the growing violence, Helen Suzman found herself defending the entire range of its opponents, from the jailed activist Nelson Mandela (whom she often visited in prison) to Communists and Jehovah's Witnesses. It did her little good in the eyes of her enemies to claim that she did not necessarily agree with these people's views, but spoke up for them only because nobody else would.

When the Prime Minister, Henrik Verwoerd, was stabbed to death on the floor of the House by a parliamentary messenger, Botha shook his finger at her, yelling: "It's you who did this. It's all you liberals. You incite people. We will get you." Eventually Botha had to make an ungracious apology.

To their credit, a series of Speakers defied the wrath of their party leaders by calling her to speak regularly, permitting her a day in which to introduce a critical Private Member's Bill every year and persuading her to stay within the procedural rules. Occasionally she had to apologise for such offences as calling the government "that bloody mob"; but in her 36 years as a member she was ordered to leave the chamber only twice.

Although the regime remained unblinkingly defiant in the eyes of the world, the apartheid system slowly started to founder because whites and blacks remained economically interdependent, just as Helen Suzman had always predicted.

It was ironic that her international reputation as a doughty fighter against apartheid was soon tarnished by criticism of her refusal to support demands for an economic boycott of South Africa. This, she argued, would make recovery harder, and badly affect neighbouring countries which depended on the South African economy.

Liberal opinion, identified particularly in her eyes with the anti-apartheid campaigning of former Australian Prime Minister Malcolm Fraser, dismissed the white opposition in South Africa as irrelevant. One consequence was that, although she was to be nominated twice, the Nobel Peace Prize was awarded to Archbishop Desmond Tutu of Cape Town; he declared that a trade boycott could not make things much worse for the blacks.

Helen Suzman did, however, win the public admiration of that stalwart opponent of a boycott, Margaret Thatcher. They had a series of meetings in London, and while Helen Suzman was no Thatcherite, she restricted her criticism to the reflection that Mrs Thatcher had no sense of humour. When they met later in South Africa some thought it appropriate that the otherwise well-behaved Suzman family Labrador bit the Iron Lady's ankle.

In 1974 five other Progressives were elected, and Helen Suzman was relieved to have their company, as she had been contemplating announcing her resignation; but she did not become leader, and found it difficult to function as part of a team again.

She was also encountering increasing criticism from the left at public meetings, though she was quite prepared to be as acerbic to black hecklers as to white. At the funeral of the murdered activist Steve Biko, she received a widely publicised rebuff by being refused entry, though she was eventually made welcome. In 1989, by which time the Progressives were part of an uneasy opposition coalition and the Afrikaner regime was clearly creaking, she thankfully resigned her seat.

Although Helen Suzman could not have been pleased after her retirement by the photographs of her embracing Winnie Mandela, she was a firm friend to Nelson, to whom she used to send classical music records at Robben Island penitentiary for Christmas; in later years she could be seen rebuking him for his thoughtlessness in making sexist remarks.

In 1989, shortly after giving up her seat, Helen Suzman was appointed an honorary DBE. She continued to lecture abroad and to play golf and bridge, but had no illusions about her importance after Mandela's "rainbow coalition" took power in 1994, the year in which her husband died. "Peripheral, dearie," she once explained. "I am just an old bag – an old-age pensioner."

Three years later she was appointed to the Order of Merit (Gold) South Africa. But in 2004 Helen Suzman was outspoken about the failings of Mandela's successor, Thabo Mbeki, citing his support for Robert Mugabe in Zimbabwe, his anti-white speeches and his failure to improve the lot of black citizens. The government made no response.

# Burma

## Stuart Macdonald

STUART MacDONALD (who died in Sydney on May 3 1999, aged 92) was the last manager of that great imperial enterprise, the Irrawaddy Flotilla Company, and had the melancholy tasking of handing it over to a newly independent Burma.

*MacDonald burned, scuttled and demolished his company's property as he retreated from the Japanese advancing up the Irrawaddy.*

The IF Company, as it was known, was founded in 1865 to provide transport in a country where rivers were the highways. In 1890, Rudyard Kipling, who had visited Rangoon, paid it tribute: "Come you back to Mandalay / Where the old Flotilla lay: / Can't you 'ear their paddles chunkin' / From Rangoon to Mandalay?"

The company fleet, built for the rivers and estuaries, was said to be the largest in the world: 644 vessels, 258 of them powered craft. Express and cargo steamers, up to 326 feet long, plied the River Irrawaddy from Rangoon to Mandalay, and smaller craft ran on to Bhamo. Special shallow-draught steamers were employed on the Irrawaddy's great tributary, the Chindwin. Some 9,000 staff were employed in the fleet, the five dockyards, the *godowns* (warehouses), the office and more than 50 agencies in river towns.

Stuart Thomson Macdonald was born at Greenock on February 20 1907. The elder son of a Glasgow coal merchant, he was educated at Trinity College, Glenalmond, and began with Paddy Henderson's shipping company before heading east to join the Irrawaddy Flotilla Company in 1927 as a shipping assistant.

If the sun was soon to set on the Empire, it was not clear to Macdonald. The tropics suited him: he fell in love with Burma and embraced colonial society. Six feet two inches tall, lean, black-haired and handsome, he was a popular figure at Scottish balls, parties, and government receptions. He golfed, played tennis, and was a splendid swimmer.

In 1936 he married, with the company's permission, Brenda Groves of Herne Bay, Kent, whom he had met in Burma.

By December 1941, when the Japanese bombed Rangoon, he was well up the management ladder. As the city fell to the Japanese Army less than four months later, the IF Company was stretched to the limit, evacuating civilians and supplying the defence of Burma. Company headquarters were now in Mandalay, and the Japanese advance up-river from Rangoon, taking port after port, was steadily reducing the Irrawaddy fleet's movements. Macdonald worked with the company's rearguard units as they burned, scuttled or demolished any property that might be useful to the enemy.

There were some close calls. At Monywa, on the Chindwin, the company was out by 6.30 a.m. on May 1, the British forces were gone by 8.00, and by 8.30 the Japanese were taking possession.

In the last few days at Mandalay, on the main Irrawaddy, Macdonald's group sank more than 100 powered boats and many other craft in the harbour. Finally, they burned the dockyard. At Katha, almost the last port on the Irrawaddy and 900 miles from Rangoon, they heard that the Japanese were ahead of them as well as behind. But Macdonald was satisfied with the job he had done. He calculated that during the campaign the company had carried at least 150,000 evacuees, 30,000 troops and tens of thousands of tons of food and army stores. Almost nothing of the great fleet remained for the Japanese; of the powered craft, fewer than 20.

From Katha, the only escape lay in Assam, a 250-mile trek westward. For three days, Macdonald and his party of a dozen drove, dragged and otherwise persuaded two small cars to crawl along bullock tracks and jungle paths, across streams and paddyfields, further than any car had ever reached in Burma. They kept up their spirits with tea, cocoa and choruses sung to a ukulele. Abandoning the cars, they tramped through thick jungle, struggled down rivers, and narrowly escaped disaster from a herd of charging water buffalo. Then it was into hill country, climbing 5,000 feet and descending exhausted down steep valleys. They had eked out their rations with food from villages, and with the plains of Assam in sight they sat down, bearded and unkempt, to eat the last Army biscuits. With some of the party in their fifties, they had nevertheless come through in less than a fortnight.

All Macdonald's hopes were pinned on a return to Burma. Immediately after the war he did return, now as manager, but in an uncertain climate of nationalism. His fate was to negotiate the transfer of the company, in 1949, to the government of an independent state.

Next year he returned to Britain. He was not afraid of starting again from scratch, and took a job packing eggs for a small company in Sussex. Before long he was managing director and proceeded to expand the company, Stonegate Farmers, into a substantial operation. On retiring in 1968 he emigrated with his wife to Sydney, where he did clerical work for stockbrokers and insurance brokers into his late seventies.

Macdonald believed firmly that young men should make their own way, as he had, and he turned out his two sons at an early age to do just that. To the end of his life his favourite song remained "On the Road to Mandalay", Kipling's poem set to music, in which the old soldier in London longs for the Burma he knew: "For the temple-bells are callin', / An' it's there that I would be …"

Stuart Macdonald was survived by his wife and a son; another son predeceased him.

# Malaya

~

## William Stafford

WILLIAM STAFFORD (who died in March 1992, aged 85) was known as "The Iron Broom" for his stalwart service in tracking down criminals and terrorists in Malaya in the 1940s and 1950s, and as "Two-Gun Stafford" for his habit of carrying two automatics whenever a gun-battle was pending.

Still a captain in the Army when appointed chief of the detective branch of the Malayan Police in January 1946, he was confronted with many opponents who had been his comrades in Force 136, the anti-Japanese guerrilla force established by Special Operations Executive in the jungles of Burma and Malaya.

As soon as the Japanese surrendered, many of these had either embarked on a life of murder and pillage, or become Communists bent on establishing a Soviet-backed Malaya. When offered a $600 bonus to return their arms, many claimed to have "lost" them. Nevertheless some among the criminal riff-raff resented being dragooned into the Malayan Communist Party; and from these Stafford set up a network of informers and agents. Since they refused to be seen in daylight talking to a European, he had to meet them in a darkened cinema in Kuala Lumpur to learn of huge dumps of arms buried in the jungle; one cache contained 257 handguns, 350 grenades and 30,000 rounds of ammunition.

Armed gangs, such as the Green Dragons, were highly organised for their trade of robbery, murder and kidnapping, which led Stafford to become engaged in many close encounters with them, including gunfights to the death. One testing experience was his arrest of a man who had run amok with a *kris* (a wavy Malay sword), killing more than 20 complete strangers and wounding many more, including some British servicemen; the man was hanged at Kuala Lumpur's Puda gaol afterwards. Another experience was being chased in his Jeep along a jungle path by a wild elephant.

When the Emergency was at its peak, Stafford enlisted the help of aborigines in capturing bandits, with the result that a young Sakai appeared in his office with a large sack, explaining that he had come for his reward. He opened up the sack and three Chinese heads rolled out, complete with hats. The bearer was overjoyed to be rewarded with a sack of rice and three cartons of cigarettes.

William Frederick Stafford was born at Margate, Kent, on September 15 1906. His great-grandfather had fought in the Battle of Trafalgar and then was town crier of Margate for 46 years; his father served in the Royal Navy, and was drowned at sea soon after young William was born. After attending local schools, the boy worked as an assistant cellarman in the mornings and assistant billiard-marker in the afternoons. He then joined the Navy as a stoker, serving in Hong Kong and China.

During one flood, he went 800 miles up the Yangtse in a motor boat to rescue Charles Lindbergh and his wife, who had flown in from China in a seaplane to drop supplies to beleaguered villages; but it had then turned over when they landed on the strong current.

After buying himself out of the Navy, Stafford joined the Admiralty Police. He learned Chinese and some dialects, and was transferred to Singapore, where well-deserved promotion rapidly followed. For recreation he went crocodile-hunting, learning to catch the reptiles with his bare hands – "not as dangerous as it sounded if you knew how to do it," he recalled. Although crocodiles can move quickly, they can only go forwards; so the trick was to make them bite on a stick and then secure their jaws. The hunters then sold their catch to the Chinese in Singapore for $1 per foot, to be used for handbags and medicines. Stafford also received $1 a foot for boa-constrictors, which he claimed were not really dangerous unless they secured a purchase round a tree: "The first thing you should do therefore is to grasp the tail and put it in a bag; this then enables you to club it on the head."

When the Japanese invaded he hid in a large iron pipe, before escaping on one of the last ships to leave. After a hazardous journey he reached Ceylon, where he joined the Army. After being gazetted as a captain, he was asked to volunteer for SOE.

For his first assignment he had to acquire a deep suntan and dress as a native in order to take a sloop with a Burmese crew and land 10 agents in Burma. Next, he was sent with his section to Poona for training in sabotage, explosives and silent killing. But the visit was cut short when the men put too much plastic explosive under a railway line and blew up a large section, which landed on the colonel's office. No one was hurt, but Stafford and his men were promptly returned to Britain for further training. They also had to test various forms of experimental equipment; these included midget submarines, in one of which he was nearly drowned at the bottom of Fishguard harbour.

Afterwards Stafford went to India to complete a course in parachuting, ready for dropping into the Malayan jungle. But peace intervened. He and his wife arrived in Kuala Lumpur by train in 1946, and were rather alarmed to be allotted a house which had no fewer than 38 lightning conductors. It seemed there was something in the soil which attracted lightning, but the house, though often struck, was never seriously damaged.

That the potentially explosive situation in Malaya was cleared up undoubtedly owed much to Stafford's cool, quick-witted approach.

On one occasion he was en route to an isolated police station in the jungle of Raub when his party encountered a tigress. Everyone opened fire and, after the kill, three week-old cubs were discovered. Stafford took them home, where he and his wife nursed them, and their children took them for walks on leads. When the animals grew too big and expensive to look after, they ended up in Whipsnade, Dublin and Edinburgh zoos.

Stafford retired from the Malayan Police in 1957 and then worked for 17 years, in absolute secrecy, as a field investigating officer in Britain. He was awarded the King's Police Medal and the Colonial Police Medal for Gallantry.

William Stafford was survived by his wife, Margaret, a son and a daughter.

~

## Sir Anthony Abell

SIR ANTHONY ABELL (who died on October 18 1994, aged 87) was an outstanding Governor and Commander-in-Chief of Sarawak.

Ruled by the Brooke family from 1842 until it was captured by the Japanese in the Second World War, Sarawak had been a British colony for only four years when Abell took over in 1950. His predecessor, the second governor, had been in the post just a few days when he was stabbed to death.

*Abell was offered a river specially stocked with trout if he would stay on in Sarawak after retiring as Governor.*

Abell soon established himself as a genial but firm leader. Judicious and tactful, he won the respect of the colony's people, among them the head-hunting Dayak tribes. On visits to their longhouses he would admiringly inspect the shrunken heads of Japanese invaders; one, he recalled, still bore its teeth and a pair of steel-rimmed spectacles. The governorship was supposed to be a five-year appointment, but Abell was asked to stay a further five, to help to prepare the colony for independence; he was simultaneously High Commissioner to British North Borneo and Brunei.

When he retired in 1959 the Malaysians offered him a house and staff in Sarawak, imagining he would want to stay there rather than return to the cold of England. Not wishing to offend, Abell explained that the real reason he was going was that he had a house in Gloucestershire on the banks of the River Test, one of the best trout streams in the country. This produced an immediate offer to stock the Sarawak rivers with trout for him.

Anthony Foster Abell was born on December 11 1906, and educated at Repton and Magdalen College, Oxford. He then joined the Colonial Service and was posted to Nigeria, where he served for nearly 20 years, training his pet monkey to smoke a cigar and sit on a lavatory.

During the Second World War a German submarine took refuge at Fernando Po, a Portuguese possession off the Nigerian coast, and Abell helped to organise a highly alcoholic cocktail party for all the local diplomats, while a group of colonial staff and planters clandestinely boarded and scuttled the vessel. Abell took a swastika flag as his trophy.

After Sarawak he worked in London for the Civil Service Commission and the Police Appointments Board for many years. He was appointed CMG in 1950 and KCMG in 1952, and from 1972 to 1979 was Gentleman Usher of the Blue Rod of the Order of St Michael and St George.

In retirement at his unheated house, he used to invite friends to join him on the Queen's birthday each year in drinking Her Majesty's health. He also liked to hold shooting competitions with his nephew, using a blow pipe with poisoned arrows he had brought home. There was some unease when one hit the nephew's girlfriend, but she survived despite the arrow being tipped with black toad poison.

## Toh Puan Bunny Suffian

TOH PUAN BUNNY SUFFIAN (who died on October 9 1997, aged 81) was a Norfolk farmer's daughter married to one of Malaysia's most distinguished judges.

Pre-independence Malaya was an uncomfortable, dangerous place during the Communist Emergency. When she and her husband, Mohamed Suffian, arrived in 1948 for him to start as a district magistrate in remote towns, social life was restricted to other government servants and the European managers of local rubber and tea estates. Prejudice against mixed marriages was common. But Bunny Suffian mixed easily with people of all ranks and stations, never attempting to disguise the broad Norfolk accent which remained with her all her life. She taught needlework to village women, and her command of the Malay language gave her entry to the highest echelons of local society, where she befriended the wives and daughters of sultans and chief ministers. Freed from the distraction of having any children, she acquired an encyclopaedic knowledge of the inter-relationships of Malay princely families, which she imparted to all with wit and infectious gaiety.

As Suffian advanced to Lord President of the Federal Judiciary in 1974, his wife became a leading light in Kuala Lumpur society. Her house was furnished with antiques and curios from Malacca and fittings which, like her hats for the grandest occasions, she took pride in making herself. Her salon was a haven of lively conversation and gossip in Malaysia's increasingly restrained political atmosphere. And when her husband was awarded the title Tun, the highest non-royal rank in Malaysia, she became Toh Puan Bunny Suffian, equivalent to countess.

Dora Evelina Grange, always known as Bunny, was born on January 11 1916 and grew up in north Norfolk, before the family moved to Cambridge where her mother had a boarding house. There, in 1939, she met her future husband, an undergraduate of Gonville and Caius College.

Called up for war service, Bunny Grange worked first at Marshall's Flying School in Cambridge and later in Coventry, inspecting repairs to the canvas fabric of aircraft damaged in raids over Germany.

After Mohamed was called to the Bar by Middle Temple in 1941 he set off for Malaya but was stranded in Ceylon, where he found work for the duration of the war with All-India Radio. He then returned to London in 1945, to become briefly head of the Malay Section of the BBC at Bush House before undertaking a course in colonial administration.

Bunny married him in 1946, and began to learn Malay at the School of Oriental and African Studies in London. As part of a group campaigning for Malayan independence, which included two future Prime Ministers, Tunku Abdul Rahman and Tun Razak, the couple were involved in the political ferment which affected the Malay student community in London. Bunny made the flag of the United Malay National Organisation (still the dominant political party in Malaysia), which hung behind the rostrum at their first meetings.

~

## Tun Mohamed Suffian

TUN MOHAMED SUFFIAN (who died on September 26 2000, aged 82) was Malaysia's most distinguished judge, with an international standing that enabled him to speak freely without fear of repression.

As Lord President, the presiding judge and administrative head of Malaysia's federal judiciary from 1974 to 1982, he had a concern for the dignity of the ordinary citizen, which ensured that he never let legal technicalities prevail over justice.

Until Mahathir bin Mohamad became Prime Minister in 1981, Tun Suffian's tenure as a judge coincided with the premierships of three successive lawyers – Tunku Abdul Rahman, Tun Razak and Tun Hussein Onn. They were British-trained like him, and showed complete respect for the judiciary's independence.

Mahathir, however, leaned towards a more autocratic Asian tradition, and showed

*Suffian commended the English for teaching him that "law is made for man, not man for the law".*

increasing hostility towards residual British influences. Some years after Suffian's retirement, a clash between Mahathir and the judiciary developed into a constitutional crisis. The government had claimed that a series of court decisions were biased against it. Matters came to a head with a case concerning electoral practices within the ruling United Malay National Organisation (UMNO), in which an unfavourable judgment might have obliged Mahathir to resign. The Prime Minister instead prevailed on the King to dismiss Suffian's successor, Tun Salleh Abbas, on the flimsiest of grounds. This brought resistance from five other senior judges, who were promptly suspended. A one-sided public tribunal ratified the sacking of Tun Salleh, while a second tribunal removed two of the senior judges from office.

Few Malaysians dared speak out, but Suffian, to whom many turned for an impartial opinion, did not hold back. "Those who stand by and do nothing to protect the independence of the judiciary", he said, "will in the end get the judiciary they deserve, one powerless to stand between them and tyranny." In private he took to referring to Mahathir as "Papa Doc", after the Haitian dictator.

Although the title Tun, conferred on Suffian by Malaysia's king in 1975, was the equivalent of a life peerage, Suffian always retained something of the simplicity of his rural village upbringing.

Mohamed Suffian was born on November 12 1917 in the *kampong* of Kota Lama Kiri on the banks of the Perak River in the north-west of the Malay peninsula. He was the second of 14 children of Haji Mohamed Hashim, a *kathi* (Muslim cleric) of unusually broad mind who sent his sons from the village Malay school to the British-run Clifford School at Kuala Kangsar. There the schoolmaster, one Captain Preedy, immediately recognised young Suffian's abilities, predicting that he would one day be "the pride of the Malay race".

But academic brilliance was not enough at that stage to win him a place in the Malayan Administrative Service: he was advised against applying on the grounds of "insufficient social connections". Instead, he won a coveted Queen's Scholarship to Cambridge, where he read law at Gonville and Caius. The only "kampong boy" to do so, he was a rarity among a generation of Cambridge-educated Malays, who came chiefly from princely families.

When, because of the Japanese invasion, he could not go home after being called to the Bar by Middle Temple in 1941, he broadcast in Malay for All-India Radio in Delhi. His deep, resonant voice became well known across Malaya, even to the Japanese occupiers who made life increasingly difficult for his family.

After returning to Britain towards the end of the war he became head of the BBC's Malay section then, in 1946, joined the Malayan Civil Service. He studied public administration at Cambridge, the School of Oriental and African Studies and the London School of Economics, where he became involved in the first meetings of UMNO and in calls for independence which began to ferment among the Malay student community in London.

He returned to Malaya two years later to become a magistrate at Malacca. When he arrived, however, there turned out to be no provision for his salary, so he had to be given an additional paid appointment as harbour master. Suffian rose swiftly to become Solicitor-General in 1959. In 1961, at 44, he became a judge of the high court in Kuala Lumpur, becoming Chief Justice in 1973. He was a constitutional adviser to the Sultan of Brunei, president of the

Commonwealth Magistrates' Association and the author of a number of works on Malaysian law. He made the first simplified translation of the Malaysian constitution into the Malay language.

He was pro-Chancellor of the University of Malaya from 1963 to 1986 and held many other public appointments. But in later years he was cold-shouldered by Kuala Lumpur's political establishment, which he himself preferred to avoid. Mahathir, however, was thought to have visited him on his deathbed in a private act of reconciliation.

Suffian and his wife "Bunny" retained many lifelong friends in the legal community in London, where they kept a house. In a speech in 1980, Suffian commended the English for their ability to "disagree in a civilised way"; they had taught him, he said, that "law is made for man, not man for the law".

~

## Henry Stonor

HENRY STONOR (who died on February 26 2006, aged 79) was a founder member of the Vintage Car Club of Malaya and a tireless campaigner for the Karen tribesmen of Burma.

*Stonor being given a push start in his Fiat 509 by his cook boy and gardeners in 1949.*

Working first as a rubber planter and then as a palm oil estate manager in Johore and Pahang, he took happily to the colonial life, dancing the

Charleston for exercise every morning and playing the cornet and guitar in a planters' jazz band. His greatest joy, however, was his collection of cars. By 1959 these included a 1925 Rolls-Royce Twenty, a 1927 three-litre Red Label Bentley, a Sunbeam Speed Twenty and a 4¼-litre Bentley of 1934, all of which were lovingly restored before being entered in the club's various sprints, hill climbs and grand prix.

Henry Anthony Stonor was born on May 11 1926, the son of a Welsh slate-mine manager who died when his son was four. With the future test pilot Brian Trubshaw, he first drove a Bullnose Morris on the sands of Anglesey when he was 12.

Initially sent to Downside, Henry was switched by his non-Catholic mother to Shrewsbury. He was then commissioned in the Royal Welch Fusiliers and posted as a transport officer to Burma, where he went on patrols with Karen tribesmen. Stonor considered becoming a professional jazz musician on being demobbed, but decided instead to go to Malaya. He first drove a Fiat 509, then bought a Rolls-Royce Twenty tourer, which he brought home two years later after growing weary of rubber-planting. When his money began to run out, he returned to the East with Oil Palms of Malaya, arriving at the quayside in Penang to be greeted by a group of vintage car drivers, who later formed today's Malaysian Singapore Vintage Car Register. Although life was comfortable, the threat of terrorism during the Emergency added a sense of danger.

One night, on hearing some shots, Stonor leapt out of bed to grab his carbine and invited his cookboy to bring his family into the bedroom to lie on the floor for safety; when the crisis passed and the light was switched on, there were titters from the boy's wife and four daughters on seeing that Stonor's sarong had fallen off. Later, on patrol with four special constables, Stonor captured a woman with a sawn-off shotgun, earning a letter of commendation from the High Commissioner and a cash reward which went towards repairing a Bentley Speed Six. But his chairman cabled from London: "I do not pay planters to capture terrorists."

After failing to have his work permit renewed, he returned home in 1978, first to lend a hand at the family home, Stonor Park, in Oxfordshire; he drove a mower through a glass door, and repaired it with Araldite. Next he bought a bakery in Cheshire to be his home. When a chance to train as a clock repairer fell through, he decided to keep the business going with its staff of nine, using his Railton and Alvis for deliveries. But when he finally had to close it down after falling ill, the staff's redundancy claims wiped out his remaining capital, forcing him to sell both the house and his beloved Railton.

Stonor took up the cause of the Karen tribesmen, relentlessly lobbying Parliament, the UN and anyone who might listen. Smuggling himself into the Burmese jungle via Thailand, he cut a dash by singing a song in Karen. The tribesmen said he was the first Englishman they had seen since the late 1940s. When government forces launched a mortar attack, his refusal to duck confirmed their admiration for British virtues; they did not realise he was too deaf to hear the explosion.

Stonor bought a piano for their church and gave individuals money; but, thinking that he could lobby more effectively in Britain, he returned home to appear in a television documentary film about their plight.

After a final visit to Malaysia for a car rally, Henry Stonor settled at Marlborough. He lived in a flat, inherited from a sister, with his 36 clocks. He gave up driving after his last car failed its Ministry of Transport test.

～

## George Patterson

GEORGE PATTERSON (who died on January 3 2008, aged 87) began his career as a member of Malaya's self-confident administrative elite, known as the "Heaven Born", then suffered the horrors of imprisonment by the Japanese before returning from the war to serve on until the Malay States were granted independence.

The son of a senior commissioner in northern Nigeria, George Sheldon Patterson was born on July 25 1920 at Newcastle upon Tyne and went to the Royal Grammar School before reading chemistry at New College, Oxford. He decided to enter the Colonial Service, but joined the Royal Artillery on the outbreak of war and then was posted to Terengganu, in Johore. He was learning Malay and supervising a dye works when Japan invaded.

Bidding farewell to his servant and leaving his car running without oil so that the engine was ruined, Patterson led a party of Europeans on a six-day journey through the jungle. They had to pause regularly to burn leeches off their bodies, but reached the River Tembeling, where their three Malays built a raft. When a rescue launch appeared, they had one tin of corned beef left.

*Patterson wiped the diary he had kept in the war from his mind until his wife produced it decades later.*

In Singapore Patterson joined an anti-aircraft unit, became an RAF liaison officer then was posted to Army headquarters. He recorded in a 3½-inch by 4½-inch Letts diary his appointment as ADC to General Percival, the GOC, on February 11 1942. Three days later he laconically noted: "Shell lifted the car off the road today but little damage done." On February 15 he attended morning Communion before driving Percival, under a white flag, to surrender to General Yamashita. Soon Patterson and Percival were sharing a married officer's quarters at Changi with seven brigadiers, one colonel, a sergeant cook and a batman.

At first they lived off Army rations, played bridge and had little contact with their captors. Then a barbed wire fence was built, and prisoners were ordered to salute all Japanese personnel. Unlike tall prisoners, Patterson was never made to kneel down to be beaten with a rifle butt; but he was slapped in the face, and if his wife moved to touch his cheek playfully in later life he would give her a look of hatred.

Although he risked being executed for possessing his diary, he hid it in the soft walls of his hut and, when prisoners were moved, would slip it into the bags of the Japanese he was made to carry. He was briefly sent to a coalmine in Japan, and then to a camp on Formosa, where the diary recorded a daily litany of deaths. But he was lucky to obtain a job exercising a spirited horse for a Japanese NCO. When some natives gave him some bananas as he rode back to camp, he retained them by telling the guards that they were the beast's favourite food. After being finally incarcerated at Mukden in Manchuria, he was released by American paratroops, who were just ahead of the Russians, on August 16 1945.

When he returned to Malaya the following January, the Malays and the Chinese were welcoming since the British were the protecting power for the rajahs. He was appointed private secretary to Malcolm MacDonald, the Governor-General, who was to speed up independence. MacDonald deemed evening dress no longer necessary for dinner parties, and even entered one walking on his hands. Later, when Patterson visited Viceregal Lodge in New Delhi, residence of Lord Mountbatten of Burma (another proconsul in a hurry), he found that the iced butter there was inscribed "M of B".

After marrying Marie Worthington, with whom he was to have two daughters, Patterson was back in Malaya during the Emergency. As district officer in Kototingi he had to have an armed guard, but he enjoyed running a rehabilitation centre which taught trades to captured Communists. When General Sir Gerald Templer, the High Commissioner, asked why he was not doing better, Patterson replied that he needed more money, and was promised it at once. Six weeks later Templer reappeared by helicopter, saying: "You didn't expect me, did you?" "Of course I did," Patterson smoothly replied. "I've got on a new pair of slacks." Patterson's last post was in the service's establishment office. He returned home with an OBE in 1960 to work for PA Management Consultants.

In retirement George Patterson expressed regret that he had never kept his diary, and was astonished when his wife produced it, together with his letters home, which he had blotted from his memory. In 1993 he used them to write his memoir, *A Spoonful of Rice with Salt.*

# HONG KONG

## David MacDougall

DAVID MacDOUGALL (who died on May 13 1991, aged 86) played a key role in reviving Hong Kong after the Second World War. In September 1944, as the tide was turning and Britain was preparing to recover the colony, he was appointed head of the Hong Kong Planning Unit.

Less than a year later MacDougall was given the rank of brigadier, to head the civil adminstration of Hong Kong under Rear-Admiral Cecil Harcourt, whose forces recovered Hong Kong from the Japanese in the face of strong Chinese irredentism. He was instrumental in persuading the Chinese Nationalist forces to disarm and the Chinese Communist guerrillas to keep the peace. Above all he ensured that the people of Hong Kong, whose number had been reduced by starvation from two million to 450,000 under the Japanese, were properly fed once more.

In the interim, MacDougall worked out a general outline for a new Hong Kong which could meet the requirements of the postwar era. Having quickly won the support of Harcourt, he prepared to liquidate the darker side of prewar imperialism, such as the reservation of the Peak for whites and the government's opium monopoly. He also fought hard to give the Hong Kong people "a fuller and more responsible share" in their own government.

With the restoration of civil government under the Governor, Sir Mark Youngs, in 1946, MacDougall became the colony's first postwar Colonial Secretary, an appointment in which he excelled. But less than three years later, much to the chagrin of his colleagues, he resigned from the service to return with his family to Britain, where he farmed for many years in East Anglia.

David Mercer MacDougall was born at Perth on December 8 1904 and educated at Perth Academy and St Andrews University.

After joining the Colonial Service he went out to Hong Kong as a cadet in 1928. When the colony was invaded by Japanese forces on Christmas Day, 1941, it fell to MacDougall, then seconded to the Ministry of Information, to escort the one-legged Admiral Chan Chak, the senior Chinese officer in Hong Kong, in a daring escape across the Japanese line.

They set out in a small launch, which was soon sunk by machine-gun and shell fire. The admiral was wounded in the wrist and MacDougall shot in the back; but they managed to swim to a nearby island. MacDougall attributed his survival to a curious chance. Taking refuge in a Chinese shop, he saw a phial of sulphanilamide, and by taking two tablets daily for the next eight days he kept his wounds clean until he reached hospital.

He then worked for the Colonial Office in London before being posted to the British embassy in Washington and then was appointed director of the Political Warfare Mission in San Francisco before another spell back in London to prepare for the return to the colony.

David MacDougall was appointed CMG and awarded the Chinese Order of the Brilliant Star in 1946. He was married, with three daughters.

~

## Lord MacLehose of Beoch

THE LORD MacLEHOSE OF BEOCH (who died on May 27 2000, aged 82) was one of the outstanding governors of Hong Kong.

His period of office, from 1971 to 1982, coincided with Hong Kong's development from a colonial trading post to a modern city-state. It was marked by progress in the battle against internal corruption, improvements in housing and the amelioration of relations with mainland China, but not by a movement towards democracy.

Tall, commanding and inclined to punctuate his speech with long, thoughtful silences, MacLehose was a figure of unmistakable authority. Yet he also introduced a new informality, dismantling much of the pomp favoured by his predecessors. He covered the short distance from Government House to the Legislative Council Chambers on foot, rather than in the official Rolls-Royce, and took to making walkabouts in crowded areas in short-sleeved, open-necked shirts. A diplomat and sinologist, rather than a colonial officer, he was the first of a new breed of Governor picked by the Foreign Office with an eye

*MacLehose doggedly opposed a move towards constitutional democracy in Hong Kong.* (AP)

to the approach of 1997, when the New Territories lease would expire and a new settlement would have to be struck with Peking.

MacLehose did much in practical terms for the ordinary people of Hong Kong. In the 1960s the colony had prospered unevenly on *laissez-faire* principles, but the MacLehose era was characterised by central planning and sharp increases in public spending on education, social services, housing and transport.

On his arrival, he was shocked to find more than 300,000 refugees from the mainland living in "squatter huts" and many thousands of others in inadequate re-settlement estates. He established a housing authority, which set out to build five high-rise new towns in the New Territories. Some 960,000 people were rehoused in 10 years, and the new towns eventually accommodated 2,500,000. As government funds grew through sales of land, many other projects were embarked upon, including the Mass Transit Railway.

But perhaps MacLehose's most important initiative was his action against corruption. During a posting to Hong Kong in the early 1960s, he had observed rampant police corruption – and a lack of will in Westminster or Hong Kong to tackle it. Early in his governorship the issue came to prominence when an inquiry into the activities of Peter Godber, a well-respected former chief superintendent, found him to have taken bribes of several million dollars from vice racketeers.

Concluding that the police could not be relied upon to clean out their own stable, MacLehose set up the Independent Commission Against Corruption. This was embarrassingly successful: 59 sergeants were arrested in a single division, three senior British officers were jailed and another took his own life. Threatened policemen finally stormed the commission's offices and assaulted its staff. MacLehose had to allow an amnesty for all but the most serious offences. Nevertheless his warning of severe action against future misdemeanours turned the tide and boosted public confidence.

In external relations, he was determined to move away from the confrontation between Hong Kong and China that had reached its height in the Cultural Revolution of 1967. He recognised, albeit unofficially, the Hong Kong director of the New China News Agency as Peking's de facto consul-general in the colony, and even had him to dine. MacLehose was the first Governor to celebrate China Day, and he made a point of signing the book of condolence on the death of Chairman Mao in 1976.

Under the pragmatic leadership of Deng Xiaoping, China was for the first time keen to welcome foreign investors. It was against this background that MacLehose received an invitation from the Chinese foreign trade minister to visit Peking in 1979, the first official visit by a Hong Kong Governor since the Communist takeover.

Conditions seemed propitious for the broaching of the question of Hong Kong's future after 1997, but MacLehose opted for a sidelong approach, in which Chinese approval would be sought for the sale of individual land leases in the New Territories extending beyond 1997. But the Chinese refused to be drawn on lease technicalities, and Deng wrong-footed the British delegation by going straight to the bigger question.

As summarised by Sir Percy Cradock, the British Ambassador to Peking, Deng's message was: "Of course Hong Kong will return to China. Sovereignty belongs to China. But 1997 is quite a long way off. Don't worry down there, you'll be all right." A phrase from the official translation, that Hong Kong investors should "set their hearts at ease", was widely proclaimed on MacLehose's return to the colony. But MacLehose was convinced that China would eventually reclaim Hong Kong *tout court*, and that attempts to discuss continued British administration after 1997 were pointless. There, in effect, matters rested until Margaret Thatcher's stormy visit to Peking in September 1992, shortly after MacLehose's retirement.

In the meantime, he opposed any significant move towards constitutional democracy in Hong Kong, a topic neglected since the departure of the first postwar Governor, Sir Mark Young, in 1947. When a group of senior civil servants sketched out plans for reform in 1979, MacLehose declined to support them; in the same year, a group of backbench MPs (including Chris Patten, later to be the colony's last Governor) arrived to harangue him on the same theme. It was to no avail: the introduction of partial direct elections for district boards – the equivalent of parish councils – was his only concession. He remained convinced that full-scale elections could not be other than provocative to China. "If the Communists won," he said, "that would be the end of Hong Kong. If the nationalists won, that would bring in the Communists."

Crawford Murray MacLehose was born on October 16 1917 and educated at Rugby and Balliol College, Oxford, where he developed a love of sailing.

He joined the Colonial Service in Malaya in 1939, and during the Second World War held consular posts at Amoy and Foochow in China, and served briefly as a lieutenant in the RNVR. In 1948, he was appointed acting Consul-General at Hankow. These early encounters with the Chinese had a deep effect on him. Later, he spoke of "the thrill of that different world". He found the Chinese, "provided you take them on their own terms, very rewarding".

But his career took him elsewhere first. He was transferred to the Foreign Office to work on Marshall Aid, and went on to serve in Prague as Commercial Secretary and in Wellington as Head of Chancery. In 1956, he moved to Paris where, as Commercial Counsellor, he began to be noticed by visiting ministers. Three years later he was appointed political adviser to the Governor of Hong Kong, Sir Robin Black.

In 1965, MacLehose became Principal Private Secretary to the Labour Foreign Secretary, Michael Stewart, and then to his successor, George Brown. Coping with the volatile, sometimes drunken Brown provided useful training for the stresses of his next posting, as Ambassador to South Vietnam at the height of the Vietnam War. In Saigon he developed close relations with the Americans, who saw him as one of the few foreign diplomats who really understood the military situation in the context of the tensions of the region.

It was a disappointment to MacLehose that his next posting was as Ambassador to Denmark. But the interlude was brief, and he returned to Hong Kong, to succeed Sir David Trench as Governor in November 1971.

MacLehose was created a life peer in 1982, before his departure from Hong Kong. He took his seat on the crossbenches, and was, by some distance, the most authoritative of the mixed bunch of peers who spoke out against democratic reform in Hong Kong. In a debate on the Legislative Council elections of November 1991, in which pro-democracy campaigners scored notable successes on a low turn-out, he was dismissive of the results on the grounds that 80 per cent of those entitled to vote had not done so.

MacLehose spoke again in the Lords in November 1992, during a debate on the electoral reforms introduced by Governor Chris Patten in the teeth of furious opposition from mainland China. When there was so much common ground with China about the future of the territory, he said, it was a pity to have provoked a "major confrontation". In a later interview, MacLehose admitted that it sounded "remarkably feeble" that the fear of provoking Peking led him both to sidestep the pressure for democracy during his governorship and to oppose it later in the House of Lords. But, he explained, "I felt my job was to make Hong Kong as contented and prosperous and cohesive as possible. Insofar as I don't sleep at nights, this is the sort of thing one looks back at and wonders whether one should have done it. I still think I was right."

MacLehose joined a group of British grandees, including Sir Edward Heath and Lord Howe, at the official swearing-in ceremony, boycotted by the British government, of the Hong Kong Special Administrative Region chief executive on July 1 1997.

MacLehose was appointed KCMG in 1971, KCVO in 1975 and GBE in 1976. Seven years later he was made a Knight of the Thistle, an honour which he held with special pride as a loyal Scot. He was a Deputy Lieutenant of Ayr and Arran.

In retirement, he was a director of the National Westminster Bank, chairman of the governors of the School of African and Oriental Studies in London and chairman of the Scottish Trust for the Physically Disabled. He took to sheep farming at his home near Maybole in Ayrshire.

Murray MacLehose married, in 1947, Noel "Squeak" Dunlop; they had two daughters.

# Sir Oswald Cheung

SIR OSWALD CHEUNG (who died on December 10 2003, aged 81)
worked for British Intelligence in southern China during the Second
World War; later he became the first Chinese to be appointed QC in
Hong Kong as well as a loyal and judicious member of the Legislative
and Executive Councils. He was also a respected businessman, the first
Chinese chairman of the stewards of the Hong Kong Jockey Club and
co-owner of the colony's most famous racehorse, River Verdon.

The son of a Chinese agent for Shell and his Eurasian wife, Oswald
Victor Cheung was born in Hong Kong on January 22 1922 and went
to the Diocesan Boys' School before going to Hong Kong University
to study mathematics and chemistry at 16.

After Japan occupied the colony in 1941, young Ozzie and his
family fled for the nearby Portuguese enclave of Macao. Determined
to help drive out the Japanese, he travelled with two schoolfriends to
Kwangsi University in southern China. The journey took six days and
involved walking in the mornings, stopping for a large lunch, then
travelling for the rest of the day by sedan chair. But when they arrived
he was unable to continue his studies because he spoke Cantonese,
not Mandarin.

Instead, he found a job as a cipher clerk in the British General
Liaison Office which, as part of British Intelligence, was charged with
monitoring Japanese activity in southern China. At first this involved
working as a courier, travelling by train, lorry and on foot, often in
considerable danger. But in time he also took over much of the office
administration, preparing for rapid withdrawals in the face of Japanese
advances, briefing agents, encoding messages and keeping the
accounts.

One of his strongest memories was of making a drink from ethyl
alcohol, which was used in lorries. Purified with charcoal and flavoured
with orange peel, it was potable when diluted; but at one party some
Americans insisted on taking it neat, so that Cheung remembered half
a dozen of them sliding to the carpet before the end. As the course of
the war improved, he was posted to his office's scientific laboratory in
Calcutta, where he saw the results of the first German experiments in
microdot printing.

He then returned home to Hong Kong, to witness the surrender of
Communist guerrillas and the warm welcome given to the old and

familiar British administration. After being stood down, he was first asked by the Bishop of Hong Kong to help re-establish the Diocesan Boys' School and briefly became acting headmaster, until the colony's Director of Education was horrified to discover that he had no teaching qualifications.

Cheung was awarded a scholarship to University College, Oxford, and was called to the Bar at Lincoln's Inn before returning to Hong Kong, where he married Pauline Cheng, later appointed the colony's first Director of Legal Aid, with whom he had a son.

Settling down, he served briefly as a magistrate, was called to the local Bar and built up a busy general practice. While he could be extremely rude about people in conversation, he proved a genial head of chambers who ignored the traditional obsession with taking the best candidate into chambers. "If everybody takes the alpha, what about the beta?" he would ask. His booming voice and fund of jokes went with a taste for fine wine and a love of making chicken liver pate, which he liked to hand round.

In addition to his busy practice, Cheung was asked by the Governor, Sir Murray MacLehose, whom he had first met during the war, to serve on the Legislative and Executive Councils during the difficult negotiations with the Communist government on the mainland. He was a director of the Mass Transit Railway Corporation, Hong Kong Electric and Ciba-Geigy (HK); he was also chairman of the Criminal Injuries Compensation Board, a member of the court of Hong Kong University and of the University Grants Commission, and honorary colonel of the Royal Hong Kong Regiment.

With Ronald Arculli, Cheung owned River Verdon, which, in the early 1990s, won all the colony's major races, including the Hong Kong Cup and the Hong Kong International. Although by then rather old for a flat horse, River Verdon competed in America and also at Moonee Valley in Victoria, where he ran well in the Melbourne Cup and Cox Plate without winning.

On becoming the first Chinese chairman of the stewards of the Jockey Club, Cheung demonstrated a concern for the employees, which differed from the Olympian style of his predecessors. When the race course experienced a spate of accidents he arranged for a busload of Buddhist monks to drive round the track, sprinkling holy water. Although he was not a Buddhist himself, the jockeys appreciated his concern; and the accidents ceased.

Ozzie Cheung was appointed OBE in 1972, CBE in 1976 and knighted in 1987. He died in hospital three months after he had set fire to his pyjamas while trying to light a cigar.

~

## K. C. Yeo

K. C. YEO (who died on May 24 2004, aged 101) gave up a chance to escape from Hong Kong in order to keep the colony's medical services running after the Japanese invasion in 1941.

*Yeo became a staunch Anglophile after he was given the wrong contract as an Assistant Medical Officer of Health in Hong Kong.*

Yeo and his wife were planning to join relations in China when Sir Selwyn Selwyn-Clarke, Director of Medical Services, implored him to stay. Selwyn-Clarke said that he was going to be imprisoned soon, leaving Yeo the only man capable of running the colony's health and hygiene, a field in which the Japanese had no expertise and little interest.

After Selwyn-Clarke's arrest, on a charge of being the head of British espionage, two members of the Kempei, the Japanese secret service, barged into Yeo's bedroom with a large Alsatian demanding that he come with them to "identify a body". He was taken to a police station for questioning, and thrown into a bare windowless cell, eight feet by five feet. For more than two months Yeo was held in solitary confinement. He was then moved to a cell next to the Reverend George Shea, an Anglican chaplain with whom started to pray and sing hymns. Eventually he was released to work at the Bacteriological Institute, although shadowed wherever he went. With his family he was baptised into the Church of England.

Kok Cheang Yeo was born at Penang, Malaysia, on April 1 1903, the eldest of a Chinese rubber plantation worker's nine children. One of his youthful memories was of borrowing his father's bicycle, which was so large that he fell off into a waterway where a crocodile crept towards him as he lay in the mud. The experience taught him the importance of not borrowing people's property without permission.

Young Kok Cheang was an excellent gymnast and weight-lifter; for some years, he claimed, he held the world record for sit-ups for his body weight. Following school in Penang he did his medical studies at Hong Kong University, then came to Britain to study tropical medicine in Liverpool and public health at Cambridge.

After qualifying with honours in both subjects, Yeo applied to the Colonial Office to become an assistant Medical Officer of Health in Hong Kong. On his arrival in the colony, the local government discovered he had been given a British doctor's contract, which included nine months' leave in Britain with full pay and first-class travel every four years, rather than the fortnight's holiday a year for local staff. But when the Colonial Office realised their mistake, they insisted on sticking to their word, thereby turning Yeo into a staunch Anglophile.

After the war, Yeo was promoted to deputy director of Health Services, when he helped to plan the 1,000-bed Queen Elizabeth Hospital at Kowloon, then was the first Chinese to become director of Medical and Health Services. It was under his directorship that the BCG vaccination against tuberculosis was introduced and malaria was stamped out. He also helped to found a leper colony on Hayling Chao Island.

In addition he was appointed Professor of Social Medicine at Hong Kong University, and became a member of the Legislative Council. In 1956, Yeo was delighted to be appointed CMG before retiring to Britain two years later. For the next 10 years, he practised as a psychiatrist at St Ebba's Hospital at Epsom in Surrey, before settling in Sussex.

K. C. Yeo married, in 1933, Florence, the daughter of the comprador Sir Robert Ho-tung. She survived him with their son and two daughters.

# SOUTH PACIFIC

~

## Dan Leahy

DAN LEAHY, the New Guinea explorer (who died at Mount Hagen on November 24 1991, aged 79), was the last of four brothers whose names are part of that country's history.

When he first journeyed among its Stone Age people in 1933 their existence was unknown to the outside world, but he lived to see them adapt to roads and supermarkets. New Guinea was a territory administered by Australia for the League of Nations, with huge blanks on the map when he arrived. With his brother Mick and the surveyor Charles Marshall, he came upon the hitherto unknown Wahgi, greatest of the Highland valleys, while looking for gold. Jim Taylor, an Assistant District Commissioner, then took charge of an expedition with the two Leahy brothers and 60 carriers: this was the historic Bena Bena–Mount Hagen patrol.

They found a thickly peopled land of agriculturists, whose gardens were laid out neatly in chessboard patterns, with parks and trees and shrubs. The various clans were armed with bows, spears and fine battle-axes of grey or blue stone. For the most part the explorers were met with wonder and awe; some regarded them as people returned from the dead. Taylor walked hand in hand with two youngsters who thought him their dead father. They built a rough airstrip to allow a light aircraft to land. When the pilot, Ian Grabowsky, climbed out, a tall figure in white flying suit and green goggles, the crowd prostrated themselves. Persuaded this was not magic, they grew bolder, and Grabowsky was rather disconcerted to find dozens of hands probing his genitals to find clues to the mystery.

The patrol took seven months. The outward journey had been occasionally tricky, but the return one was dangerous. Crowds had become hostile, shouting insults, drawing bows and raising spears. On two occasions Taylor fired and killed a native. The next year, prospecting near Wabag in the Highlands, the Leahy brothers and their party survived an attack by shooting the enemy leader and wounding others. Then they patched up their assailant's wounds and resumed friendly relations.

Daniel Leahy was born at Toowoomba, Queensland, in 1912, one of nine children of a railway guard of Irish extraction. Four of the sons Pat, Mick, Jim and Dan were to make their names in New Guinea.

After the Japanese invasion in the Second World War, Dan Leahy made journeys on foot to rescue Europeans trapped on the north coast, and led one party of middle-aged nuns over tracks 10,000 feet up. He had to persuade them to forget modesty, and wear shorts or turn their skirts into rompers; when the going was particularly heavy the nuns were pulled up by two natives, while two more shoved from behind.

Leahy stayed on in the Western Highlands after the war, at first working a gold lease, later farming cattle and pigs, growing crops and trading. Of good height and solidly built, he was firm of purpose and straight as a die. He had a renowned temper, which could flare suddenly, but also a good sense of humour. In his last years he was almost blind, and extremely deaf, as a result of wartime privations.

The discoveries in which the Leahys participated were recognised by the Royal Geographic Society in 1936 and the New York Explorers' Club in 1959.

Dan Leahy had three wives, whom he married by tribal custom. When the first died, he took two, one of whom, Mants, survived him. There were 10 children, whom he educated at good schools in Australia.

~

## Sir Len Usher

SIR LEN USHER (who died on August 26 2003, aged 96) was the "eyes and ears" of Buckingham Palace during the constitutional crisis which saw the loyal Fijians abandon the Crown and leave the Commonwealth in the 1980s.

When Lieutenant-Colonel Sitiveni Rabuka entered the Parliament at Suva to declare that he had taken over the country from the recently elected government on May 14 1987, Usher sat down at his computer to write a letter to Sir William Heseltine, the Queen's secretary. Usher had known Her Majesty the Queen since acting as official press officer on her first visit in 1954, and he had also corresponded with Heseltine for

*Usher was not the first strong supporter of the British connection to be exasperated by the Commonwealth.*

some years. As the crisis developed, and the country drifted towards becoming a republic despite the Fijians' strong personal attachment to the Queen, Usher wrote daily, and then weekly, accounts which were dispatched through the mail to Buckingham Palace.

When his book, *Letters from Fiji*, was published in 1992 it contained few surprises, not least because Heseltine's replies were not included. Nevertheless, Usher recorded in matter-of-fact prose how first the newspapers were halted and the radio stations prevented from broadcasting news, and then how a misleading air of calm settled on the streets.

As the Governor-General attempted to resume control by bringing all the parties together, a sense of the ridiculous began to emerge. People started to refer to Rabuka as "Rambo" in private conversation. But the imperial role in the peace between two peoples, which was once hailed as "the Pacific way", had been irredeemably destroyed.

The Indians had been imported to harvest the sugar crop in the 19th century because the Colonial Office wanted to reduce the British subsidy. But the suspension of democratic government in 1987, and the imposition of a regime guaranteeing a Fijian majority over the Indians, meant that the country had become an international pariah.

It earned not only the disapproval of the Australian and New Zealand governments, but also threats to suspend trade links by their countries' trades unions and a calamitous decline in tourism. A visit to London by Fiji's deposed Indian Prime Minister did not aid the country's cause. Some Indians, who had made matters worse by closing their shops, were harassed by hooligans, and the Methodist Church did little to attract international sympathy by halting bus travel on Sunday mornings. In the end, a large number of Indians left the islands.

Usher was not the first strong supporter of the British connection to be exasperated by the Commonwealth. He considered the comments made throughout the crisis by Sir Shridath Ramphal, the Secretary-General, distinctly unhelpful. He was also nagged by Sir Philip Moore's remark that, had he still been the Queen's private secretary at the Commonwealth conference in Vancouver shortly after the coup, Fiji might not have been forced to leave. As he observed the re-emergence of those tribal divisions which had prompted the Fijians to seek British rule in 1874, Usher wryly reflected on those benefits afforded by life under the Crown.

Leonard Gray Usher was born on May 27 1907 at Paeroa, New Zealand, and educated at Auckland Grammar School, before training as a teacher. At 23 he arrived in Fiji to take up the post of an assistant teacher at Levuka School, which was within sight of where the Fijian chiefs voluntarily ceded sovereignty of their islands to Queen Victoria in 1874. During the next seven years he moved to other schools and became a town councillor before achieving the headmastership of the prestigious Queen Victoria College. Although he failed to obtain a post with the elite colonial administrative service in 1943, when Fiji was making limp preparations to resist a possible Japanese invasion, Usher became the first head of a Fijian public relations office and also a founding member of the Fijian Broadcasting Corporation. Fourteen years later, he became editor and publisher of the moribund *Fiji Times*, which he nursed back to a healthy profit.

In time, few major institutions believed they could manage without retaining Usher on their boards. He was Mayor of Suva from 1966 to 1969 and 1975 to 1977. He became chairman of the Suva Stock Exchange and the Fiji Development Bank; deputy chairman of the National Bank of Fiji; and organising director of the Fiji Islands News Association. He even saw a street in Suva named after him.

Usher published a collection of his speeches and writings, *Mainly About Fiji*. The book, which concluded with the ringing assertion that "democracy, clearly, was alive and well in Fiji", came out in 1987 on the very day that the coup took place. He learned of the government's overthrow from Ratu Sir Penaia Ganilau, the Governor-General. Sir Penaia explained that since Colonel Rabuka, third in command of the armed forces, had assumed power and had locked up the Prime Minister, he (the Governor-General) could not attend the launch party for Usher's book.

Disappointed at the turn of events, Usher still hoped that the Fijians might turn to the Crown again. When Paul Keating, the Australian Prime Minister, drew parallels between Australia's aspirations and the Fijian revolution, Usher pointed out the islands' continuing loyalty to the Queen, whose portrait still appeared on the national currency, in a letter to *The Daily Telegraph*.

Although discreet about his relations with the Palace, when his Maltese terrier died, Usher wrote to Heseltine's successor, Sir Robert Fellowes, and received back the sympathy of the Queen who had just lost one of her three "dorgis".

Len Usher was appointed CBE in 1971, a Companion of the Order of Fiji in 1977 and KBE in 1986.

In 1940 he married Mary Gertrude Lockie, with whom he had a son and a daughter. After their divorce he married Jane Hammond Derne, who died in 1984.

~

## Ratu Sir Kamisese Mara

RATU SIR KAMISESE MARA (who died on April 18 2004, aged 83) became President of Fiji in 1995 after earlier serving as a district officer and then the first Prime Minister of the South Seas dominion.

In all these roles he remained committed to ensuring the continuation of amicable relations with Britain, which stretched back to the Fijian request to be enrolled among Queen Victoria's possessions in 1874. The Fijians only reluctantly gave up colonial rule in 1970, after sustained pressure from the United Nations.

Mara cut a formidable figure at Commonwealth prime ministers' conferences, not least because he was six feet six inches tall and wore the *sulu* (knee-length skirt); his statesmanlike qualities were immediately apparent. When the Her Majesty the Queen visited Fiji in 1982, he assured her that the Fijian islanders' "hope and desire" was that their loyalty to the Crown would remain for "all time".

But five years later, when he was out of office, a coup was led by Lieutenant-Colonel Sitiveni Rabuka in protest against the election of a government dominated by Indians. Mara made efforts behind the scenes to restore the political situation. But, after a second coup which ousted a legitimately elected Indian Prime Minister, he realised that Fiji would not be readmitted to the Commonwealth as a republic, because of determined opposition by the government of India.

However, in 1994 Mara became Fiji's second President; and during his term of office he saw his nation readmitted to the Commonwealth family. Throughout his life, Mara never lost his affection for Britain; and the Fijians have been happy to retain the Queen's head on their currency and to see their young men join the British Army.

Kamisese Kapaiwai Tuimacilai Mara was born on May 13 1920 into one of Fiji's four important chiefly families. His father was Ratu Tevita Uluilakeba, Tui Nayau; his mother, Lusiana Qolikoro, was the daughter of a Tongan who was himself descended from a European missionary. Mara exhibited some marked European features.

A Roman Catholic in a population that was 90 per cent Wesleyan, young Kamisese was educated at Sacred Heart College, and then the Central Medical School, in Suva. He was studying medicine at Otago

*Mara with the British minister Anthony Greenwood; Mara hoped Fijians' loyalty to the Crown would remain for "all time".*

University, New Zealand, when the greatest of Fijians, Ratu Sir Lala Sukuna, Tui Lau, decided that Mara was destined to become his successor. In consequence Mara was sent, against his wishes, to Wadham College, Oxford, where he read history and was years later elected an Honorary Fellow.

He gained a Blue for the high-jump, and showed a talent for both fast bowling and straight batting, which had become apparent when he was coached at the Central Medical School by Philip Snow, brother of the novelist C. P. Snow. A leg injury prevented Mara from obtaining a Blue at cricket, but he had played first-class matches for Otago Province, and later became vice-captain of the Fijian team which toured New Zealand in 1954. In the same year he also captained a Suva team which defeated the West Indies – the tourists had not yet found their "land legs". On opening the bowling, Mara had what he described as "a blinding flash of insight", and immediately took himself off; this, he insisted, enabled the Fijians to win. In later life, he liked to play pre-breakfast golf.

Mara was selected for the Colonial Service in 1950, and appointed a district officer. He became a member of the Legislative Council in 1953 and of the Executive Council in 1959, before embarking on a political career; with Ratu Sir Edward Cakobau, he founded the Alliance Party, which was predominantly Fijian in its composition. After a term at the London School of Economics, he became Minister for Natural Resources in 1964 and, the following year, led the Fijian delegation at the London constitutional conference on the colony's future.

When Britain announced its intention of joining the Common Market, relations between Britain and Fiji rapidly became strained. Mara, by now Prime Minister, realised that Britain was not prepared to offer sufficient protection for Fiji's sugar industry, even when he pointed out that France's colonies had received guarantees. So, saying that he wanted to make the break while the two countries were still friends, he pushed through swift constitutional changes which ensured that Fiji received the deeds of independence a year later. However, when the Prince of Wales arrived in Suva in 1970, Mara greeted him with the traditional Fijian salute, clapping as he knelt on one knee.

At his first Commonwealth prime ministers' conference in London, Mara had what was regarded as a singular piece of luck when he obtained the number FIJ1 for his official car. But although all seemed to go well, storm clouds were gathering. In 1977 he was defeated at the polls by a party dominated by Indians. But they could not agree on a prime minister, and he was brought back to power by Governor-General Cakobau, a dynastic rival who, on this occasion, saved Mara's career.

After a further decade as Prime Minister, Mara lost the 1987 election to a coalition headed by a Fijian, Dr Timoci Bavadra, but consisting principally of Mara's Indian opponents. The change of government offended extremist anti-Indian Fijians, and Bavadra and his Cabinet were kidnapped in an Army coup led by Rabuka, a Fijian commoner and Wesleyan lay preacher.

Following the exploration of alternatives by the Governor-General, Ratu Sir Penaia Ganilau, Bavadra agreed to form a bipartisan caretaker government with Mara. But Rabuka was dissatisfied; he led a second coup, and imprisoned Bavadra. These actions hazarded Fiji's future and led to its exit from the Commonwealth, as well as to a severe slump in the tourist industry.

Thirteen years later, in 2000, Mara's presidency ended with a third coup. He was flown to the safety of a Fijian warship in Suva Bay; but the coup leader, George Speight, captured one of Mara's daughters, who was paraded on television in the grounds of Parliament House with a pistol to her head. As a result, a disillusioned Mara agreed to retire to private life, in which he suffered increasing ill health.

Ratu Mara's character was a mixture of the forthright and the diplomatic, the inflexible and the dexterous, the imperious and the tolerant. But with all these went a strong, dignified nature accompanied by a dry, English sense of humour and an ability to forgive his opponents.

In 1951 he married Adi Lala Tuisawau, the Paramount Chief of Rewa. Since he was Paramount Chief of Lau, together they controlled a wide area of Fiji.

Mara received honorary doctorates from Guam, Delhi and Otago Universities, and was also Chancellor of the University of the South Pacific at Suva, a new institution with which he was not enamoured. He was appointed OBE in 1961; KBE in 1969; and GCMG in 1983. In 1973 he became the only Fijian to be sworn of the Privy Council.

His wife survived him with two sons and five daughters; one son predeceased him.

~

# King Taufa'ahau Tupou IV

HIS MAJESTY KING TAUFA'AHAU TUPOU IV OF TONGA (who died on September 10 2006, aged 88) was the benign feudal ruler of the South Pacific kingdom, known since the days of Captain Cook as the Friendly Islands.

The son of Queen Salote, who endeared herself to Londoners when she drove smiling through the rain in an open carriage at the Coronation in 1953, he was the world's only Methodist sovereign and for many years, according to the *Guinness Book of Records*, the heaviest. A jovial man-mountain of energy, he was six feet four inches tall and, at

*King Taufa'ahau: "I'm a bit of a Pooh-Bah, you know, except that I don't cut off any heads".*

his peak, weighed some 35 stone. Although he belonged to a people famous for feasting, he was sometimes troubled by his size. "In his heart", as one of his aides once put it, "His Majesty is a thin man." But cutting down did not come easily. "My doctor's put me on a diet," the King said in 1999. "I'm only allowed to eat three yams a day. But a yam can be six feet long." When the King, who succeeded his mother in 1965, came on visits to London he would sometimes decline the use of his embassy's Mercedes (number plate TON 1), preferring a more commodious Rolls-Royce with "more leg room".

The kingdom of Tonga is a group of some 150 palm-fringed, coral-decked Polynesian islands in the South Pacific about 1,000 miles north-east of New Zealand. Captain Cook first visited Tonga in the 1770s, and until gaining independence in June 1970 they constituted a self-governing British-protected state under the terms of a Treaty of Friendship concluded in 1900.

In a foreword to *The Friendly Islanders* (1967) by Kenneth Bain, the King described how Tongans have trouble with time. While their days of the week are calculated on the 180 degrees meridian, so that the same days are maintained as in Australia and other parts of the eastern hemisphere, the hours of the day are based on 165 degrees west longitude. Instead of Tongan time being 11 hours behind Greenwich Mean Time, it is 13 hours ahead. "All this tends to confuse strangers," the King wrote, "but it is the normal Tongan way of life."

While other South Sea island groups have experienced political turmoil this century, Tonga has remained stable; in 1990 there was widespread consternation in the islands over rumours of a plot to topple the King. And the King, who ruled through his Privy Council and whose family occupied a third of the seats in the Legislative Assembly, realised that the system of Tonga's government appeared archaic. "Some might think that our constitution seems at first sight a trifle unfair," he once conceded. "But you have to remember that when our first King George united the islands in 1845, he was doing so on behalf of the people themselves. He was not grabbing power on behalf of other aristocrats. He was ridding the islands of the despots and the villains and the robber-barons. And he installed a kindly and caring royal line, of which I have the honour to be the latest. My people love me. I love them and care for them. It is as simple as that."

The King was born Crown Prince Tupouto'a Tungi on July 4 1918 at the royal palace in Tonga's capital Nuku'alofa on the sacred island of Tongatapu. He was the eldest son of Queen Salote Tupou III and Prince Uiliami Tupoulahi Tungi, Prime Minister of Tonga from 1923 until his death in 1941.

The Crown Prince belonged to the 43rd generation of direct descendants of Aho'eitu, the first Tui Tonga (supreme ruler) who lived in the 10th century. More distantly, he descended from the sky god Tangeroa. But it was his great-great-great grandfather King George Tupou I who, in the 19th century, gathered the Tongan tribes together and, with the help of Methodist missionaries (who converted him in 1831), founded the kingdom in 1845.

As a small boy Crown Prince Tungi attended Tupou College, where he was influenced by a Methodist missionary minister, Dr A. H. Wood. He then went to Newington College, a Methodist school in New South Wales, where he showed himself a fine sportsman and broke the pole-vault record. After graduating from Sydney University with a law degree, he introduced surfing to Tonga and became a keen diver.

Following the Second World War, during which he leased tracts of his land to the British government for airfield construction, the Crown Prince married, in 1947, the beautiful Princess Mata'aho. Two years later Queen Salote appointed him Prime Minister, and also assigned him the portfolios of foreign affairs, agriculture, education and works. Subsequently, he also served as head of the Justice and Auditing department, Minister of Radio and Telephonic Communications, chairman of the Broadcasting Commission, and chairman of the Copra and Produce Boards, established to oversee the marketing of the country's principal products. "I'm a bit of a Pooh-Bah, you know," said the Crown Prince in 1962, "except that I don't cut off any heads."

He was crowned King on his 49th birthday, July 4 1967, in the royal chapel in Nuku'alofa. The ceremony, the first coronation in Tonga since Queen Salote's in 1918, was part Methodist and part Tongan, with elements derived from the Coronation his mother had attended at Westminster Abbey. He was crowned by the royal chaplain, the Reverend George Harris. The crown was adorned with a carved, six-pointed star cut from the koka tree under which all the old Kanokupolu kings, Taufa'ahau's tribal ancestors, were installed.

Originally, the King had wished to be crowned wearing the traditional *tapa* (tree bark) clothes of his country, but his advisers persuaded him that European dress would be more appropriate. Under his European-style coronation robes he wore a uniform, based on a British general's full-dress uniform, made by Gieves in Savile Row. His Queen wore a dress of cream and gold brocade with a short train, made by the two sisters who ran the Bond Street salon, Madame Raie.

In the days beforehand islanders poured into the capital, bringing pigs of all sizes, crates of chickens, and tons of yams and kava roots for the week-long feasting. The daily menu consisted of around 1,000 pigs and 1,000 chickens, saddles of mutton, barons of beef, turtle steaks, fish, crayfish and crabs, which were all cooked in vast earthenware ovens. The food was served on woven palm stretchers called *polas*, each one 14 feet long and four feet wide and piled nearly three feet deep with food.

As well as the feasting, there was tremendous dancing and music-making. For weeks before, dancers had been rehearsing the *laka laka* (a conga-style dance) to produce a display, in supple body and hand movements, telling the story of the coronation. Nose flautists had been practising the haunting melodies with which they awoke the King and Queen in a dawn serenade on Coronation Day.

At the ceremony, where the Duke of Kent represented the Queen, there was the sacred *taumafa kava*, at which the 33 nobles of Tonga installed their monarch as the 21st T'ui Kanokupolu. For this, a seven-hour ceremony, the King wore a 700-year-old *ta'ovala*, the traditional Tongan grass or tree-bark mat worn around the waist.

Like his mother, the King was a passionate believer in education, and helped to ensure that his people were among the most literate in the South Pacific. He was also a great believer in the use of the abacus to teach mathematics. "I teach my own children on the abacus," he once said. "They enjoy it and are far ahead of their fellow pupils." He himself enjoyed reading Western literature, preferring scientific works to fiction, and was always interested in new technology. He even wrote a textbook of music, which was for many years used in Tongan schools.

He considered the monarch's right to appoint one third of the Legislature as the only certain means of ensuring that the better-educated Tongans got into the government. "The intelligentsia", he said some years after ascending the throne, "are not the best campaigners. We have not had one person with a degree elected. They have all been appointed by me." The King was careful, too, to protect his other rights. In 1969 he was swift to annul the marriage of his daughter, Princess Siulikutapu, to a Tongan commoner, Siosiva (Joshua) Liaivaa. It was, the King declared, unlawful for a member of the royal family to marry without his consent. Shortly afterwards, the Princess married the King's ADC, Major Kalaniuvalu Fotofili.

In his last years the King was seen as increasingly autocratic, and a pro-democracy movement was formed calling for constitutional reform following the collapse of Royal Tongan Airlines and the waning fortunes of Millenium Asset Management, a company set up as a receptacle for money raised from the sale of Tongan passports to Chinese from Hong Kong.

The King had great admiration for Britain and friendship for the Royal Family. After he and Queen Mata'aho made their first trip to London after Queen Salote's death in 1967, they became regular visitors. The Queen, Prince Philip and Princess Anne visited Tonga in March 1970, and in 1981 the King came to Britain for the wedding of the Prince of Wales to Lady Diana Spencer, bringing presents of dumb valets made to his own design and a bedspread worked by Queen Mata'aho.

The King had a daughter and four sons, the eldest of whom, Crown Prince Tupouto'a, succeeded to the throne. He passed out of Sandhurst in 1968 and for a time studied economics at Oxford.

# AUSTRALIA

~

## Sir Henry Bolte

SIR HENRY BOLTE (who died on January 4 1990, aged 81) was Premier of Victoria for a record 17 years and a Knight Grand Cross of the Order of St Michael and St George; but he was better known Down Under as "Billy from the Bush" or "Pud" (short for Pudding).

A politician naturally blessed with the common touch, the bulbous-faced Bolte proved a great populist leader, a species otherwise unknown in the rather superior Liberal Party of Australia. He could dance with a waitress, get himself up in fancy dress, deny himself potatoes when prices were hurting the people; and he could also, in the face of a furious campaign, carry through the last execution of a criminal in Australia.

This was the biggest crisis of Bolte's life. In 1965 Ronald Ryan shot dead a warder while escaping from Pentridge jail, and Bolte, calling it "murder against authority", resolved to hang him. For the previous 16 years, Victorian governments had commuted all death sentences, though Bolte on one occasion did so only after a public outcry. It was widely supposed that this defeat explained his iron determination later. As the furore over Ryan mounted and a mob tried to invade Parliament House, Bolte feared for his own life. He kept a special police guard, restricted his public appearances, and at one stage evacuated his farm. Politically, he knew he had nothing to fear. In later years he summed up public attitudes with brutal realism: "If you want to win an election, have a hanging."

Before Bolte, Victorians had endured 10 governments in 10 years. He had the good luck to come to office in 1955, just as the Labour Party suffered a disastrous split. He brought with him political stability, industrial development and an unerring instinct. "The fewer controls the better," he would say, and "We want the people of Victoria to be little capitalists – home owners."

His most important struggle, which he could not win, was fought against Sir Robert Menzies and other Liberal Prime Minsters, to regain the income-taxing capacity which Canberra ("that dreamland") had stolen from the states. Bolte was hostile to the High Court, and outraged by the nakedly centralist policies of the Prime Minister, John Gorton, whom he helped to destroy.

Of largely German descent, Henry Edward Bolte was born at Ballarat, Victoria, on May 20 1908 and educated at the local grammar school. From the age of 16 he frittered away his youth in the rural backwater of Skipton, as a roustabout in shearing sheds, a draper (failed), and a gold fossiker. He preferred to indulge in sport and amateur theatricals. At the age of 26 he married Edith Elder, the girl next door, and settled on "Kialla", a rundown farm with no water, sewerage or electricity.

Bolte's Army service in the Second World War broadened his horizons, and as Menzies created the new Liberal Party of Australia in 1944 he was drawn to active politics. When no other Liberal would try, he volunteered as a candidate for the state seat of Hampden, which he won at his second attempt in 1947. A year later, "Billy from the Bush" (as a newspaper labelled him) was a minister in the Hollway government. In 1953, with the party in opposition, he was pitchforked into the leadership to replace Trevor Oldham, who was killed when the Comet taking him to the Coronation crashed near Calcutta. Bolte became the fourth leader in 19 months, inheriting 10 followers from a riven party. After a particularly savage election campaign in 1955 he emerged with 34 seats, exactly enough to govern, and in five subsequent general elections he won safe majorities.

Sink or swim, Bolte was never other than himself. Blunt, shrewd, decisive, a rugged, often far-sighted farmer, he saw life in black and white. He could also be dictatorial, intolerant and vengeful, with scant time for minorities. Angered once by striking railwaymen, he growled: "They can march up and down until they're bloody well foot-sore! It's nothing to do with me." His quick wit rarely let him down. When he was a guest at the opening of New South Wales House in 1972, an occasion with overtones of rivalry, Her Majesty the Queen teased him with the question: "Sir Henry, what are you doing here?" "I am the poor relation," Bolte replied.

With the Turf as a ruling passion, he once interrupted a deputation that was earnestly discussing superannuation, to switch on the radio to hear the commentary of a race in which one of his horses was running. On Melbourne Cup Day he always wore a yellow carnation, a buttonhole he had once observed Prince Philip sporting at Epsom.

Business prospered from Bolte's policies, Melbourne sprawled and reached up. His imperative of "Victoria-over-all" found its most controversial expression when he used Parliament to save the airline of his old friend, Sir Reginald Ansett, from takeover by New South Wales interests. He brought in more liberal drinking hours, set up legal off-course betting, relaxed trading regulations, took a hard line on law and order and maintained censorship of literature. Bolte had no coherent philosophy of social justice. He allowed public transport to run down, and he was not squeamish about his ministers acting as company directors.

He was appointed KCMG in 1966 and GCMG in 1972, when he chose to retire undefeated, knowing that his day had passed.

His wife, Dame Edith ("Jill") Bolte, a pillar of the Girl Guide movement and the Red Cross in Victoria, died in 1986.

---

# R. M. Williams

R. M. WILLIAMS (who died on November 4 1992, aged 84) founded the eponymous clothing company which became a worldwide purveyor of "Outback Chic"; its products included everything from sturdy, elastic-sided leather boots, saddles and whips, to moleskin trousers and flannel shirts. The success of the enterprise, which spawned stores across Australia as well as in London and New York, turned Williams, a former ranch hand and gold panner, into a multi-millionaire. Having established the business in a shed at Adelaide in 1934, he sold it to Bennett & Fisher 53 years later for $14 million.

Reginald Murray Williams was born on May 24 1908 at Belalie North, 125 miles north of Adelaide. His father worked and trained horses in the bush, and the family had no running water or electricity. But when R. M. was 10, they moved to Adelaide. Education did not inspire him, however, and aged 15 he packed his swag and left home, working first as a lime burner and then as a stockman on cattle ranches. By the age of 18, he was a camel driver for a missionary. For three years, the two men trekked across thousands of square miles of desert, living with Aborigines, who taught them how to survive in the bush. At one camp, a bushman instructed Williams in how to plait, using a single strand of kangaroo leather.

After a period selling dingo hides, Williams then returned to Adelaide, where he married Thelma Mitchell. The couple decided to live in the Flinders Ranges, where they ground their own wheat and dined off rabbits and kangaroos. It is said that one day a horseman called "Dollar Mick" stopped by, and taught Williams how to make leather bridles, pack saddles and boots.

Then, in 1932, their second child contracted an eye disease, and to pay for his treatment Williams took some of his leatherwork to Sir Sidney

*Williams's business was saved when gold was found in a mine he had bought from an elderly woman.*

Kidman, who owned a large number of cattle stations. Kidman bought some of his saddles and, with the money from these commissions, Williams bought leather and equipment and set up a small factory in his father's shed in Adelaide. It was the beginning of R. M. Williams Country Outfitters.

The business prospered; but, as orders flooded in, Williams borrowed money to expand and was soon deep in debt. His saviour turned out to be an elderly woman who owned a gold mine in the Northern Territory which she could no longer work alone. When she offered to sell it to Williams, he succeeded in raising the money, and eventually struck gold. Nobles Nob, as the mine was called, became one of the richest small gold mines in Australia. It turned Williams into a multimillionaire, and guaranteed the survival and expansion of his clothing business.

But, despite the large house in Adelaide, the parties and the polo matches, his marriage collapsed, leaving him yearning for the simple life of the bush. Accordingly, he decamped to a property called Rockbar in Queensland; and remarried to have a further three children to add to the six he had had with his first wife. Meanwhile, the hand-made goods bearing his name and longhorn cattle logo were selling around the world.

In the New Year's Honours list for 1985 R. M. Williams was appointed CMG for services to the Outback community. He was appointed AO in 1992.

## Sir Sidney Nolan

SIR SIDNEY NOLAN (who died in London on November 28 1992, aged 75) did more than anyone to invigorate Australian painting and put his country on the artistic map in the 20th century.

*Nolan felt suspended between two continents.* (Sidney Nolan Trust)

Conveying the heat, light and space of the vast continent in works of startling power and beauty, he was best known for his series of paintings based on Australian historical and legendary figures. These included the bushranger Ned Kelly, who became a folk hero for his defiance of the police; the explorers Burke and Wills; and the ship-wrecked Mrs Fraser, who lived with the Aborigines, was rescued by an escaped convict and then betrayed him. Of all Nolan's symbols, the most celebrated is the helmet in which he portrayed the outlaw Kelly: a heavy black box with a wide slit for the eyes. In one painting, Kelly sits on his horse like a centaur, dominating a flat, enigmatic landscape while nothing but the clouds above can be seen through the slit.

At first Nolan received little local recognition, but in the late 1940s he was described by Kenneth Clark, the British critic, as "the first artist to give us the real flavour of that strange continent. He has extracted its essences: the red desert, the dead animals, the stranded, ridiculous towns." Nolan recalled that Clark told him that he could either stay and paint all the birds and animals of Australia, or he could come to England "and I'll help you do an exhibition. But you have to realise," Clark added, "that if you leave Australia perhaps you'll never go back." "So now," Nolan reflected in an interview with *The Daily Telegraph* shortly before his death, "I'm suspended between the two."

After he settled in Britain in the 1950s, success came quickly, and within a decade he had pictures in the Tate Gallery and in the Royal Collection. Subsequently, however, he felt that the critics had turned against him.

His paintings on the theme of Oedipus in 1975 caused particular controversy. In *Notes for Oedipus (XXIV)*, for example, the detached head of a blinded African, wearing white spectacles, lolls nonchalantly in front of a large Sphinx, with an elongated neck, shaped like a stone phallus. On the horizon, an ominous pyramid probes the vastness of a blue-and-rose sky while the lone, level sands in the middle distance are dominated by an inquisitive cockerel whose comic crest is painted with all Nolan's familiar verve.

These paintings shocked even Nolan's most ardent supporters. Terence Mullaly, *The Daily Telegraph*'s art critic who had earlier described *Leda and the Swan* (1960) as "among the greatest things produced in recent years", called them "an unmitigated disaster ... with no redeeming qualities". At the private view, Kenneth Clark (now Lord Clark) inquired plaintively: "But what do they all mean, Sidney?"

A tram driver's son of Irish descent, Sidney Robert Nolan was born in Melbourne on April 22 1917. He left school at 14, and educated himself at night school and by voracious reading at the public library. Enjoying bicycle racing and athletics, he worked in a hamburger joint, a pie shop and on an asparagus farm. Then, while painting posters for a hat factory, he started night classes at the National Gallery School, Melbourne.

In 1937, Nolan stowed away in a ship for Europe, but was discovered and returned ignominiously in the pilot boat. The next year he became a foundation member of the Contemporary Art Society, and contributed to its early exhibitions. In 1940 John Reed, a

Melbourne solicitor interested in contemporary art, staged Nolan's first one-man show. It revealed interest in collage, Rimbaud and the derangement of figuration. Similar themes were discernible in his designs for Serge Lifar's ballet *Icare*, which sprang from his fascination with children's art.

When it became clear after he was called up that he was to be sent to the front in New Guinea, Nolan decided to opt for art rather than the Army. He deserted, and lived under an alias. Obtaining a dishonourable discharge after the war ended, he joined the publishers Reed & Harris, where he illustrated poetry and fiction and provided editorial assistance for *Angry Penguins* and *Angry Penguins Broadsheet.*

In 1946, he travelled throughout north-eastern Victoria, visiting places associated with Ned Kelly, whom he had talked about with his policeman grandfather. Nolan's arresting mixture of sunlight and colonial legend reached its zenith in the paintings inspired by a visit to Fraser Island, Queensland. These, together with the Outback and Interior series completed in the late 1940s, marked the final stages of his development as an Australian landscape painter.

In 1949, Nolan exhibited his Kelly paintings at UNESCO in Paris, and the next year showed his Central Australian work at the Redfern Gallery in London. He then visited France, Spain, Portugal and Italy, and exhibited some Mediterranean studies on his return to Australia in 1951. The next year the Brisbane *Courier Mail* commissioned him to draw Central Australia during a severe drought; the resulting depictions of animal cadavers in arid spaces achieved new heights of severity. He also helped John Heyer on the film *Back of Beyond*, which won the Grand Prix at the Venice Film Festival, and exhibited at the Venice Biennale.

Nolan's later work included the Gallipoli series (1957–8); *The Riverbend* (1960), which, with its opalescent light slanting down through a tall eucalyptus on a shimmering, purple-brown snake of water, he regarded as "a vision of heaven"; the African paintings (1962); and depictions of Shakespeare's sonnets (1967). Based in England, he travelled to Africa, Antarctica, America and China in search of new ideas. In his eighth decade he took up sculpture again.

Nolan had an enormous output, and worked quickly, often listening as he painted to the same slow movements of the late Beethoven quartets 30 or 40 times a day. His last years were clouded by a feud with his former friend, Patrick White, the Australian Nobel Prize-winning novelist. In 1983, White declared that Nolan would "bite the dust. He already has as far as his talent goes." He thought Nolan had fallen in love and remarried too soon after the suicide of his second wife, Cynthia. Accusing Nolan of "flinging himself on another woman's breast when the ashes were scarcely cold", he wrote darkly of "the chase after recognition by one who did not need it, the cameras, the public birthdays, the political hanky-panky …" Nolan retaliated with *Nightmare*, which showed White standing by the hindquarters of a dog, whose head resembled a former lover. There were also drawings of White in that part of Hell where Dante had placed sodomites.

This distasteful quarrel was unworthy of both of them, and Nolan later regretted that he had expended so much time and energy on it. He was certainly not a man given to savage gestures. Normally quietly spoken, patient and obliging, he increasingly appeared in dress and manner the country gentleman. At his Jacobean house in Hereford-shire, The Rodd, his third wife, Mary, kept a herd of prize-winning Welsh Black cattle and organised art exhibitions and music recitals in the old barn.

But he continued to visit Australia for exhibitions and to refresh himself with the Outback and the brilliant, bleaching southern light. "I find it wonderful," he said. "I watch anything on television to do with Australia. I even watch *Neighbours* to hear the magpies. I still feel Australian … I'd like to spend my last minutes there." Latterly he had been working on the sets for the Victoria State Opera's staging of Wagner's Ring cycle.

While his reputation rose in Australia, thanks, particularly, to a major retrospective at Melbourne during the Australian bicentenary celebrations, it dipped in Britain, where there were repeated complaints about over-production, technical mannerisms and the populist subject matter.

However, this was only a temporary reversal. Renewed enthusiasm was sparked in Britain by a 75th birthday show at Harewood House's Terrace Gallery in Yorkshire, and a roomful of his work in the Tate proved a revelation for a modern audience, largely unaware of the continuing relevance and extraordinary originality of his artistic gifts. Much of the ambivalence towards Nolan came from a constant misunderstanding of his artistic intentions. These centred on his profound belief in the value of 20th-century European culture and his equally strong feelings for the historical experience of Australia.

Better than any painter of his generation, Nolan saw that, paradoxically, the only way the Australian story could be told was by a total immersion in the most advanced and sophisticated aspects of European culture. From a deep study of literature, philosophy, music and art he moved unpredictably towards a decade of confrontation with the Australian Outback and Interior before embarking from England, on the final, lengthy process of fusing these two traditions.

It was never an easy balancing act to sustain. His art took on an autobiographical quality, powerfully mirroring the intellectual and emotional events of a life lived at full pitch right up to the end. His images linger in the memory with an almost physical presence which eludes both time and geography. As he once explained, he wanted Australian art to be filled with a naturalness, comparable to the relationship between the Aboriginals and the land.

"Somewhere in our painting," he wrote, "their fundamental simplicity is going to tell. Perhaps that, and the pure mornings here with the big grey trees and green parrots flying up from burnt grass, will help us to break through to something clean and brittle that will belong."

Sidney Nolan was appointed CBE in 1963 and knighted in 1981; he received the Order of Merit in 1983, was appointed a Companion of the Order of Australia in 1988 and elected a Royal Academician in 1991.

He married first, in 1939, Elizabeth Patterson; after a divorce he married, in 1948, Cynthia Reed, the novelist and sister of John Reed; following her death in 1974 his third wife was Mary Perceval, who had been married to the artist John Perceval and who was sister of the artist Arthur Boyd.

## Oodgeroo Noonuccal

OODGEROO NOONUCCAL (who died in Brisbane on September 16 1993, aged 72) did much through her writing and campaigning to make white Australians acknowledge the injustices perpetrated on the Aboriginal people. A teacher, painter, actress and environmentalist, she was the first Aboriginal poet to be published in English.

She was known as Kath Walker, from the time of her marriage in 1942 to Bruce Walker, a Brisbane docker of Aboriginal descent with whom she had two sons. But she renounced both her name and her MBE to show her revulsion at the 1988 celebration of the bicentenary of white settlement, which represented "200 years of sheer, unadulterated humiliation". Instead she became Oodgeroo, which means "paper-bark tree", and took the name of her tribe, the Noonuccal, who were attached to the land of Minjerribah (now known as Stradbroke Island, near Brisbane).

Once, after an Aboriginal burial ground had been desecrated by developers, she removed bones from a display in a nearby shop, telling the angry shopkeeper, "They are my ancestors' bones." After police inquiries and protests by an anthropologist, she asked: "Tell me, why is that they love our

*Oodgeroo Noonuccal successfully campaigned for a referendum on whether Aborigines should be given the vote and be counted in censuses, but was left penniless afterwards.*

bones, but they hate our living bodies? It has always perplexed me, that question."

Fiercely resisting the assimilation of Aborigines into the white community, which at one point was official Australian policy, she wrote in *Assimilation No*: "We would be one with you, one people, / We must surrender now much that we love / The old freedoms for new musts ..."

She was born Kathleen Jean Mary Ruska on November 3 1920 to Aboriginal parents at Stradbroke. Her father, the foreman of a gang of council workers, passed on the knowledge of their tribe and its totem, Kabool, the carpet-snake. With the sea and the bush at hand, she learned to fish and catch crabs, and to understand the small fauna of her island.

At 13 she left school to work as a domestic. When the Second World War broke out she joined the Australian Women's Army Service, despite being warned that she might encounter racism in the armed forces: she said that a racist in uniform and a racist in civilian clothes were all the same to her.

While in the Army she caught an infection, leading to a permanent hearing handicap and later to the loss of all her teeth. After discharge she briefly joined the Communist Party, since they were "the only ones that didn't have the White Australia policy". In the rum town of Bundaberg she led a demonstration which persuaded a shopkeeper to take down a sign declaring "We serve whites only" and to sell a shirt to an Aborigine. Later she was to stand unsuccessfully for the Queensland Parliament as a Labour candidate and later as a Democrat.

When her poems *We Are Going* were published in 1964 they proved a phenomenal success. Oodgeroo herself described some of the work as propaganda. In *Son of Mine*, she denounces: 'heartbreak, hatred blind ... / crimes that shame mankind". Yet she could also write such lines as: "Pour your pitcher of wine into the wide river / And where is your wine? There is only the river."

Her later works included *The Dawn is at Hand* (1966), *My People* (1970), *Stradbroke Dreamtime* (1972), *Quandamooka: The Art of Kath Walker* (1985) and *Kath Walker in China* (1988).

In 1967 she crossed Australia to win support for a constitutional referendum on whether Aborigines should be given the vote and be counted in censuses. By the time the referendum was passed (with a 93 per cent "yes" vote), she was exhausted and penniless. Two years later, the World Council of Churches asked her to be a delegate to their London conference on racism.

One of her dreams was to educate white children in the ways of Aboriginal culture and concerns. Many thousands of people visited her at her *moongalba*, or "sitting down place", on Stradbroke.

~

## Sir James Darling

SIR JAMES DARLING (who died on November 1 1995, aged 96) was Headmaster of Geelong Grammar School, Victoria, and the founder of Timbertop, the unorthodox educational institution attended by the Prince of Wales.

Jim Darling was an enemy of philistinism and materialism, and an ally of intellectual heterodoxy. In 31 years at Geelong, he turned out a string of dazzling pupils who went on to lead Australia in politics, the arts, the law and industry. A socialist in his youth, he determined that Geelong boys, who included the sons of Australia's wealthiest families, should atone for their privileged status by developing a social conscience. He counted Sir John Gorton, the Prime Minister, and Sir Rupert Hamer, Premier of Victoria, among his successes. But he feared he might have to answer on the Day of Judgment for Rupert Murdoch and Kerry Packer.

In 1930, Darling arrived at Geelong from England to find a school full of lazy, bored boys who worshipped sport and skived their studies. Run as a boarding school on English lines, it seemed exotic and rather snobbish to Australians. From his earliest days, the gaunt, hawk-like figure of "The Boss" (or, as detractors preferred to call him, "The Beast") embarked on all-encompassing changes. He gave full status to literature, art, music, carpentry and mechanics. Lewis Casson and Sybil Thorndike visited the newly formed Shakespeare Society. The historian Manning Clark was allowed free rein for his progressive ideas.

*Darling was known as "the Boss", and sometimes "the Beast", to his pupils at Geelong Grammar School.* (Tyler, Little)

When Darling began, the school had only 330 pupils; when he left there were 1,250. During his headmastership his socialism finally evaporated, but not his Christianity, his liberalism or his sense of high moral purpose. In the Depression, he pushed his pupils into working for schemes to help unemployed people and distressed families.

By his retirement from the school in 1961 Darling was one of the most respected figures in Australia. As a member of the Australian Broadcasting Control Board in 1954, he had helped to draw up standards for commercial television broadcasting, and to hear applications for the first Australian licences. Seven years later he put aside the chance of a new career in the Church or Parliament to serve six hard years as chairman of the Australian Broadcasting Commission, where he found himself under severe political pressure.

Prime Minister Robert Menzies, whom Darling counted a friend, tried to interfere with ABC's political and fiscal independence, and sometimes succeeded. After Menzies's retirement, the government of Harold Holt decided not to appoint Darling for a third term, and inexcusably made a public announcement to this effect before it had officially notified him. Darling was deeply disillusioned. He had once believed that television might be an instrument of democracy; now he discovered that he had been dropped from ABC because some programmes opposed government policy.

James Ralph Darling was born at Tonbridge, Kent, on June 18 1899. His father ran a prep school; his Scottish mother fostered a devotion to public service.

Young Jim won a scholarship to Repton, where he edited *The Reptonian* and was president of the debating society. Both his headmasters later became Archbishops of Canterbury; he blossomed under William Temple, the Christian Socialist, but withered under Geoffrey Fisher. In Darling's final year, Victor Gollancz, the future publisher, arrived as a teacher. Only 23, Gollancz horrified his elders with his liberal ideas, but made a lasting mark.

Darling had barely left the classroom when he was commissioned into the Royal Field Artillery, in which he served in France towards the end of the First World War. He found the experience of warfare bruising, but toughening. He counted himself fortunate to have survived, and resolved to live life at the double in memory of those who had died.

Going up to Oriel College, Oxford, his contemporaries in the Union included Anthony Eden, Leslie Hore-Belisha and Malcolm Macdonald. Among the debating society's visitors were the former Prime Minister, H. H. Asquith, and Winston Churchill, though, as an active member of the Labour Party, Darling thoroughly disapproved of the latter. His literary interests made him a friend of Hilaire Belloc, G. K. Chesterton, Robert Graves and Siegfried Sassoon, and he recalled seeing W. B. Yeats with flowing hair and cloak in the High.

Darling decided that the world could be saved by education, and after Oxford threw himself into schoolmastering. He shunned schools for the rich, and spent three years at Merchant Taylors', near Liverpool. Offered George Mallory's post at Charterhouse after he had been killed on Mount Everest, Darling overcame his scruples and went to teach under Frank Fletcher, then considered the best headmaster in England. He was inclined to believe that Charterhouse was smug, devoid of social conscience and isolated from the world. But the school authorities scarcely blinked when Darling became a Labour member of Godalming Borough Council and chairman of the local party. When he left after just five years to take up the headmastership of Geelong, he was given membership of the Old Carthusian Society.

In 1952 Darling started Timbertop, a branch of Geelong 160 miles distant in the bush, at which boys could learn independence and acquire a sense of responsibility not possible in the main school. In 1966, five years after Darling's retirement, Prince Charles attended Timbertop.

In his later years Darling was chairman of the Australian Road Safety Council, a member of the Immigration Advisory Council, president of the Elizabethan Theatre Trust and chairman of the Australian Frontier Commission. He was also founding secretary, and later chairman, of the Australian Headmasters' Conference; and founding president of the Australian College of Education.

For 14 years, until his 95th birthday, he wrote a regular weekly article on social topics for the Melbourne *Age*. His books included *The Education of a Civilized Man* (1962); *Richly Rewarding* (1978); and *Reflections for the Age* (1991).

At the heart of Darling's success was the belief that though most children do not want to learn, they can be lured into liking it, or driven to put up with it. He held that those who advocated the freedom of their pupils to decide for themselves or preached the equality of teacher and pupil, were abrogating their responsibilities. To control a class, Darling recommended the deployment of humour and a quick tongue, but warned against a thirst for absolute justice. Lessons should be carefully prepared, but the teacher should not be tied to the preparation. To forestall boredom, there should be things for a class to do as well as to listen to. Above all, Darling counselled, never shout: if things do get out of hand, lower the voice, and the little dears will nearly always quieten down to hear you. Then the teacher should try to say something devastating.

Jim Darling was appointed OBE in 1953 and CMG in 1958. He was knighted in 1968. In 1935 he married Margaret Dunlop Campbell. He was 36, and she only 20, but she had such dignity and sense that it never occurred to him that she faced a difficult role. They had a son and three daughters.

## Dudley Magnus

DUDLEY MAGNUS (who died in Winnipeg on July 31 1997, aged 86) proved the truth of the journalistic adage about every reporter having a novel in him when his autobiographical tale of the Australian Depression found a publisher more than 40 years after he wrote it.

*Magnus had lived abroad so long that he asked: "Don't people still dress for dinner?"*

*Hanabeke*, which achieved remarkable success Down Under on its publication in 1983, is a crisp thriller about a young Englishman who comes to Australia to look for a missing heir. He promptly loses his money in a brothel and ends up "on the track" as a bagman, one of the amateur sheep station-hands who swarmed the Outback in search of work during the 1930s. The novel lacks a dramatic climax, but it gives a vivid impression of playing in a crooked game of two-up, jumping on a moving cattle train and living by the strict bagman's code. When Magnus returned to Australia after some 50 years, he irritated several communities by recalling how rough their towns had been, and sometimes still were. But he attracted the attention of historians and philologists at a time when many were producing memoirs of the Depression, by offering a long work that had been written when the memory was fresh in the mind.

Dudley St John Magnus was born at Richmond, Surrey, on May 27 1911, into a family with better connections than finances. His father, a clerk at Coutts Bank, was sent out to Madeira for his health, only to return home and be killed in the First World War.

When young Dudley came home by boat in 1918, he was so shaken at being parted from his black nanny that he refused to speak English. A cure was effected by a fellow passenger who began to address him in

English, then said to his mother: "Oh, I'm sorry, I forgot. He's a little Portuguese boy." "I'm not a Portuguese boy, I'm not a Portuguese boy," came the immediate protest, "I'm an English boy"

While his mother took on a boarding house and then a hotel in Torquay, Magnus was sent to Christ's Hospital at Horsham, Sussex, where he displayed a journalistic eye for opportunity when he found himself alone with the visiting Prince of Wales. He asked him for an autograph, a serious breach of etiquette. The Prince hastily looked around to see that no one was watching, before signing "Edward P" in the proffered book.

With the help of a family friend, the 1st Lord Glendyne, Magnus was then enrolled in the Big Brother Movement, which helped young men to emigrate to Australia. Landing at Melbourne in 1927, he was told that the only difference from home was that the weather was hot and the beer cold. For the next two years he worked on a variety of farms in Victoria and New South Wales, until thrown out of work by the Great Depression. Without a word to his sponsors he set off in search of adventure and casual work. Powerfully built and wearing a light tweed jacket and a trilby, he learned to "hump his bluey" (trek) up to northern New South Wales, with his "swag" (bedding) packed like a swiss roll on his back and his "tucker" (food) bag suspended over his shoulder. An old cake tin, used for making damper, was slung behind.

As a "baggie", one rung down from both the professional "sundowner", who only did part-time jobs on stations, and the "swaggie", who did any jobs going, he worked on a railway construction contract, once spent three days in prison for trespassing, and collected the five shillings a week dole authorised by Jack Lang, the Premier of New South Wales. Eventually he saw a notice in a police station asking him to get in touch, and found that his mother had sent him the return fare to England.

While helping at the hotel, Magnus had some difficulty in adjusting to English life. His habit of drinking heavily, then hailing a taxi with the words "I'm as drunk as a dingo, mate, where's the next pub?" was not always well received. He peddled vacuum cleaners, sold advertising space and wrote copy for book jackets.

By the late 1930s, he had married the wealthy Bunty Gordon-Dickson, with whom he had a son. Although it would have been strongly frowned upon if known, he sold advertising space for *The Times*, and also wrote features on related topics for Anthony Hurd, the paper's agriculture editor and a future MP who was a friend of Magnus's brother-in-law and the father of Douglas Hurd, the Tory minister under Margaret Thatcher and John Major.

Magnus joined the ranks of the Honourable Artillery Company in 1938, and was commissioned into the Royal Ulster Rifles after war broke out. In 1941 he whiled away six months as adjutant at the regimental depot at Ballymena by writing *Hanabeke*. No British publisher was interested, though years later he discovered that Kylie Tennant's *The Battlers*, about nomads in New South Wales, had won great acclaim in Australia in the same year.

Two years later Magnus was sent out to India, where he was seconded to run a gossip column in the Bombay *Evening News*, then was briefly under fire in Burma before the war ended.

After coming home to find that his marriage was over, Magnus became a magazine writer with the Allied Control Commission in Germany, and became friendly with Lale Anderson, singer of the German desert campaign favourite "Lili Marlene". Conscious of cutting a dash in evening dress with the eyeglass he sported at the time, he was glad to have the blonde vocalist on his arm. She was receiving threats of reprisals when the Nazis returned to power, and once suggested that Magnus, only eight years her junior, might marry her. In the end he married her daughter Carmen-Litta, who had been looking after his small son.

After living for a while in Switzerland, Magnus headed for Canada, where he and Carmen-Litta had a son and three daughters. An uncle found him a job as an axeman, and then a clerk, with a logging company in northern Manitoba. When he tired of this, he presented to the editor of the *Winnipeg Tribune* a letter of recommendation from the bestselling novelist Nicholas Monsarrat (who had once been engaged to Magnus's first wife). Fortunately, six of the paper's reporters had just resigned.

For the next 24 years on the *Tribune* and then the *Free Press*, he earned a reputation as Canada's most respected labour correspondent. While never an elegant writer, he was accurate, thorough and able to impress trade unionists with his experiences of the Depression. He never disguised his Tory leanings, which led him to advise the Manitoba Progressive Conservative Party on the province's labour code and also to file monthly reports to the American Department of Labour, which was concerned about a supposed threat to the nuclear early warning system.

On retiring to England after two more divorces, he made a fourth match to a cousin, Meg Holcroft, and settled at Witham, Essex, where he met Jack Lindsay, the Australian writer, at a meeting of the local poetry society. He showed his manuscript to Lindsay, who was so impressed that he wrote an enthusiastic letter to the publishers Angus & Robertson, who published it as the book's foreword.

By the time of its publication, Magnus had moved back to Canada, partly because of his dollar pension, where he lived in a mobile home in southern Ontario and wrote *Uneasy Lies the Word* (1982), a study of the English texts of the King James, Revised Standard and New English Bibles, which did not stint on criticism. He spent his last years toying with his memoirs and writing occasional letters about swagmen and Red Indians to *The Daily Telegraph*.

Dudley Magnus had spent so long abroad that he never completely settled in England. But like others born at the apogee of the Empire, he retained sunlit memories which no subsequent experience could extinguish. On being introduced to a journalist from Britain in the late 1960s, he asked: "Don't people still dress for dinner?"

~

## The Right Reverend Howell Witt

THE RIGHT REVEREND HOWELL WITT (who died on July 8 1998, aged 77) began life as the son of a Welsh docker, and became one of the most colourful figures in the Anglican Church in Australia.

He took up the post of Bishop of North West Australia in 1965, with some reservations. "When the good Lord made me," said Witt, "he made me a clown. And, a clown, he called to the priesthood. But to the episcopate? That surely was another matter." The North West see, which covers 720,000 square miles, or nearly a quarter of the Australian continent, was the largest diocese by land area in the Anglican communion. In consequence, Witt spent seven months of the year travelling, while his wife and children remained at the Bishop's Palace, formerly a boarding house, at Geraldton, 250 miles north of Perth.

The bishop not only learned to fly an aircraft; he became expert in such arts as sheep-dipping, catching crayfish and rounding up wild goats. In the absence of proper church buildings he would improvise places of worship in dance halls, railway sidings and shearing sheds. He liked to recall the occasion when he was visited in the back of beyond by Prince

*Witt once opened a fete dressed as "Deborah, Dowager Duchess of Dingo Creek", complete with hooped skirt, tiara and false bosom.*

Philip, who found himself reading the lesson from the witness box of the local police court. For Witt, the long hours of travel afforded the best time for his devotions; as he put it, he prayed in transit rather than in transept, bellowing Anglican hymns and passages from *The Book of Common Prayer* into the passing wilderness.

He remembered arriving in the port of Dampier, then under construction, and officiating in a mess where the all-male congregation was drawn from 65 nationalities. They thrust foward to shake his hand; clasped him to their bosoms and kissed both cheeks; knelt at his feet and kissed his ring. "I don't think that they're all Anglican," the local priest whispered.

Howell Arthur John Witt was born on July 12 1920 near the docks at Newport, Monmouthshire, where his grandfather as well as his father had worked. His father, a Methodist, was a man of saintly character; his mother taught in Sunday School. Early in life Howell Witt felt himself called to the ministry. This never prevented him, however, from developing his comic streak and indulging his flair for the stage. And though he used to describe himself as a midget, he was big enough to play rugby for London Welsh.

He took a degree at Leeds University, and then prepared for Holy Orders at the College of Resurrection, Mirfield. He was ordained in 1944 and served as a curate first at Usk and then at Camberwell, south London. In 1949 he married Doreen Edwards, with whom he had three sons and two daughters, and became Anglican chaplain at the Woomera rocket range in the deserts of South Australia.

This afforded Witt an introduction to the arts of improvisation. He conducted his first Sunday service at Woomera in a spare room used by the barber. Having lost his luggage, he called for a bottle of port and a slice of bread and made do with a pewter beer mug as a chalice, and a cheese dish as paten. A sheet served as altar cloth and blankets as kneelers.

Later he was to open the Woomera fete dressed as Deborah, Dowager Duchess of Dingo Creek, complete with hooped skirt, tiara and false bosom. That was only after a drama involving two camels, their Aboriginal minders and much dashing about the desert in costume. The Dowager Duchess also opened a fete at St Peter's College, the leading boys' school in Adelaide.

In 1954 Witt went to St Mary Magdalene in Adelaide, but, after three years, volunteered for the post of priest in charge of Elizabeth, a new satellite town largely peopled by British migrants, where social work seemed to make more immediate claims than spiritual care. Witt complained that he spent more time standing up to hire purchase companies than on his knees. He remembered answering a call from a woman who said she was about to put her head in a gas oven. It was not until he was halfway to her house that he remembered that Elizabeth was an all-electric town.

Witt put his church, St Theodore's, to a multitude of uses, as youth club, theatre, pensioners' club and gymnasium. His energy seemed inexhaustible. He built two churches; coached a junior rugby side; scripted and took part in programmes for the South Australian Christian Television Association; acted with the Adelaide repertory theatre; and wrote columns for two newspapers. When he became a bishop he took with him a firm idea of the parish as the centre of the Church's operations, and saw his main episcopal duty as simply sharing in parish life.

Witt's reminiscences, *Bush Bishop* (1979), reflect his dynamic and popular preaching style. In 1981 he left the North West diocese to become Bishop of Bathurst, in New South Wales; and although badly hurt in an accident, he stayed in this post until 1989. When he died he was listening to his favourite hymn, *Cwm Rhondda*.

~

# The Earl of Lincoln

THE 18TH EARL OF LINCOLN (who died on July 7 2001, aged 88) was enjoying a comfortable retirement in Western Australia in 1989, after a career as a manual worker, when *The Daily Telegraph* diarist Peterborough telephoned to congratulate him on succeeding to the 16th-century earldom.

*Lord Lincoln wielding the broadsword of his ancestor, the 1st Earl, at Lincoln.*

"Lord Lincoln," began Peterborough, "if I may be the first to address you so ..." During the ensuing conversation, Ted Fiennes-Clinton said that he had known about the possibility of the title but had rather forgotten about it while earning a living and bringing up a family. When Peterborough remarked that he did not seem very excited, the new Earl shot back: "Young man, I have lived for 75 years and I have learned to take things as they come."

His lordship was glad to receive Peterborough's offer to help him to establish his title but was disappointed to hear that there were no rolling acres to inherit. The 10th and last Duke of Newcastle, from whom he had inherited the earldom, was a bachelor lepidopterist who lived in a terraced house at Axminster, Devon.

This made no difference to the Australian press which recognised a real-life fairy tale (that would soon be fictionalised in the popular soap opera *Neighbours*). The gentle routine of the retirement flats at Elanora Villas, Bunbury, soon underwent sharp change. Three camera crews appeared on the Lincolns' lawn and a posse of reporters arrived, one by helicopter. When, however, an Australian journalist was refused an interview for a London paper, she made up a story which Lincoln roundly denounced as "a farrago of spiteful and petty nonsense". Lincoln spurned a British tabloid's offer to finance a trip to England, and a couple of months later he paid out of his own pocket for a visit with his wife.

The new Earl and Countess were feted by the city of Lincoln and made warmly welcome by old friends in the West Country, with whom they had stayed during the Queen's Silver Jubilee in 1977. Lincoln also visited the College of Arms in London, where he managed to lodge a small sum with a herald in order to launch formally his generally accepted claim to the title, which was expected to cost about £8,000.

When the couple arrived in Docklands for lunch with Peterborough and his staff, Lord Lincoln apologised for wearing a cardigan; he had left his jacket in Perth by mistake. His countess, a former waitress at the Savoy in that city, whom he addressed affectionately as "Mum", confided to Peterborough's secretary, Maureen O'Leary: "We're really working class."

But although the Earl was lame, he had an upright bearing and a natural charm and dignity which told of his noble ancestry. He liked shooting, fencing and fishing as a young man, preferred whisky to beer and planned to sit in the House of Lords as a Tory. "I thought of going into politics in Australia, but decided I was too honest," he explained. After lunch and a briefing on the working of the House of Lords from Lord Deedes, the *Telegraph*'s former editor, Lord Lincoln emerged from the office at South Quay to discover the taxi waiting for him had run its bumper up on to the top of a low wall. As the driver revved up, the practical Earl put a broad shoulder to the back of the vehicle and pushed it free.

Edward Horace Fiennes-Clinton was born in Melbourne on February 23 1913. His claim to the Earldom of Lincoln, which was created in 1572 for Queen Elizabeth I's first Lord High Admiral, was through a cadet line of modest barristers, Army officers and clergymen descended from the third son of the 2nd Earl. The Earldom became a subsidiary title of the Dukes of Newcastle when the 9th Earl inherited the Dukedom by special remainder from an uncle in the 18th century.

Young Ted's father, a mate in the merchant navy, had emigrated from England to Australia in 1912. But he was killed in France with the Australian Army during the First World War, leaving a wife and three-year-old son with few advantages. The boy went to Hale School, Perth, where he proved able with his hands, and was apprenticed to a blacksmith in the local railway workshops. At 21, he received his father's estate of £646, the equivalent of two years' wages, and took a series of jobs as a boilermaker, welder's assistant and butcher. He then became a "bogger", a machine-minder's assistant who had to shovel broken ore into underground trucks at a gold mine in Kalgoorlie.

Despite his qualifications as a dinkie-di digger, Fiennes-Clinton retained sufficient traces of his origins to win the gruff attentions of a Slav miner at a dance. "My wife says you're a gentleman," said the Slav. "I try to be polite," replied Fiennes-Clinton. "If my wife says you're a gentleman, then you are," persisted the Slav. "She's been in service with some of the best families in Europe, and she knows a gentleman when she sees one."

Shortly after marrying in 1940 Leila Millen, a nurse whom he had met through their mutual interest in fencing, Fiennes-Clinton left the mines to join the RAAF, but was turned down because he was needed more as a skilled worker. Instead he helped to build swivels and chains for a boom at Fremantle, then returned to the mines where he was involved in platelaying, timbering, pipe-fitting and underground maintenance. When a badly injured man had to be brought up from 600 feet below ground, Fiennes-Clinton's steady handling of the crisis led to the offer of the job of first aid and safety officer.

The flexible working hours involved proved a boon after his wife died in 1947, leaving him to bring up their six-year old daughter and three-year old son. Seven years later Fiennes-Clinton married Linda O'Brien, a widow, and moved to Bunbury to work first as a welder. He tried selling water filters, then took a job with the local public works department.

After returning from his trip to England to claim the title, Lord Lincoln set to work on his *Memoirs of an Embryo Earl* (1992). This 74-page autobiography, which he published himself, was wrought with little literary skill; but it explained his belief in the dignity of manual work and described his life in the neighbourly but self-reliant atmosphere of Western Australia.

His grandson, Robert Edward Fiennes-Clinton (born 1972) has not established his legal right but is the accepted claimant to the peerage.

~

## Bill Wentworth

BILL WENTWORTH (who died in Sydney on June 15 2003, aged 95) was an Australian MP with a brain that teemed with endless schemes, all meant for his country's good; but he was never a man for half-

*Wentworth named his cockatoo "D'Arcy" after an ancestor accused of highway robbery and murder.* (Sydney Morning Herald)

measures or for guarding his tongue, and these characteristics told against him.

In his long public career, which included almost 30 years as a Liberal member of the House of Representatives, Wentworth seemed to affectionate colleagues to be an eccentric genius; to others a crank. His passionate anti-communism made him a special target of the left. During the Cold War, it was one of the sights of the Federal Parliament to see him in action on the government backbenches, a stumpy red-faced figure outrageously denouncing opposition members while they yelled "Liar" and "Fascist". Once, a Labour frontbencher left the chamber, donned a long white coat and, returning through another door, gravely tapped Wentworth on the shoulder in mid-speech, as if summoning him back to the asylum.

Wentworth was an irrepressible know-all with firm opinions about everything and an enormous capacity for both detail and action. He was saved by an underlying geniality. His humour ran to naming his white, sulphur-crested cockatoo "D'Arcy", after the able young rogue who founded the family fortunes.

Charged with highway robbery and murder in London, D'Arcy Wentworth reached New South Wales with the second fleet in 1790 as a free man, and made a notable career and great wealth there;

possibly he escaped the law in England through the influence of the 4th Earl Fitzwilliam, a distant family connection. D'Arcy's eldest son by the convict Catherine Crowley was Bill Wentworth's great-grandfather, an explorer and statesman.

William Charles Wentworth, the fourth member of the family to bear these names, was born in Sydney on September 8 1907, and educated at the Armidale School. He went on to New College, Oxford, where he read Greats and won a Blue for athletics.

In 1929 he was returning to Britain from a tour of America with an Oxford–Cambridge athletics team when he met Montagu Norman, Governor of the Bank of England, who was sailing under the alias "Mr Skinner". The Governor forecast (according to Wentworth) that the world would experience a bit of a shakeout, which would be a little unpleasant for perhaps six months, then know an unexampled prosperity. Three months later came the Wall Street Crash; Wentworth never trusted central bankers again.

The Depression also aroused his sense of social justice, and Wentworth, who had private means, was to the right in foreign affairs but left-leaning on economics and social policy. From 1933 to 1937 he was economic adviser to the New South Wales Treasury.

His service with the Australian Army in the Second World War was notable for one incident. In order to demonstrate that the country's eastern seaboard was vulnerable to Japanese invasion in 1942, Captain Wentworth led 70 soldiers in a simulated landing at Cronulla, a seaside suburb of Sydney. They penetrated the beach barriers; seized vehicles; stopped all train movements; threw the local army, police and fire brigade into confusion; made off with Bren-gun carriers; and captured the unit headquarters. They then carried out a token demolition of Sydney's main munitions depot. The Army's counter-attack was to transfer Captain Wentworth to the reserve.

In 1949, Wentworth entered Parliament. But he enjoyed poor relations with the Prime Minister, Robert Menzies, whom he once told to his face that the best service he could render Australia might be to "leave politics". Without any hope of preferment, Wentworth embarked instead on the project that was to become his monument. This was Australia's standard-gauge rail system, which eventually replaced the three different gauges adopted by the separate colonies before federation. He published his plan in 1949, but it was not until 1962 that the first single-gauge train departed from Sydney for Melbourne.

Wentworth was unable to attend this ground-breaking event, being detained on political business in Canberra. But his wife Barbara was so outraged by this that she paraded up and down the platform at Sydney station in front of Menzies with a placard bearing the legend: "Where's Wentworth?"

It was not until his friend John Gorton became Prime Minister that Wentworth was rewarded with office, in 1968 taking on the ministries of social services and Aboriginal affairs, and holding both posts for four years. He chafed to find how little scope he had under Gorton, but warned in 1969 that one Aboriginal dialect was being lost on average every month, and took enormous pride in establishing the Institute for Aboriginal Studies.

Eventually, in 1977, Wentworth resigned from Parliament and from the Liberal Party, complaining that its economic policies relied too much on the free market. He twice more contested elections as an independent, the last time at the age of 87. When he was nearly 90 he was struck by a car, bouncing off the windscreen; but he recovered well.

Wentworth was appointed AO in 1993, and was the author of *Demand for Defence* (1939) and *Time and the Bomb* (1954).

In 1935 he married Barbara Baird, of Sydney, at Reno, Nevada. Together they wore out generations of vehicles exploring the Outback and observing Aboriginal culture. They celebrated her 82nd birthday aloft in a hot-air balloon, drinking champagne, but soon afterwards he was crestfallen at having to be rescued while rock-climbing.

Bill Wentworth was survived by his wife and their four children, among whom he planned to divide his estate regardless of their sex. This was intended to break Wentworth tradition of property descending in the male line.

~

# Queen Susan of the Albanians

QUEEN SUSAN OF THE ALBANIANS (who died in Tirana on July 17 2004, aged 63) was the level-headed Australian wife of King Leka I, claimant to the Albanian throne.

It is unusual, though not unknown, for middle-class girls to marry into the fading respectability of dispossessed monarchs. But when the petite Susan Cullen-Ward married Leka, son of King Zog I in 1975, she became consort to a six feet nine inches tall, six-gun-toting giant who has never shaken off the aura of his country's bandit culture.

*Queen Susan would call herself Mrs Smith or Mrs Jones because shop assistants were so bamboozled by her title that they would ask "Queen? That's a funny name, Mrs Susan".* (Sydney Morning Herald)

Leka was born at Tirana just before the Second World War and left with his family two days later, when Mussolini invaded Albania. After his father's death in 1961, he was crowned in Paris, from which he was expelled because of the ill-effects he was having on French relations with Albania's Communist regime; he was once arrested on suspicion of arms smuggling in Thailand. In the course of his restless travels, he met Susan Cullen-Ward at a dinner party in Sydney.

They discovered that they both had claims of royal lineage; she was descended from King Edward I and he was a ninth cousin once removed of Queen Elizabeth II. When later she was on holiday in London, a courtier suggested that she visit the King in Madrid. Leka's mother, Queen Geraldine, realised that the couple's friendship was turning into love, and proceeded to groom the Australian girl as her royal successor. This involved teaching her to speak Albanian and steeping her in the history and customs of the country.

Leka and Susan were married in a civil ceremony at Biarritz, then held a reception at a five-star Toledo roadhouse, which was attended by members of other exiled royal families, loyal Albanians and Spanish friends. An Anglican clergyman flew from Australia to give the couple a blessing. Queen Elizabeth II sent a telegram of congratulations. Queen Susan looked suitably regal in a 200-year-old gold embroidered Royal Albanian shawl and the guests cried "Long Live the King". At the reception she told he press: "I don't feel like a queen. I feel a happy bride. Nothing has changed except I have the responsibility of helping His Majesty back on to the throne of his country."

A grazier's daughter, Susan Cullen-Ward was born at Waverley, a suburb of Sydney, on January 28 1941. She was brought up on a New South Wales sheep station, where she remembered practising to curtsey to Her Majesty the Queen before a royal visit, and also being taken with the achievements of Colonel Harry Llewellyn and his showjumper Foxhunter, which won a gold medal at the 1952 Olympics. Young Sue went to the Presbyterian Ladies' College at Orange, then Sydney Technical College, before teaching art at a private studio and contracting a brief marriage.

After their marriage, Leka and Susan returned to Madrid, where they were befriended by King Juan Carlos and continued to enjoy the attentions of Albanians, while awaiting what they knew must be the fall of Communism. But when it was discovered that Leka not only retained some Thai bodyguards but had what was claimed to be an arms cache in their home, the Spanish government asked him to leave.

That Leka had some reason for his fears was proved when he arrived at Gabon to find his plane surrounded by local troops, who were said to have been hired to capture him by the Albanian Communist government; he saw them off by appearing at the plane's door with a bazooka in his hand. The couple went on to Rhodesia. But after Robert Mugabe took power they settled in a large compound at Johannesburg, where they were given diplomatic status by the apartheid regime. There were always questions about how Leka lived. Such good friends as the Shah of Persia, President Richard Nixon (a distant cousin) and the CIA are thought to have helped.

The royal couple enjoyed a close personal relationship. They both had a keen liking for smoking. He affectionately called her "Roo", and showed some signs of allowing her to check a few of his more outlandish instincts. For over a decade she tried to lead as ordinary a life as her roles of housewife, mother and queen permitted.

Out shopping, she often called herself Mrs Smith or Mrs Jones because shop assistants were so bamboozled by her title that they would ask "Queen? That's a funny name, Mrs Susan." When her son, also called Leka, was born, her hospital room was declared part of Albania for an hour. The boy used another name at school, though she once heard him tell a friend: "You can't say that to me, because I'm a prince." Entering the room, she said: "Well, I am queen, so I outrank you. Bend over." But as Communism looked increasingly shaky in Eastern Europe, she felt lonely with Leka so frequently away; and she was always delighted to receive visits from old Australian friends, replete with gossip.

Her relationship with the dominion's government proved a problem when she wanted a passport. The Australian authorities declined to recognise her as a queen, and eventually, after a friend had a word with the Foreign Minister, Andrew Peacock, the document described her as "Susan Cullen-Ward, known as Queen Susan". There was also trouble when her son, aged four, wanted to visit a dying grandfather whom he had never met. He was asked to sign an undertaking not to address any dissident groups.

By the time it was clear that Leka's dream of returning to his country had a chance of being fulfilled, Susan showed signs of preferring the simple life, saying she had no desire to live in a castle, and she was sometimes tempted to laugh when grown men, in their confusion, curtseyed to her. But she duly went to Albania where a referendum was held on his offer to become king in 1997; it was lost. Nevertheless Leka was invited to return by 74 members of parliament in 2002; and it was thought for a time that the royalist party could have joined a government after a general election, thanks to proportional representation.

Following her death, Queen Sue lay in state at the royal palace outside Tirana. Hundreds paid their last respects before she was buried in a grave next to her mother-in-law and bridge partner, Queen Geraldine.

~

# Michael Thwaites

MICHAEL THWAITES (who died on November 1 2005, aged 90) was the poet responsible for masterminding the defection of Vladimir Petrov, a Soviet intelligence officer in Australia during the Cold War.

As head of counter-espionage in the Australian Security Intelligence Organisation (ASIO) he had been hired in 1950 to bring a more

*Thwaites's* Anzac Graves at Gallipoli *is read at the dawn service on Lone Pine overlooking Suvla Bay every Anzac Day.*

"intellectual approach" to spy hunting after the Venona decrypts of Soviet intelligence messages by the British and Americans had revealed Communist activity in Canberra. A Polish doctor and part-time ASIO agent was already a drinking companion of the Soviet Union's secret service *resident*, whose wife was the cipher clerk. The Petrovs had been sent to Canberra by the Soviet security chief Laventri Beria. But after Stalin's death and Beria's summary execution in 1953, Petrov feared that he too would be purged if he returned home.

While ASIO wondered uneasily whether the defection could be a KGB plot, Thwaites masterminded the coup. During six weeks' negotiations largely carried out in King's Cross, Sydney's red-light district, Petrov was offered £5,000 and asylum in exchange for documents. When he defected without telling his wife, Soviet agents tried to take her back to Russia by force until she was removed from a plane at Darwin in front of a noisy crowd.

Ten days later, Robert Menzies, the Liberal Prime Minister, announced a royal commission to investigate evidence of Soviet espionage, which Petrov had turned over to Thwaites. The matter became an issue during the bitter federal election in which the Labour leader, H. V. Evatt, alleged a right-wing conspiracy, and Menzies ruthlessly exploited the situation. Nothing was said at the time about the Venona findings which were added to the material supplied by Petrov, who also revealed that the missing diplomats Guy Burgess and Donald Maclean were in Moscow. The conspiracy claims and dismissals of Petrov's value rumbled on until much of the royal commission's evidence was declassified in 1984 to show that the defection and the election were coincidental.

Thwaites dealt with the subject in two books. One was *Empire of Fear* (1956), the Petrovs' life stories, which he ghost-wrote while staying with them in safe houses during the royal commission hearings. The other was his own account *Truth Will Out* (1980), which explained much more without being permitted to mention Venona. In it he declared that the agents exposed, including one in Evatt's private office, were "true believers" in Communism, and that Petrov's defection had led to the unmasking of 600 Soviet spies worldwide.

Michael Rayner Thwaites was born in Brisbane on May 30 1915. A love of poetry was kindled by his father reading him Kipling at the age of eight, and his facility with verse was encouraged at Geelong Grammar by the headmaster, Sir James Darling. He recalled being beaten by Darling for throwing a ball into a window, and thinking between each stroke what "a wonderful mind" the head had.

Young Michael helped to translate the *Aeneid* for a pageant around the school's lagoon for the bi-millennium of Virgil's birth, and also took part in a performance of Thomas Hardy's *The Dynasts*. He went on to Trinity College, Melbourne, and then to New College, Oxford, as a Rhodes Scholar. There he was tutored by Lord David Cecil, and won the Newdigate Prize for his blank verse poem *Milton Blind*.

After the outbreak of war, Thwaites married Honor Scott-Good, and joined the RNVR, with which he was to serve on Atlantic convoys. On returning to Belfast from one patrol, he was astonished to receive a gold-embossed letter from John Masefield, the Poet Laureate, declaring that he had won the King's Medal for Poetry; the young poet had never heard of it. When he arrived back from another patrol, his wife urged him to write about the armed merchant cruiser *Jervis Bay*, which had been sunk attacking the pocket battleship *Admiral Scheer* to protect a convoy.

He managed to see the official record, then sent his first draft to Masefield, who made some amendments which Thwaites decided to ignore. The result is a vigorous patriotic ballad of a kind currently out of fashion. The little ship, under Captain Fogarty Fegen (who was awarded a posthumous VC), is likened to a sheepdog attacking a wolf, with inevitable consequences when the battleship fires back: "A flash, and she staggers, as through her egg-shell plates / Tear the eleven-inch projectiles, malevolent as the Fates." The Admiralty censors insisted on one change, to a disparaging remark about workshy dockyard mateys, and the piece was included in Thwaites's first book, *The Jervis Bay and Other Poems* (1943); it has been much anthologised ever since.

In another work included, he reflected young people's haunting knowledge that they were being called to repeat the experience of their fathers' generation, "Who died without the hero's throb, / And if they trembled, hid it, / Who did not fancy much their job / But thought it best, and did it."

Thwaites was first lieutenant of the converted trawler *Wastwater* and then captain of the sloop *Guillemot*. More than 50 years later he wrote a memoir, *Atlantic Odyssey*, in which he vividly evoked life at sea.

After the war Thwaites returned to Oxford to complete his BLitt, then became a lecturer in English at Melbourne University for three years before being recruited into ASIO, when he did not even know what the abbreviation MI6 meant. After retiring in 1971, he joined the parliamentary library in Canberra.

His poetry in later years reflected Australia's growing sense of national identity. *Anzac Graves at Gallipoli* is read at the dawn service on Lone Pine, overlooking Suvla Bay, every Anzac Day, and *For Australia*, which he wrote with his wife to be set to a Purcell tune, formed part of the nation's bicentennial celebrations in 1998. The collection *Unfinished Journey* (2004) also included meditations on Mozart's clarinet concerto, his short-lived baby son and a witty *Equal Rights for Emus*, which urged: 'Come down from that crest! It's Australia Day, emu – / We just want to say, mate, how much we esteem you."

Thwaites underwent a religious experience in Belfast during the war, which led him to become a life-long activist in Moral Rearmament and later a regular worshipper at St John's Cathedral, Canberra. After his wife's death in 1993, he liked to walk with friends in Remembrance Park, which she had helped to create on Mount Ainslie in Canberra.

Michael Thwaites, who was appointed AO in 2002, was survived by three sons and a daughter, the pianist Penelope Thwaites, with whom he used to give recitals.

# New Zealand

~

### Sir Robert Muldoon

SIR ROBERT MULDOON (who died on August 5 1992, aged 70) dominated the political life of New Zealand with a combination of hard-hitting realism and engaging lack of inhibitions during almost a decade as Prime Minister.

*Muldoon said his relationship with Mrs Thatcher was simple: " 'Rob,' she will say, 'what can I do to help?' And it will be done."*
(PA)

Burly, square-jawed and pugnacious, "Piggy" Muldoon might have been mistaken for a boxer, but he was an accountant by profession with a remarkable capacity for saying what others were thinking but were too polite to say. Militant trade unionists, in his view, were "traitors and saboteurs"; President Carter was "only a peanut farmer"; Idi Amin "a homicidal maniac". When another African leader incurred his wrath, Muldoon prescribed the use of a good taxidermist.

He never hesitated to translate words into action. On being hit by a flour bomb during the 1975 election campaign he broke away from his police escort and ran towards the demonstrators, fists flailing. One youth fell to the ground. Muldoon, his clothes and face spattered with flour, shouted: "One at a time, and you're all welcome." The campaign concluded with an overwhelming victory over Labour for the revitalised National Party. "This is a tough world," he said. "You win or lose, and you don't win by smiling gently but by getting stuck into it."

On becoming Prime Minister Muldoon kept the finance portfolio for himself. But, while dedicated to lifting his country out of economic muddle and high inflation, he soon found himself in the thick of international controversy over New Zealand's sporting links with South Africa. At a dinner held at London's Savoy Hotel in 1977, he had a blazing row with Malcolm Fraser, the Australian Prime Minister (whom he found to be "some distance short of Moses, or Abraham Lincoln"); he defended his own policy on sporting contacts by attacking Australia's race record.

To the rugby- and cricket-loving New Zealanders, South Africa was an important part of the sporting world. Although Muldoon had helped to draft the declaration against sporting contacts at the Gleneagles Hotel in Perthshire, he also believed that it was up to New Zealand sporting bodies to make the final decision whether they wanted to play South Africa. Later, in 1989, he wrote a letter to *The Daily Telegraph* to advocate that the "Gleneagles Agreement" be rewritten or scrapped.

In 1981 his policy was put to riotous test when the Springbok rugby team toured New Zealand. Thousands took to the streets to protest. Muldoon, in London for the wedding of the Prince of Wales, declared that, although he abhorred the regimes of both South Africa and the Soviet Union, he would not stop New Zealanders from playing sportsmen from either country. He refused to order the tour to be called off, despite threats that New Zealand might be banned from the 1982 Commonwealth Games. Unrepentant, he attended the Commonwealth heads of government meeting in Melbourne, and let it be known that he carried a full dossier of human rights violations by African members that he would be happy to produce.

Instead of being seen to bow to pressure, Muldoon returned home on this occasion as the man who would not let his country be unfairly criticised or condemned. His National Party was returned to power for another three years later in 1981, although with a slim majority.

In 1982, with Britain immersed in the Falklands conflict, Muldoon offered the services of a New Zealand frigate to take over patrol duties in the Indian Ocean, thereby freeing a British warship to take part in the campaign. Thereafter his friendship with Margaret Thatcher blossomed; and in 1983, when Muldoon addressed the British Institute of Directors, he declared: "My relationship with Mrs Thatcher is simple. 'Rob,' she will say, 'what can I do to help?' And it will be done."

At that conference Muldoon spoke at length on the possibility of a collapse in the world banking system, a subject that had increasingly begun to attract his attention as high interest rates made it more and more difficult for Third World countries, in particular, to repay their debts. (In 1978 Muldoon had been elected for a 12-month term as chairman of the World Bank and of the International Monetary Fund.)

Robert David Muldoon was born in Auckland on September 25 1921, the grandson of an Irish Methodist missionary who had emigrated to New Zealand from Liverpool. When young Rob was five, he gashed his cheek in a fall. This left him with what friends described as a dimple and enemies a scar. He was brought up by his widowed mother in straitened circumstances which conferred on him a burning ambition. At Auckland's Mount Albert Grammar School he was credited with an IQ in the "genius" class; but shortage of cash obliged him to leave school at the age of 15 and begin work with the Electric Power Board.

During the Second World War he served in the infantry in New Caledonia, and took part in the advance to Trieste, becoming a company sergeant-major. Afterwards he took an Army bursary to study cost accounting in London. He won the Leverhulme Prize for first place in the final paper; he was the first person residing outside Britain to achieve this distinction.

Back in New Zealand, he joined the National Party, seeking a seat in two elections before arriving in Parliament as member for Tamaki in 1960. Three years later he was appointed Parliamentary Under-Secretary to the Minister of Finance, and then studied the American taxation system with a State Department foreign leaders' grant. In 1967 Muldoon smoothly carried out the changeover to decimal currency, before becoming Finance Minister. He visited London and Washington and attended the Commonwealth finance ministers' meeting in Trinidad as well as those of the International Monetary Fund and World Bank.

Muldoon's hardest year in the New Zealand Parliament was 1970, when his Budget introducing payroll tax earned Labour execration, but it enabled him to become Deputy Prime Minister two years later. Then

Labour was elected to power. On becoming his party's leader in 1974, he prepared for the coming election by taking "Meet the People" meetings around the country, in which he put up charts to show Labour's economic mismanagement which had led the inflation rate to double. He also demonstrated his mastery of the electronic media by conducting a weekly talk-back programme on television.

Labour's majority was reversed and the National Party duly returned to power. Its first moves were to cut back on immigration and government spending. But when the party retained office in 1978 many New Zealanders, including some cabinet members, were losing faith in Muldoon's approach. On returning from an extended tour abroad two years later, he found himself confronted by a party revolt, with the numbers clearly against him. He agreed that there should be a vote on his continued leadership but asked for it to deferred for a week. He then launched a public "Save Muldoon" campaign that produced a flood of messages in support. The "palace revolt" collapsed without a vote, though his position grew ever more precarious.

In 1984, while visiting Washington, he learned that one National MP had withdrawn from the party caucus; and, on the night of June 14, he called a general election because, he said, his administration had lost its majority in Parliament. That was debatable, according to many commentators, and there was a general feeling that he had seized on the opportunity to hold an election four-and-a-half months early. The first snap election to be held in New Zealand since 1951, it showed that Muldoon had seriously misjudged the mood of the electorate.

Labour obtained a comfortable majority under David Lange after a campaign in which Muldoon's handling of the economy was the dominant issue. Four months later, in November 1984, he was replaced by Jim McLay as party leader, and retired to the backbenches. But his views on the world economy were recognised by Lange, who offered to help Muldoon to project his ideas and warnings overseas. Muldoon refused.

In 1987 he was returned for Tamaki again, but the National Party lost the contest. When it returned to office in 1990, he had been critically ill with a heart condition and declined a ministerial post. He announced his retirement in 1991.

In 1977 Muldoon had broken with tradition by publishing his political memoirs when he had been Prime Minister for only two years. This autobiography, *Muldoon*, was a sequel to *The Rise and Fall of a*

*Young Turk* (1974). He also published *My Way* (1981), *The New Zealand Economy: A Personal View* (1985) and *No 38* (1986).

He was president of the New Zealand Institute of Cost Accountants, a governor of the International Monetary Fund and of the Asian Development Bank. He was sworn of the Privy Council in 1976, appointed CH in 1977 and GCMG in 1984.

Although "Rob" Muldoon was celebrated for his swashbuckling, bruising style, there was a side to him which few had the opportunity to see. Addressing a London press conference in 1983 about his worries for the world banking system, he was asked by one journalist, clearly out of his depth, exactly what he was talking about. Instead of dismissing his questioner out of hand, Muldoon asked him to see him after the conference. The journalist was then given a simple 45-minute private guide to his thinking on the world banking system, even though it meant that an official luncheon was long delayed.

Muldoon acquired an early interest in gardening when he helped his mother to grow vegetables during the Depression. A fellow of the Royal Horticultural Society, he had a large collection of lilium species and hybrids.

He married, in 1951, Thea Flyger, a builder's daughter, with whom he had a son and two daughters.

---

## Maurice Shadbolt

MAURICE SHADBOLT, the New Zealand writer (who died on October 10 2004, aged 72) made his name in London as a short-story writer, then evolved into an internationally admired author of historical novels about the 19th-century Maori wars.

His first work, *The New Zealanders* (1959), was a collection of short stories which impressed the poet Stevie Smith in *The Daily Telegraph* with its evocation of the New Zealand scenery and careful delineation of characters, such as the immigrant who cannot forget "dear Ealing Common". Her enthusiasm was echoed by both Alan Sillitoe and Muriel Spark, though the book's dark shades disturbed a New Zealand society still basking in the assurance of living in a sunlit corner of the Empire.

*Fires and Winter Country* (1963) was another admired collection of tales about young New Zealanders. Gradually, however, Shadbolt revealed an autobiographical strain. His first novel, *Among the Cinders*

*Shadbolt in Moscow, where he shed his last delusions about Communism.*

(1965), was an account of a "mixed-up teenager" which touched on the uneasy relationship between Maoris and whites. This, in turn, led him to evolve a distinctive way of treating past and present in *The Lovelock Version* (1980), a rollicking tale of the Otago gold rush in the 19th century, though it probably suffered from the author having an editor on the other side of the world in London.

From this Shadbolt progressed to his historical trilogy about the Maori wars, *The Season of the Jew* (1986), *Monday's Warriors* (1990) and *The House of Strife* (1993). Many of his countrymen regarded these as the finest examples of the genre produced by a New Zealander, though it had less appeal in Britain. But, in a review of the first for the *New York Times*, Conor Cruise O'Brien was impressed with its portrait of the Maori leader who rejects Queen Victoria but clings to the Old Testament, praising the tautness and astringency of a work which was both winsome and gory.

Maurice Francis Richard Shadbolt was born on June 4 1932 at Auckland, New Zealand, the great-grandson of a farm labourer transported to Van Diemen's Land in 1826 for robbing a drapery shop at Datchworth, Hertfordshire. After completing his sentence the convict went to Canterbury, New Zealand, where he became an upright citizen. Young Maurice used the story for his first piece of fiction, written when he was a 14-year-old pupil at Te Kuiti High School.

He went to Auckland University College, where he failed every exam and became involved in left-wing student politics, taking over the Labour Club and renaming it the Socialist Club. Various jobs followed, including road builder, proof reader for the *New Zealand Herald* and journalist on local newspapers before he became a scriptwriter for the New Zealand National Film Unit; one of his productions, about a dolphin washed up on the shore, later provided the plot of his novel *The Summer's Dolphin*.

In 1957, Shadbolt set out for Britain, travelling via Peking to Moscow, where his last delusions about Communism were shed and he met Len Wincott, leader of the Invergordon naval mutiny of 1931. On going on to Bulgaria, he was asked if E. M. Forster was still writing; when Shadbolt said that he was, his questioner commented with a sigh: "He is no Bulgarian." Arriving in London, Shadbolt settled in a basement flat close to Oscar Wilde's house at Tite Street, Chelsea, and wrote *The New Zealanders*. He posted it to Gollancz, which sent him an advance of £75.

After returning to New Zealand Shadbolt added to his reputation with *The Presence of Music* (1967), about the place of the artist in society, and *An Ear of the Dragon* (1971), a sprawling, overlong New Zealand "Forsyte Saga", which was followed by *A Touch of Clay* (1974), about an ex-lawyer potter's relationship with a drug-addled young woman. The intense *Danger Zone* (1976) drew on his experience aboard a sloop, protesting against the French hydrogen bomb explosions in the Pacific, though he turned back when it reached Tahiti, to attend his dying father at home. Shadbolt's later fiction included his *Selected Stories*, which showed how his view of life had become less bleak with age. He also wrote two volumes of autobiography, which contained strands of fantasy, including a venomous portrait of the writer Frank Sargeson.

These did not add to his popularity with New Zealand critics, who complained that his career as a successful freelance writer for *Reader's Digest* and the *National Geographic* encouraged a weakness for purple prose. His factual works included the *Shell Guide to New Zealand* (1968) and *New Zealand: Gift of the Sea* (1971) as well as *Voices of Gallipoli* (1988), based on a series of interviews with First World War veterans; his film scripts included an adaptation of his play *Once on Chunuk Bair* (1982) about Turkey in 1915.

Yet, despite the carping, he won the Katherine Mansfield Memorial Award in 1963, 1967 and 1995, and was appointed CBE in 1988.

Maurice Shadbolt was married four times and had five children.

~

## Sir Roy McKenzie

SIR ROY MCKENZIE (who died on September 1 2007, aged 84) gave away more than $100 million as New Zealand's most modest philanthropist, and was an intrepid sportsman in several fields.

Preferring to be known as a "community volunteer", he added numerous charitable trusts to one which had been formed in the late 1930s with the wealth from a family chain of department stores. But he differed from his father in not only putting up money for deserving causes but personally taking a close interest in their progress, writing handwritten letters of encouragement. Using a specially created investment company, he arranged for educational scholarships, aid for the deaf and backward children as well as the foundation of Outward Bound in the dominion. McKenzie also helped to start its first hospice after seeing the work of Dame Cicely Saunders in London.

*Sir Roy's 300-foot fall on Mount Ruapehu, in which he broke an arm, a leg and two fingers, is now commemorated on the map as McKenzie's Mistake.*

As the cracks in New Zealand's social security system became increasingly apparent he found himself approached personally for help. If he considered a cause worthwhile, he could pull out his personal chequebook, as he did when he was asked to fund a women's refuge and handed over $15,000 rather than the $1,500 for which he had been asked.

McKenzie was remarkable for maintaining both his charitable activity and the family businesses without mishap or unduly upsetting politicians, though he criticised the health service for allowing too many people to die unnecessarily.

As well as encouraging harness racing and climbing, he led the New Zealand ski team to the Oslo Olympics in 1952, though he broke his wrist in a practice run. He did more than sponsor the sport; he once lost control of his skis for 300 feet when coming down Mount Ruapehu, on North Island, and broke an arm, a leg and two fingers. The incident is now commemorated on the map as McKenzie's Mistake.

The son of Sir John McKenzie, an Australian who served with the Victoria Bushmen's Regiment in the Boer War before founding the McKenzie department stores in New Zealand, Roy Allan McKenzie was born on November 7 1922. When his father wanted a name for a new range of underwear he chose Roydon, after Roy and his brother Don, and later used it for one of his numerous trusts.

The boys were educated at Timaru Boys' High School, where Roy played wing with the first XV and excelled at tennis and long jump. He started to study accountancy at Otago University then joined the Army on the outbreak of war. However, after Don was killed while training to be a pilot with the RNZAF, Roy followed him into the Air Force. After breaking an arm playing rugby he trained to be a bomb aimer in Canada, where he once found himself suddenly called upon to play the Warsaw Concerto on the piano. Shortly before D-Day he was posted to No. 103 Squadron, RAF, with which he dropped "Window" strips of aluminium to divert the Germans on D-Day.

Qualifying as an accountant after the war, McKenzie returned to Europe, and climbed the Matterhorn before doing a training course at Marks & Spencer's head office in London; he then worked behind the counter at Reading. On the boat from New Zealand he had met Shirley Howard, whom he married in 1949; they adopted two boys and a girl.

Back in Wellington McKenzie settled into the family firm, where he was first a buyer's assistant and then concentrated on the expansion of the branches. He soon had his interest in charity fired by joining Rotary and then the family investment trust.

He continued to play tennis and to enjoy harness racing. When, at 65, he was prevented from participating in the latter, he continued as a breeder, writing a book on the subject and making several visits to see his horses race in America. After giving up climbing he enjoyed mountain walking in New Zealand, Australia and Nepal.

Roy McKenzie was appointed KBE in 1989 and ONZ in 1995.

## Sir Edmund Hillary

SIR EDMUND HILLARY (who died on January 11 2008, aged 88) made his name as the first conqueror of Everest with the Sherpa Tenzing Norgay; though just as impressive was the use he made of his renown during the remainder of his life.

*Hillary (left) and Sherpa Tenzing Norgay (right), with the expedition leader Colonel John Hunt in Kathmandu after the conquest of Everest in 1953. (PA)*

There were feats of exploration in the Antarctic from 1956 to 1958, and in other parts of the Everest region during the early 1960s (including a search for the Abominable Snowman, or yeti). In 1968 he drove jetboats up the violent rapids of Nepalese rivers; in 1977 he took them up the Ganges.

Hillary developed a deep admiration for the Sherpa people, and through the Himalayan Trust, which he established in the 1960s, oversaw the building of 25 schools, two hospitals and a dozen medical clinics as well as bridges and airfields. This work led to his appointment as New Zealand's High Commissioner in India, Nepal and Bangladesh, a position he held from 1985 to 1988.

When he first visited the Himalayas they were still very remote. Two years earlier the Chinese had closed the traditional approach to Everest, through Tibet to the northern face. Eric Shipton's 1951 expedition, which he joined, was trying to discover a route from the south-west. By forcing their way up the difficult Khumbu icefall and into the Western Cwm, which runs up to the South Col, Shipton and Hillary showed that it would be possible to climb Everest by this route.

The following year Hillary was bitterly disappointed when the British Himalayan Committee decided that Shipton, whom he greatly admired, was to be replaced as leader of the forthcoming British Everest expedition by John Hunt, "someone unknown to me personally, and a senior Army officer to boot". Rumours circulated that Hunt wanted to drop Hillary and George Lowe, another New Zealander, in favour of climbers he knew. But their reputations were already such that they could not easily be discarded. In the event Hunt handled Hillary with great tact, and was amply rewarded.

Hillary led Lowe and George Band up the Khumbu icefall, perhaps the most dangerous part of the entire climb, and established Camp III, the advanced base camp, in the Western Cwm. But he had a narrow escape when the ice gave way as he was moving loads up to this camp, plunging him into a crevasse. Fortunately Tenzing, who was following, thrust his ice-axe in the snow, and whipped the rope round it in a good belay. It tightened just in time to prevent Hillary being smashed to pieces at the bottom of the crevasse. Thereafter Hillary began to think of Tenzing as the ideal partner in a bid for the summit.

By his own admission, Hillary had been quite determined that he himself would be chosen for this honour. Together he and Tenzing climbed from Base Camp to Camp III and back again in a day. It was a pointless effort, as Hillary himself admitted, save that it showed that he and Tenzing were ultra-fit. "I was sufficiently calculating", he later confessed, "to regard it as important for Hunt to keep us in the front of his mind."

Hillary followed up by putting in mighty efforts as a load-carrier, first from Camp VII to the South Col, and then up to Camp IX at 27,900 feet. James (now Jan) Morris, who covered the expedition for *The Times*, wrote of Hillary working in the half-light, "huge and cheerful, his movement not so much graceful as unshakeably assured, his energy almost demonic. He had a tremendous, bursting, elemental, infectious, glorious vitality about him, like some bright, burly diesel express pounding across America."

When Hunt did select Hillary and Tenzing for the main attempt on the summit, they spent the night of May 28/29 1953 at Camp IX. Rising at 4.00 a.m., with the temperature minus 27 Centigrade, they proceeded to the South summit; cutting steps cautiously along the left-hand side of the summit ridge until they reached the 40-foot rock face now called the Hillary Step. Hillary managed to wriggle his way up a narrow crack. Thirty-seven years later his son Peter would ring him from the summit of Everest to express his admiration: "People have talked about the south-east ridge and the Hillary Step as though it were relatively easy, and it certainly is not easy."

Hillary reached the summit first, as Tenzing admitted in an autobiography as early as 1955. But since Hillary insisted that the matter was of no importance, and that the achievement belonged equally to them both, he refused for years to claim any primacy, even when the King of Nepal announced that Tenzing had been on the summit before him. They spent a quarter of an hour at the peak. Turning in typical Anglo-Saxon manner to shake Tenzing's hand, Hillary was enveloped in a bearhug: "With a feeling of mild surprise I realised that Tenzing was perhaps more excited at our success than I was."

Hillary remained determinedly low-key. "Having paid my respects to the highest mountain in the world," he recalled 46 years later in his autobiography *View from the Summit* (1999), "I had no choice but to urinate on it." Though he took Tenzing's photograph, he did not bother to organise one of himself. And when he met Lowe at Camp VIII on the way down, he delivered the great news in a laconic fashion deemed too shocking for publication at that time: "Well, George, we knocked the bastard off." Though Hillary claimed to feel British first and a New Zealander second, the Kiwi strain was always strong in him.

Edmund Percival Hillary was born in Auckland on July 20 1919. His sister June had arrived two years before; his brother Rex followed in 1920. Hillary's parents lived at the small town of Tuakau, 40 miles south of Auckland. Edmund's paternal grandmother had been an Irishwoman who (he recalled) "had the misfortune to meet my grandfather", a man who made friends, and money, with a well-heeled maharajah in India, then travelled on to New Zealand where he lost it all on the horses. Edmund's father reacted by adopting harsh and austere moral views. He believed that the only cure for ill-health was having no food, which meant that his children learned never to declare themselves ill. His wife, however, was concerned to mingle with the right people.

As a boy Edmund dreamed of exciting adventures, devouring a book a day, with especial concentration on the works of Rider Haggard, John Buchan and Edgar Rice Burroughs. His independent spirit led to frequent rows with his father; but, although frequently beaten in the woodshed, he never admitted being wrong.

At Auckland Grammar School he was at first a shy, scrawny figure who made few friends and provoked the despair of the gym instructor: "What will they send me next?" But he soon began to grow, and showed himself more than capable of looking after himself in fights.

His enthusiasm for snow and mountains began in 1935 on a school trip to Mount Ruapehu, on North Island. At home his father gave up his job as a journalist to concentrate on bee-keeping; and the boys were expected to help shift the 120-pound crates of honey. During two years at Auckland University, where he was supposed to be reading mathematics and science, Hillary failed to pass a single exam or make a single friend. So he returned to bee-keeping, though his father never thought of giving anything more than food and lodging for his back-breaking daily labour.

At the outbreak of the Second World War Hillary applied to join the Royal New Zealand Air Force, and was told he would have to wait a year to be called up for training. On a short trip to the South Island he scaled Mount Oliver, a modest peak but sufficient to spark an enthusiasm for climbing. His father had applied to keep him at home for bee-keeping, deemed essential work, though without telling him. It was not until the beginning of 1944 that he joined the RNZAF.

Training in the Wairu Valley on South Island, he began to spend all his money and every spare moment on climbing. He set a tough pace. "It was great fun, Ed," said an exhausted companion after one ascent, "but I'm not going to do it again." Soon afterwards Hillary used a spare weekend to make a solo climb of the 9,465-foot Mount Tapuaenuku. His confidence was growing, and having come 14th out of 260 in his Air Force exams, he was sent to navigation school at New Plymouth, and then posted to the Solomon Islands as a navigator of Catalina flying-boats. After the war ended he had a lucky escape when a petrol tank on the speedboat he was piloting fell off its mounting and set the craft on fire. Hillary suffered 40 per cent burns and much pain, but was lucky to have an excellent surgeon.

Back in New Zealand, he returned to his father's bee-keeping business (earning a modest salary) and devoted his holidays to climbing. His technique was much improved by Harry Ayres, New Zealand's leading mountain guide. In 1946 they scaled Mount Cook, at 12,349 feet the country's highest peak; and two years later they became the first men to conquer the difficult south range of the same mountain.

After being first interested in the possibility of climbing in the Himalayas by George Lowe the two were part of the first all-New Zealand team that went to Nepal in 1951, having sought the advice of Dr Noel Odell, who had caught the last glimpse of Mallory and Irvine "going hard for the summit" on the 1924 Everest expedition. Odell's counsel, that it was not necessary to take expensive equipment, proved over-sanguine, particularly in the matter of boots.

When in the Himalayas Hillary heard about Eric Shipton's expedition to the south side of Everest, and showed a ruthless determination to join him. The two men hit it off straight away, and Hillary was set on the path which led him to the peak of Everest.

The news of the mountain's conquest appeared in the British papers on June 2 1953, the morning of the Coronation, and unleashed a torrent of patriotic sentiment. Hillary was halfway back to Kathmandu when he received a letter addressed to "Sir Edmund Hillary KBE". "With sinking heart", he recalled his realisation that this was no joke. "I did not consider myself knightly material. For one thing I was far too impoverished to play the role." He was also uneasy that Tenzing (who was awarded the George Medal) had not received a knighthood.

Yet, for all his diffidence, his name had overnight become one of the best known in the world, even if he himself was not always recognised. Later that year he was climbing on Snowdon when he received a dressing-down from a member of the Alpine Club for being improperly accoutred for mountaineering. Afterwards, when introduced to Hillary, this gentleman was appropriately covered in confusion. Not that there was ever any side to Hillary. "I did a good job on Everest," he considered, "but have always known my limitations, and I found being classified as a hero slightly embarrassing." This attitude only added to his stature.

Back in New Zealand, in September 1953 Hillary married Louise Rose, daughter of the president of the New Zealand Alpine Club, with whom he was to have a son and daughter. But there was no question of a quiet domestic life. The following year he returned to the Himalayas as leader of the New Zealand Alpine Club expedition. In helping to extricate a colleague from a glacier, he broke three ribs. Typically, he tried to carry on as though nothing had happened, only to collapse completely high up on Makalu (27,790 feet). It took three days to carry him down to Camp I, and without the skill of Dr Charles Evans (another veteran of Everest) he might not have survived.

On Everest Hillary had been particularly remarkable for his ability to acclimatise quickly to high altitude, but after his near-escape on Makalu he found himself increasingly vulnerable as the air thinned. His spirit, however, was undimmed. In 1955 he was appointed leader of the New Zealand Antarctic team, in support of Sir Vivian Fuchs's Commonwealth Trans-Antarctic Expedition. His first task was to establish Scott base in McMurdo Sound, but by the time this was achieved in 1957 it was clear that there was scant empathy between Hillary and Fuchs. At Cape Crozier Hillary discovered the stone shelter where members of Scott's expedition had spent the winter in 1911. Under the snow was a film labelled: "To be developed before May 1 1911."

Hillary's next task was to reconnoitre crevassed areas, and lay out depots for Fuchs's trans-Antarctic journey from Shackleton Base on the other side of Antarctica. But he was also determined to reach the South Pole, and saw no hindrance in the lack of instructions to that end. On January 4 1958, after some hair-raising adventures driving tractors over crevasses, his team became the first to arrive at the South Pole by vehicle. In his book *No Latitude for Error* (1961), Hillary was unsparing in his criticism of Fuchs, and, some felt, less than generous in his failure to appreciate the difficulties which the Englishman had faced.

Hillary's search for the Abominable Snowman in 1960, financed by an American publisher, reached the conclusion that the animal was a myth derived from rare sightings of the Tibetan blue bear. Strange footprints were attributed to deformed Sherpa feet.

In 1961 Hillary returned to Makalu again, without oxygen equipment. At 19,000 feet he suffered a minor stroke, which for two days partially paralysed his facial muscles and affected his speech. His friend Peter Mulgrew suffered a pulmonary oedema in his lung at 27,000 feet, and as a consequence of the resulting frostbite had to have both legs amputated. "Now I realise," Hillary wrote in *High in the Thin Cold Air* (1963), "that my theories were a little too optimistic, and these long periods at high altitude without oxygen were possibly our undoing."

But caution was never in his nature. In 1967 he led a team that climbed Mount Herschel, "the Matterhorn of the Antarctic". Two years later he celebrated his 50th birthday by doing a Grand Traverse of Mount Cook, though one of the young men accompanying him fell 1,000 feet to his death. Aged 58 in 1977, Hillary suffered a cerebral oedema at 18,000 feet when he attempted Akash Parbat, on the upper Ganges. And in 1981, as chairman emeritus of an American attempt on the east face of Everest, he had to be escorted down after suffering hallucinations at 17,000 feet.

All this time Hillary had been deeply involved with his work for Sherpas. In this he enjoyed the full-hearted support of his wife Louise, who wrote two books about the family's adventures in the Himalayas, conveying the life-enhancing impact Hillary had on all who met him. But in 1975 Louise Hillary and their daughter Belinda were killed when their aircraft crashed on take-off at Kathmandu. For months thereafter Hillary was in a bad state, depending heavily on drink and sleeping pills, though he denied ever being an alcoholic. He buried himself in his work for the Himalayan Trust; all the same, he observed in 1977, "I am now operating more from a sense of duty, whereas before it was just all jolly good fun."

In the 1980s, however, Hillary was supported by his friendship with the widow of Peter Mulgrew (who had been killed in an air crash in 1979). She went with him to New Delhi as official companion when he was appointed New Zealand's High Commissioner in 1985; and they married in 1989. Hillary was much loved in India and Nepal, where he and June Mulgrew often found themselves the only foreigners at official functions. In 1986 he had the melancholy experience of attending Tenzing's funeral. His own energy seemed inexhaustible, even if he confessed to finding the hills he ascended increasingly steep. This did not prevent him from celebrating the 40th anniversary of the conquest of Everest with a trek in the Himalayas.

In 1987 Hillary was appointed ONZ , and in 1995 invested as a Knight of the Garter on the same day as Lady Thatcher. Yet his style remained downbeat. He drew satisfaction from his work in Nepal – "not, I hope, of the do-gooder sort, which I rather deplore, but the satisfaction of working with people I like and admire, and being able to give them a bit of a hand, and also getting quite a lot back from them".

He felt slightly guilty that his work, especially the airstrip at Lukla, had opened up Everest to tourists, and was appalled when, in 1992, 32 people reached the summit of Everest in a single day. "Visiting Everest now is like taking a bus tour of South Wales," he complained.

# ANTARCTICA

### David Lewis

DAVID LEWIS (who died on October 22 2002, aged 85) was a renowned amateur sailor whose most remarkable voyage saw him capsized three times and dismasted twice by hurricane-force Antarctic storms, leaving him beyond any chance of rescue – which he would never have sought.

*Lewis with his wife, Fiona, and children Susan and Vicky, before setting off for the Antarctic again.*

Lewis left Sydney in the 32-foot steel cutter *Ice Bird* on October 19 1972 to circumnavigate the Antarctic continent, where no one was known to have sailed alone. He was 55, a doctor in general practice, and thought of himself as timid though venturesome. He planned a voyage of 6,000 nautical miles, via New Zealand, to reach the Antarctic

Peninsula, but the timing and his chosen course proved unfortunate. Six weeks after setting off, he was running down the 60th Parallel – the "Screaming Sixties" – under a tiny storm jib. Wet snow filled the cockpit and festooned the rigging. He was dog-tired, tossed about and dispirited by repeated gales. In his memoirs, *Shapes on the Wind*, he recalled observing himself with clinical detachment drifting into hallucination, twice hearing voices, and making mistakes.

The pointer moved right off the barometer's scale; the wind rose to hurricane strength; the waves climbed above 15 metres high. One wave seized *Ice Bird*, hurtling her forward and slewing her to starboard. It exploded overhead and crashed the yacht down on her port side. The galley was wrecked, so was the self-steering gear; the life raft had been carried away and the jib torn across. From inside the cabin, Lewis hauled on the tiller lines to try to get the boat running without sail, but mostly she wallowed in the valleys between the waves. His stomach, he wrote, was hollow with fear; the wind now gave off the high scream of a hurricane of more than 80 knots, as the sea grew white.

In an instant all went black for Lewis, and he found himself upside down and spinning, with the cabin table coming down on his head. *Ice Bird* had been picked up, cast on to her lee side, then rolled through 360 degrees to be righted by her heavy keel. The mast had gone, but banged alongside until he could secure the remains. The cabin was wrecked and water spurted in with every roll from a crack in the steel between two portholes. The radio was destroyed, the pump out of action. The strong steel cabin trunk had been stoved in. It was 3,600 miles to Sydney, 2,500 miles to the Antarctic Peninsula. Hands numb, frost-bitten and gashed, Lewis bailed automatically for 10 hours.

When the storm abated, he managed with much pain to raise a jury mast and rig a storm jib. Two weeks later, a second hurricane turned him over again. This time he was prepared, and the damage was less, but he cried in near despair.

After six weeks he made landfall as originally planned, and soon afterwards reached the American Antarctic base of Palmer, tying up alongside Jacques Cousteau's oceanographic ship *Calypso*. The voyage had taken more than 14 weeks, the last 2,500 miles under jury rig.

David Henry Lewis was born on September 16 1917 at Plymouth, the only son of a Welsh mining engineer and an Irish doctor. The family moved to New Zealand when David was a boy, and he spent a year at a Maori village school on Rarotonga, in the Cook Islands, where he heard wonderful sagas of ancient Polynesian navigators of the Pacific who had "dared the clouds of heaven".

At 17 he built a kayak, and ended his days at Wanganui Collegiate School by travelling home to Auckland alone, 430 miles by river, lake, sea and portage, in 50 days. At medical school at Dunedin, he ascended 19 unclimbed peaks.

He completed his medical training in England, at Leeds University, graduating in 1942 as the fifth doctor in a direct family line that had begun with his Irish great-great-grandfather. He joined the Army in time to serve after D-Day as medical officer with 9th Parachute Battalion in France. Posted to Egypt, he dabbled secretly with the outlawed Arab League of National Liberation in Cairo and with left-wing Zionists in Palestine. Characteristically, he sympathised with both sides. Just after the war, in Jamaica with his Lithuanian first wife, Perle Michaelson, and their daughter Anna, Lewis became involved in the independence movement led by Norman Manley, during 18 months as medical officer at Port Royal.

Back in London, he was driven by social conscience to set up a general practice at East Ham, which angered conservative colleagues by supporting the nascent National Health Service. He sat on the executive of the London Trades Council as the representative of the Medical Practitioners' Union, and led its May Day march from Stepney to Trafalgar Square.

When his first marriage ended in divorce, Lewis turned increasingly to the sea and the mountains. In 1960 he entered the first *Observer* single-handed transatlantic race, and came third in a fleet of five, after shattering his mast with England still in sight and losing two days in repairs. The winner was Francis Chichester. That race produced the first of Lewis's dozen books, *The Ship Would Not Sail Due West*. Next he planned the first circumnavigation of the world by a catamaran, and spent all his savings on her design and construction. First, he sailed this craft, *Rehu Moana* (Maori for "Ocean Spray"), in the 1964 trans-atlantic race, finishing seventh.

At Newport, Rhode Island, his second wife, Fiona, joined him with their two small girls for the world voyage. They had sold their London home and practice, and sailed, with some rudder troubles, down to Magellan Strait and out into the Pacific. There Lewis, eschewing compass, chronometer and sextant, intended to test his theories about the navigational methods of the ancient Polynesian voyagers. At first he strayed, but then took *Rehu Moana* 1,600 nautical miles from Rarotonga to New Zealand by observing the sun and stars and other natural phenomena, fetching up just 25 miles off his intended landfall.

He was to learn much more about Polynesian path-finding by sailing with Polynesian navigators whose knowledge had very largely been thought lost. A four-year fellowship with the Australian National University supported his studies, and the Institute of Aboriginal Affairs financed research into Aboriginal desert journeyings.

It was after this that he embarked on the personal challenge of the Antarctic. When the smashed *Ice Bird* reached Palmer station, the Americans worked on repairing boat and sailor. Invited by the magazine *National Geographic* to postpone the rest of the circum-navigation and revisit the Pacific to write about the navigators, Lewis accepted, and returned to Palmer in the southern hemisphere spring of 1973. It was a hard thing to do.

This time, ice smashed his self-steering gear and a gale capsized and again dismasted him. He had to abandon the circumnavigation and make for Cape Town, 800 nautical miles north, under jury rig.

His voyage inspired the establishment of a non-profit organisation, the Oceanic Research Foundation, which he led at the outset. It marshalled finance and expertise for expeditions, which he led at first, to fill small gaps in south polar knowledge. Later, his interests turned to the north Pacific and Arctic regions, and he helped unite Eskimo families split for 40 years by the Bering Sea and the Cold War, some in Alaska, some in the Chukotka region of Russia's Far East.

At 75, with a short third marriage behind him, Lewis concluded that he was certainly not too old to pick up the pieces and start again. He continued to sail small craft on long voyages, sometimes alone, to win over good-looking and clever women, and to lecture and practise medicine when he needed money. It was his version of what John Masefield in *Sea Fever* called "the vagrant gypsy life".

He was 80 and a naturalised Australian, when *Australian Geographic* named him their 1998 Adventurer of the Year. His other awards included the Gold Medal of the Royal Institute of Navigation and the Bernard Fergusson Trophy as New Zealand's Yachtsman of the Year in 1965. Leeds University gave him an honorary MSc for his research into exposure and reactions to fatigue and solitude. His eyesight failed off the Queensland coast, but with help he continued to cruise until his death.

Apart from his former wives, David Lewis left a son and three daughters.

~

## Ray Adie

RAY ADIE (who died on May 14 2006, aged 81), was the geologist responsible for introducing the Antarctic explorer Sir Vivian Fuchs to the joys of dog sledging.

A South African, unacquainted with snow before arriving at Hope Bay, northern Antarctica, in 1946, he learned to drive sledges, then made a successful 700-mile trip to Stonington Island, the southernmost station of the Falkland Islands Dependencies Survey, when Fuchs arrived there to take command two years later.

Since Fuchs had never used dogs on previous expeditions, Adie instructed him in every aspect of human–husky relations: the way to steer teams by cracking a 40-foot whip to their left or right; how to avoid treating the dogs like pets; and when to let a lead dog show the best route to an objective.

*Adie came up with the red stripe line in Gibbs SR toothpaste.* (International Glaciological Society)

Adie and Fuchs made numerous journeys to study the geology of George VI Sound, including one 220-mile crossing of Alexander Island during which Adie's sledge once turned over 25 times in the course of a mile. After Adie had been in the Antarctic for two years, a relief ship failed to reach Stonington, and the party there was condemned to remain another year, earning headlines at home about "The Lost Eleven". But he and Fuchs used the time to make a 90-day journey of more than 1,000 miles south to Eklund Island.

Forty-four days out, they were worried by dwindling supplies of food for the dogs until the sudden appearance of 11 Adelie penguins, which provided a restorative meal. Adie's dog, Mutt, then fell 20 feet through the ice, and waited without moving while his master, speaking softly amid the sound of tinkling icicles, climbed down to attach a line which Fuchs hauled up.

The two men were fortunate to get on well. In his memoirs Fuchs noted Adie's imperturbability and meticulous attention to detail: "At the end of each day's long and often weary march he always gave me a written statement of exactly how far we had travelled, how much food and fuel we had left, and the actual weight carried by each sledge. Despite his youth he had already developed the habit of precise thinking which was later to make him one of the best scientific editors in the country."

When they had read and re-read the two books they had with them, Fuchs found himself listening to an account of the virtues of a brand of sausages, then of some pea flour, and next peaches as Adie read aloud the labels, including every full stop and comma. "To such is one reduced when, during months of isolated travel, everything has been said, and each man knows every detail of the other's family and the nooks and crannies of his home," Fuchs later recalled.

They also discussed the logistics for Fuchs's proposed crossing of Antarctica. But when that expedition was finally launched in 1958, Adie decided that he could not spare the necessary time. Fuchs deeply regretted this, as he would have liked to pay his debt for the dog-driving lessons by teaching Adie to ride a Sno-Cat.

Raymond John Adie was born on February 26 1925, and went to Maritzburg College before gaining his BSc in Geology and Chemistry at Natal University.

A few months after joining the Falkland Islands Dependencies Survey section in Birmingham University's geology department he set off for Hope Bay, where he was soon on a month-long survey and geological journey under the mountaineer Frank Elliott. Further field work was followed by a 350-mile depot-laying journey to Seal Nunataks, on the east coast, before they set off for Stonington on a 71-day trip, during which 200 miles of new coastline were mapped; they also found fossil tree trunks embedded in volcanic rocks. It was a journey that has been repeated only once. The names allocated along the way (Shiver Point, Exasperation Inlet and Delusion Point) reflect the party's mood as they encountered high winds and dense mist, and found their sledges breaking as they hurried along too quickly for Adie's taste.

On his return from the Antarctic, Adie married his wife Aileen, with whom he had two daughters, and spent three years at St John's College, Cambridge, writing up the geological results for his PhD. During this time he joined a Cambridge summer expedition to Arctic Norway, where he studied ice petro-fabrics and developed a lifelong interest in glaciology. He then joined a Birmingham-based chemicals firm, prospecting for phosphates in the tropics and coming up with the red stripe in Gibbs SR toothpaste.

Adie then returned to the Falkland Survey section at Birmingham University until it was moved to the British Antarctic Survey's new headquarters in Cambridge. He encouraged some 100 young scholars to work in the field, though they did not always find him easy, since he believed that their research should be based on original work, and not be over-influenced by that of their predecessors.

During this time Adie was responsible for the Survey's scientific reports, and helped to initiate the *British Antarctic Survey Bulletin* and its annual report, demonstrating meticulous attention to convention, phraseology and punctuation while stopping short of pedantry. He also edited the *Journal of Glaciology* and landmark volumes of proceedings of two international symposia on Antarctic geology and geophysics.

As the Survey's deputy director from 1972 until his retirement in 1985, he had to deal with disasters such as the loss of three members' lives on Mount Peary in 1976; and when Argentina invaded the Falklands he was summoned to brief Margaret Thatcher at 10 Downing Street on the role that the Survey's two ships could play. Adie returned to the Antarctic some 20 times and took part in the first international conference in the Antarctic, organised by the Chileans.

He was appointed OBE in 1970, and received the Polar Medal (Antarctic Clasp) in 1953 and the Fuchs Medal in 1985. He is commemorated in Adie Inlet on the east coast of the Antarctic Peninsula.

# WHITEHALL

—

## Sir Algernon Rumbold

SIR ALGERNON RUMBOLD (who died on October 23 1993, aged 87) was a champion of Tibet, from his time as a young desk officer at the India Office dealing with the Northern Frontiers.

In 1943, he was responsible for drafting Anthony Eden's statement recognising the suzerainty of China over Tibet but reserving to it considerable autonomy, not least in foreign relations. However, during 1950 and 1951 Chinese Communist forces established a stranglehold over Tibet. For the next 40 years "Algy" Rumbold did all he could, through letters to *The Daily Telegraph* and *The Times*, to counter Chinese propaganda about the nature of their rule. The best measure of events, Rumbold commented in 1978, was that 100,000 Tibetans had braved the Chinese Army and the snows of the Himalayas to seek sanctuary in India.

After the Lhasa riots in 1959 he was instrumental in creating the Tibet Society of the United Kingdom, which he served as president from 1977 to 1988. Dry and precise in style, persevering in temperament, he strove to curb the Sinophile tendency in the Foreign Office. On meeting the Dalai Lama, he enjoyed his giggly nature, and was exasperated that he did not receive that political status awarded him in other countries. However, it was a considerable success when, shortly before Rumbold's death, Douglas Hurd, the Foreign Secretary, who was himself a former China hand in the Foreign Office, received the Dalai Lama.

A soldier's son, Horace Algernon Fraser Rumbold was born on February 27 1906. His uncle was the xenophobic diplomatist Sir Horace Rumbold who, as ambassador to Berlin from 1928 to 1933, was one of the first to take the measure of the Nazis.

Young Algy was educated at Wellington and Christ Church, Oxford. In 1929 he began his career in the India Office, and during the early 1930s he served as private secretary, first to the 2nd Earl Russell (Parliamentary Under-Secretary of State for India in Ramsay Macdonald's government and Bertrand Russell's brother) and then to the Permanent Under-Secretary. By 1943 Rumbold had become Assistant Secretary; on the day India was granted independence four years later he was transferred to the Commonwealth Relations Office. Between 1949 and 1953 he was Deputy High Commissioner, under Lord Howick, in South Africa.

His health, though, could not endure hot climates, and the rest of his career was spent mainly in Whitehall. In the efficient discharge of business Rumbold was a quintessential mandarin, but he was never cowed in his views. In 1954 he became Assistant Under-Secretary at the Commonwealth Office, and in 1958 Deputy Under-Secretary,

*Rumbold fell foul of the Macmillan government's pro-European views.*

with special responsibility for economic affairs.

Rumbold was concerned with the negotiation of Commonwealth preferences in the European Free Trade Association, and in 1961, when Britain first attempted to join the European Economic Community, he helped establish that New Zealand butter should be given special treatment. Since he was hostile to Britain's entry to the Common Market he soon ran foul of Duncan Sandys, who shared Harold Macmillan's pro-European views.

With the break-up of the Central African Federation in 1962–3, Rumbold was appointed chairman of a commission to arrange for continuing joint administration of certain services.

He retired in 1966, but five years later found himself involved in a controversy with Harold Wilson. In *The Labour Government 1964–70* (1971) Wilson claimed that he had been given misleading advice about events in the Indo-Pakistan War of 1965. As a result, he had issued a statement deploring the extension of the fighting from Kashmir to the Punjab and calling for an immediate cessation of hostilities. It was Wilson's complaint that, since India was winning the conflict at the time of his statement, he had been made to look as if he was supporting Pakistan. He even implied that the official concerned had been forced into early retirement. His remarks on television rendered this official easily identifiable as Rumbold – although Wilson unreservedly withdrew the slur about early retirement.

Wilson's breach of confidence stung Rumbold to a general rebuttal. He pointed out that there were "powerful international reasons ... well known to Mr Wilson even if he has now forgotten them" why it was important in September 1965 to bring the fighting to an end as quickly as possible. These reasons, Rumbold went on, would be available to historians in 1996. Meanwhile he had no intention of discussing them publicly. Later the papers were held back for a further 10 years.

Rumbold continued to be active in retirement. Besides his work for Tibet, he was an adviser to the Welsh Office in 1967; deputy chairman of the Air Transport Licensing Board in 1971–2; and a member of the governing body of the School of Oriental and African Studies from 1965 to 1980. In 1979 he published *Watershed in India, 1914–1922*.

Algy Rumbold was appointed CIE in 1947, CMG in 1953 and KCMG in 1960. He married, in 1946, Margaret Hughes; they had two daughters. He was the heir of his cousin Sir Henry Rumbold, 11th Bt.

～

# Henry Hall

HENRY HALL (who died on October 30 2004, aged 91) was a colonial service "troubleshooter" called in to deal with the problems involved in Britain's divestment of its empire after the Second World War.

Over 40 years, he served in the Indian Army and the Indian Political Service; he was a Colonial Office official and Deputy High Commissioner for Eastern Malaysia, Kuching and Sarawak. In the course of his travels, he identified the shortcomings of district commissioners in Kenya, helped draw up a power-sharing constitution for Mauritius that was to serve as a model for Northern Ireland, and was trusted as a genial, discreet adviser to ministers, Commonwealth governments and members of the Royal Family.

After retiring in 1973, he spent nine years as director of studies at the Royal Institute of Public Administration. By the time Hall gave this up he was increasingly conscious, like many other former public servants, of his successors' shortcomings, which stemmed from a belief that the accumulated wisdom of the past was no longer relevant. As a consequence he was a spirited letter-writer to *The Daily Telegraph* until shortly before his death.

*Hall got on well with seven Labour secretaries of state and six Tories because he was "totally impartial and they knew it".*

Hall was disappointed by the Foreign and Commonwealth Office's often cavalier lack of concern for any remaining imperial responsibility. He criticised Britain's timidity in agreeing to give up Hong Kong; was deeply unimpressed by the way Australia and New Zealand drove Fiji out of the Commonwealth; and dismissed Argentina's specious claims to the Falkland Islands. He saw no reason to suppose that the failure of the Central African, West Indies and Nigerian federations meant that the creators of a European state would do any better.

The son of an Indian Army officer, Harold Percival Hall was born in India on September 9 1913 and educated at Portsmouth Grammar School, before going to Sandhurst. He represented the academy at hockey, soccer, cricket and rifle shooting; he won the sword for tactics and the prize for electricity and wireless. Coming top of those whose fathers had served in the Indian services, he became King's India Cadet.

Young Henry, as he was known, was attached first to the 22nd Cheshire Regiment near the Khyber Pass before transferring to Abala in the Punjab. He commanded the Dogra company of the 3rd/15th Punjab Regiment on operations in Waziristan, when he was involved in a skirmish that resulted in two men being killed and two wounded. While stationed at Fort Sandeman, in mountainous Baluchistan, Hall was so impressed by the freedom that members of the Political Service enjoyed in running their areas that he obtained a transfer to the Central States Residency. He was sent to Meerut as a tax collector and assistant magistrate, with the duty of witnessing hangings to ensure that the right man was executed.

Hall was back in the Army when he married Majory Dickson, with whom he was to have three sons, before joining the planning staff for the war against Japan. Three years later he returned to the Political Service in the Loralai agency. Over four years, he had responsibility for exports to Persia and was director of food supplies for more than two million people in an area the size of England and Wales. He was once held up by bandits, who let him go on discovering that he was not the garrison engineer carrying pay for tribal workers; his Indian deputy was in much more danger, and had to prove he was circumcised and therefore a Muslim.

After Independence, Hall returned home to bring his experience and self-reliance to the Colonial Office. He persuaded Jim Griffiths, the Colonial Secretary who did not believe in capital punishment, to accept it for murder and possession of a bomb in Hong Kong when the Communists and Nationalists were fighting. Visiting Kenya during the Mau Mau insurrection, he realised that the district officers were handicapped by knowing only Swahili, not the languages of their districts; and he arranged for reports of troublemaking speeches to be referred to the local department of African Affairs instead of to the Attorney-General, who usually did nothing because no offence had been committed. On a Pacific tour, he impressed the Fijians by being able to talk in Urdu to the wife of the Indian government's representative, who spoke neither Fijian nor the local Indians' dialects. He also made a firm friend in Queen Salote of Tonga, which meant that when he returned some years later he was treated as the VIP while his minister, Julian Amery, was regarded as his junior.

Such visits taught him things that were not always welcome in London. His explanation of why the Gilbert Islands could never manage without British aid drew the retort from one newly appointed Labour Minister that his party wanted to get rid of them.

While acting as secretary to the Commonwealth royal commission on Malaysia's constitution, he was astonished to hear a former Chief

Justice of Pakistan say that if his countrymen held a referendum they would vote for the return of the British. The commission had almost completed its work when the Indonesians attacked Brunei. To the astonishment of all, Hall had an amiable working relationship with the fiery Major-General Walter Walker, in charge of the Borneo operations, thanks to their earlier acquaintance in India.

One of his duties as Assistant High Commissioner for Eastern Malaysia in the 1960s was to accompany the Duke of Devonshire, a Foreign Office minister, on a tour which included a St John Ambulance ball. After the Duke left, Hall's cook found a raffle ticket which had won a car in his bedroom. Since Hall had bought the Duke the ticket he therefore felt a right to the vehicle, which would have been useful for his office, but the departed Duke sent a telegram giving it to the cook.

When trouble broke out on Anguilla, Hall arrived to find that some disgruntled members of a party which had lost an election had disrupted a beauty contest and let off stink bombs. The party's leader warned Hall that he might be shot; but he hired a taxi and persuaded the four culprits to give themselves up. Afterwards, when he found that his minister, Judith Hart, feared that he had been shot, he reassured her that if there was a shot it had missed badly.

In 1966, Hall negotiated his ministry's merger into a new Commonwealth Relations Office. Two years later he moved to the Ministry of Defence, where he helped to upgrade pensions, and was instructed to prevent any changes which were impracticable.

By his retirement, with an MBE and CMG, Hall calculated that he had worked with seven Labour secretaries of state and six Conservatives. "I was entirely impartial and they knew it," he recalled. "That was why I got on with them so well."

# ABBREVIATIONS

## Sovereign's Honours and Awards

| | |
|---|---|
| ADC | Aide-de-camp |
| AO | Officer of the Order of Australia |
| Bt | Baronet |
| CB | Companion of the Order of the Bath |
| CBE | Commander of the Order of the British Empire |
| CC | Companion of the Order of Canada |
| CH | Companion of Honour |
| CIE | Commander of the Order of the Indian Empire |
| CM | Member of the Order of Canada |
| CMG | Companion of the Order of St Michael and St George |
| DBE | Dame Commander of the Order of the British Empire |
| DSO | Distinguished Service Order |
| GBE | Knight Grand Cross of the Order of the British Empire |
| GCMG | Grand Commander of the Order of St Michael and St George |
| KB | Knight Bachelor |
| KBE | Knight of the Order of the British Empire |
| KCIE | Knight Commander of the Indian Empire |
| KCMG | Knight Commander of the Order of St Michael and St George |
| KCVO | Knight Commander of the Royal Victorian Order |
| MBE | Member of the Order of the British Empire |
| MC | Military Cross |
| OBE | Officer of the Order of the British Empire |
| OC | Officer of the Order of Canada |
| ONZ | Order of New Zealand |
| QC | Queen's Counsel |
| VC | Victoria Cross |

# INDEX

~